LAST CALL
SOUTH FLORIDA

A HISTORY OF 1001 LGBTQ-FRIENDLY TAVERNS, HAUNTS & HANGOUTS

FRED FEJES
&
RICK KARLIN

RATTLING GOOD YARNS
PRESS

Rattling Good Yarns Press
33490 Date Palm Drive 3065
Cathedral City CA 92235
USA
www.rattlinggoodyarns.com

Library of Congress Control Number: 2024946087

ISBN: 978-1-955826-71-6

First Edition

DEDICATION

Last Call South Florida is dedicated to Norm Kent (October 18, 1949–April 13, 2023), bar owner, lawyer, publisher, humanitarian, and activist.

*Norm Kent (October 18, 1949–April 13, 2023), photograph
courtesy of OUTSFL publisher Jason Parsley*

TABLE OF CONTENTS

FOREWORD

THE GOLDEN AGE OF SOUTH FLORIDA'S LGBTQ BARS

BY JESSE MONTEAGUDO

Although there were bars that attracted people whom we now would identify as LGBT or queer as far back as the 1930s, the Golden Age of LGBTQ bars in the State of Florida spanned the last three decades of the twentieth century. Though police raids continued sporadically—the most famous ones being the raids that Broward County Sheriff Nick Navarro conducted against Club 21 and the Copa on May 3, 1991—they eased somewhat to the extent that bargoers could expect to enjoy a night out without fear of being arrested. A series of court cases repealed archaic laws that barred LGBTQ people from congregating, being served alcoholic beverages, or "wearing clothes that pertained to the opposite sex." LGBTQ people were tolerated if we remained in our closets.

Soon business owners realized that queers had disposable income and were willing to spend it. Not even AIDS, which led to the closing of many baths and sex clubs, could keep many of us from enjoying a night out on the town, at a pub or a club. Bars served as de facto community centers, where LGBTQ people could meet friends, find lovers, seek support, and learn about their community in a discrete setting. Though newly established groups like the Sunshine Cathedral (1972) and Congregation Etz Chaim (1974) began to attract community members, they could not compete with popular pubs and clubs.

I came out in 1973 when South Florida had more LGBTQ bars than there are today. In his 1972 directory, *The Gay Insider USA*, author John Paul Hudson (writing as John Francis Hunter) listed fifteen gay or mixed pubs and clubs on the mainland (including Coconut Grove and Coral Gables), eight bars on Miami Beach, and seven in Fort Lauderdale. There were also bars in Hallandale, Hollywood, Key West, Lake Worth, and West Palm Beach. Though queer bars came and went, like they do today, some stuck around for much of the 1970s. One of them was Warehouse VIII. Located on SW 8th Street (Calle Ocho) and 36th Avenue in Little Havana, this former warehouse (hence the name) boasted a huge dance floor, a Levi-leather bar in the back, a cruise bar upstairs, and a rooftop where anything could happen. Another favorite of mine was the Second Landing, on the second floor at the corner of Calle Ocho and Le Jeune Road (SW 42nd. Ave.).

The number of queer watering holes has markedly declined. Although big mega-discos like the Copa or the Warsaw Ballroom continued to attract large numbers of community members during the eighties and nineties, interest and investment in bars declined in the new millennium. As businesses whose primary goal was selling alcoholic beverages, gay bars contributed their share to a silent epidemic of substance abuse that raged in our community. And bars are no longer necessary. As more of us came out as openly LGBTQ people, we did not need the bars to be queer in; we could do so anywhere. An increasing variety of support groups gave us new opportunities to express ourselves, meet people, and take care of our needs. Virtual community centers, which is what bars were, could not compete with the real thing. We found other ways to meet people, online and on apps like Grindr. Even so, bars continue to be a rite of passage among a new generation of LGBTQ people. In South Florida, LGBTQ bars continue to flourish in places such as South Beach and Wilton Manors, where tourists and residents mingle.

Last Call South Florida is a valuable resource for those of us who remember South Florida's LGBTQ bars, during their golden age and beyond. My friends and scholars Fred Fejes and Rick Karlin did an amazing job listing all the pubs and clubs, past and present, even those that no one has heard of or remembers. South Florida's queer history is a rich one; *Last Call South Florida* takes us back to both the good times and (sometimes) the bad times. Despite the violence and the prejudice, we all had fun.

CRUISING SOUTH FLORIDA'S GOLD COAST with sky masters

SOUTH FLORIDA—The beaches in Ft. Lauderdale, Dania and Singer Island are packed with all those beautiful college boys and servicemen on leave during the holidays. Now that the season is here, the jet-setters, the rich sons-of-corporation-executives and those groovy yacht captains are lingering in the sunshine on the goldcoast.

Rent yourself a little 19-foot outboard and go for a cruise on the Intracoastal and Lake Worth for a real fun time. There's easy docking facilities at Spanish River Park in Boca Raton where you'll find you can get tied up in no time at all . . . even for an inexperienced motorboat captain.

A cruise around the yacht basins can be fun too. There's a lot of big ones down here at this time of year. Oh. Wow!. . . The Navy cooperates too (for those who like navel vessels) by sending some of their ships' crews to Port Everglades for R & R.

There's no business like show business, so the saying goes and nothing brings in business like having a show. The performance at the **Venture Inn** in Ft. Lauderdale is such a success that a number of other area bars are venturing into on-stage theatrics.

Kieth's Cruise Room in Hallendale may be a little hard to find, but it's worth the effort when you get there. You're always assured of good entertainment and the Sunday buffet is sumptious just like the go-go boys.

The tourists in south Florida bars are very impressed with David. It's a sell-out within a few short hours after it hits the display rack.

The **Music Box Lounge** in Lake Worth was the recent scene of a ceremony for the Knights of Juvenis, an international honorary fraternity. Three new members were tapped for the group at the affair attended by an estimated 150 persons.

When the owners of the Music Box, Bill and Jerry, had their lounge completely remodeled, they decided not to stop there. . . They hired Excalibur, a new party decorating service, to change the decor of the lounge to compliment the seasons and holidays. The orange and yellow theme of October and November gave way to a dazzling snowstorm in December. Glittering silver and white snowflakes suspended from the ceiling dance in the breezes created by the mingling crowds standing around silver trees sprouting red roses. A "King of Hearts" theme is being readied now and will give way to Kelly green decorations in March for the **Music Box's** annual St. Patricks party. . . always an S. R. O. affair.

If you haven't been to Top's or the Annex in Hollywood lately, you're in for a big surprise. The wall between the two places has been removed creating one big fun palace. You used to be able to stand in the doorway between the two and get zonked on the music blaring from the juke boxes in each room. . . now there's just one music system. . . and the beat goes on!

As we move farther south we hit the magic city of Miami that casts an evil spell of promiscuity on all who visit. After a few turns through Coconut Grove we refresh ourselves at **Warehouse VIII** or **Mother's Lounge.** The Warehouse, located between lucrative Coconut Grove and glittering Miami Beach is groovy and cruisey with both an indoor and outdoor roof top bars.

The Sun and Fun Capital of the world is Miami Beach and which ever is your preference, both are in abundance. The Alley Kat on the Alton strip offers both mystery of a speak easy with its seductive back entrance and the excitement of life with its lively interior. The Pin Up near 21st Street offers visual enticement that make the bar circuit more interesting. You don't know on which to concentrate, the clientelle or the pin ups. Around the corner is the plush **Ambassadors III** in which a replica of David greats you on your arrival. The Go-Go Dancers are as nice as the surroundings in which they must perform.

Ted Larson reports that his Pantomaniacs of '71 are all set to go with a weekly show at **Kieth's Cruise Room.** Showtime will be every Sunday at 11:30 p.m. starting the first week in February.

The Turf in West Palm Beach plans a Valentine party for February 13. Nominations and voting are in progress for the "King of Hearts" who will be crowned at midnight.

Miami Beach's **Ambassadors III** is really pulling in the crowds with their Go-Go Boys. Wow, how those boys can move.

The Gym in Ft. Lauderdale has come a long way, baby, since it opened less than two years ago. It you stay away for a few weeks you won't recognize the place when you return. . . they make improvements and additions so fast and furious. . . only problem is the light in the sauna may need rewiring. . . it keeps going out. . . pity!!!

The Everglades Bar in Fort Lauderdale has done a beautiful job of redecorating since the change of management in December. The blue color theme is carried out throughout the club in a very attractive manner.

The Saloon is conveniently tucked in an arcade (it can be reached from either end) in downtown Fort Lauderdale. The resulting feeling of seclusion and privacy is marvelous and the friendly, intimate bar has been enjoying very good business.

The Coconut Grove section of Miami has a lot to offer by itself. From elegant homes and shops gracing beautiful parks to the modest. One could wander all day through the art galleries, arcade shops showing their wares from wigs to leather; psychedelic posters to coffee houses. The sidewalk art shows always attract attention, and prove a profitable source of revenue for local talent.

Truly if its excitement, glamour, variety and action for which you are looking, the Gold Coast of South Florida is rich with treasures for you to discover—Come on Down.

David, February, 1971

INTRODUCTION
FROM SWAMPLAND TO DANCE CLUBS: THE EVOLUTION OF LGBTQ LIFE IN SOUTH FLORIDA

Until the late 1800s, there was nothing in South Florida that would attract the farmers or factory workers that moved to and populated the other American states in the 19th century. Although the area had pleasant, warm, winter weather and sandy beaches warmed by gulf stream currents, aside from the beaches and a thin strip of land along the Coast, most of the area was a mosquito-infested swamp filled with alligators.

That changed in the 1890s when Henry Flagler laid the Florida East Coast railroad through the region, connecting the luxury hotels he and others were building in South Florida. In short order, swamps were drained, native habitats were destroyed, and palm trees and other foreign plants and creatures were imported to create a tropical paradise. Along with this physical transformation, South Florida was reinvented as a site of exotic adventure for those wishing to escape established rules and regimes. While other parts of the country produced foodstuffs, minerals, and factory goods, South Florida was now producing something very, very different: pleasure, leisure, and fun.

Although tourism in some form has existed since the Roman times, only in the 20th century did it become a form of business that could propel millions of people to visit a region, some even to move there, to experience the unique pleasures of its environment. While many came to avoid the frigid winter weather of the North, others came to escape and find a place with less rigid rules and structures that governed desire and pleasure up North. Many were looking for a queer place, where the lines defining sexuality and gender were blurred.

From the beginning of that time, there were signs of a queer presence in South Florida. In 1912, James Deering, bachelor, the scion of a wealthy Midwest family, a barely closeted homosexual, began building Vizcaya, a Renaissance fantasy estate and garden complex along Biscayne Bay. He, and his artistic design director, Paul Chaflin, also a bachelor, would visit European palaces where they would buy entire rooms of furnishings and bring them to Vizcaya. Deering invited his friend John Stewart Sargent, a prominent 20th-century painter to visit. Sargent was enthralled with Vizcaya, calling it the equal of any Venetian palace. In addition to paintings of the lavish Vizcaya interiors, he also did highly erotic drawings of the nude muscular Bahamian estate laborers lounging by the water after work. Sargent was also a bachelor.

The queerness of South Florida is also reflected in the architectural works of Addison Mizner in Palm Beach. A barely closeted homosexual (and the subject of Steven Sondheim's musical *Road Show*), he designed numerous homes for the county's wealthy winter residents, employing a truly queer mishmash of Gothic, Romanesque, and Renaissance styles to produce a faux Mediterranean-colonial look. He had a pet monkey, JB, who sat on his shoulder and went everywhere with him. The monkey even ran for mayor of Palm Beach and lost by only four votes.

Entertaining the winter crowd was a big part of South Florida life. Clubs, bars, and saloons were a central element in the South Florida landscape. By 1920, the Miami newspapers ran more than 10,000 ads for saloons.

The proximity of South Florida to the British Bahamas alleviated any negative effects of national prohibition on alcohol as numerous private gatherings and garden parties kept the social life active.

After Prohibition ended, the number of public bars grew. Miami looked to New York for inspiration. One newspaper columnist called Miami "Broadway Under the Palms." A popular kind of bar at the time in New York was the pansy bar with a highly effeminate staff and entertainment by female impersonators. Although female impersonators were popular entertainers both in Miami and Palm Beach since the 1910s, where they often appeared at garden parties and socials, it was in the 1930s that they began appearing in bars. For many bars in the 1930s-1950s, having a female impersonator as entertainment was one sure way to tell the public that this was a "femmic bar" (as one newspaper called them), or as we would say today, a gay bar.

In the years after World War II, the population of South Florida exploded, growing from 401,000 in 1940 to 2,002,000 in 1970, and it has kept on growing. Florida is now the fastest-growing state in the country. With the many new residents came new cities and suburbs, interstate highways, and airports. The core business of the region is tourism. The warm winters and beaches attracted crowds during the winters and, thanks to air conditioning, many year-round residents.

Along with this growth came large new communities of LGBTQ people. Although they lived in all areas of the region, the main communities were concentrated in the Southeastern and Southern tip of the state from Palm Beach through Fort Lauderdale, Miami, and Key West, where bars, restaurants, and entertainment emerged to serve them. Their presence changed the overall social fabric, making South Florida one of the most LGBTQ-accepting areas in the country.

For South Florida's queer community, bars were the key institution in community-making. The queer bars first appeared in Dade County, then concurrently in Broward, Palm Beach, and Monroe. They were the first places that provided the space where LGBTQ people could gather safely, meet each other, socialize, and have fun. Often, it was in bars that the seeds of many of the later community social, political, and advocacy organizations and efforts were planted. During the AIDS crisis bars were important places of education, organizing, and fundraising.

Most of the cities in South Florida have similar origin stories, but today, they each have very distinct personalities. Key West is a relaxed, laid-back place, similar to Provincetown, Massachusetts, where it is unlikely to meet anyone who is "not gay." West Palm Beach retains the small-town vibe of central Florida. Miami, once referred to as the sixth borough of New York City, is now the northernmost city in Latin America; Fort Lauderdale now stakes a claim of a borough of New York City but is also home to many ex-Bostonians, Midwesterners, and Quebecois.

Also, the number of bars has remained relatively stable, despite the impact of social media. The need for a specially designated queer space is not as great anymore. Still, LGBTQ bars and LGBTQ-friendly spaces play a significant role. As one gay man, a former Catholic seminarian said, "The bars are like our churches. We don't go to them every day like we used to. But they're there to remind us of who we are and where we go when we need to get in touch both with ourselves and with our community."

As Lucas Hilderbrand states in his book *The Bars Are Ours: Histories and Culture in Gay Bars in America 1960 and After*, "What we call 'gay bars' are many things, and that capricious term encompasses numerous venues." He then goes on to point out that some places attracted large numbers of gay people but did not identify as gay venues, some "straight" bars became queer on certain days or certain times (from the gay nights at straight clubs to hotel bars that were often gay later in the evening) and some turned gay when queer people came and kept showing up." All of these and more, are included in *Last Call South Florida*.

Notes About This Book

In listing the bars, clubs, and occasional supper clubs that we have included, we have chosen to divide our list by county. We start with Palm Beach County to the North and traveling down the coast to Broward, Miami/Dade to the South, and then South and West to Monroe County following the demographics of the majority of the LGBTQ population in South Florida. While there may well be LGBTQ communities along the West Coast of Florida and in the Central region, it is simply not part of the region of our study. Also, we are aware there is a strong LGBTQ population centered in Tampa/St. Pete as well as in Orlando, and we encourage them to create their own "Last Call" book. In fact, the authors hope that this book stimulates research for a "Last Call" book in any area with an active LGBTQ community, for it is truly in the bars that our history is written. How many community agencies and events started with an idea jotted on a bar napkin? The queer bars were the community centers of our past and we must record their histories.

A Few Words About Terminology

Obviously, the acronym LGBTQ did not come into widespread use until the 21st century. Before that, it was either "gay" or "lesbian," or when the two communities worked and played together it was "gay and lesbian." Trans and bi people were folded into gay or lesbian groups. Gay has been used as a code word for those who were "queer," which was often used as a pejorative term, but also used by members of the community itself. In the late 1980s and '90s, the term queer was reclaimed and now many people use that term to include almost everyone on the spectrum of LGBTQI (Lesbian, Gay, Bisexual, Trans, Queer and/or Questioning, and Intersex). For our purposes, we use queer as an all-encompassing word and use gay to refer to men, lesbians to refer to women, and trans to refer to anyone on the trans spectrum, from transgender to transsexuals, to drag queens. None of these are used pejoratively, but to match the terminology of the times. For the most part, when referring to the entire community, we use LGBTQ.

PALM BEACH COUNTY
MORE DIVERSE THAN YOU KNOW

Say "Palm Beach," and images suddenly appear of white beachfront mansions, elegant parties around the pool with handsome people dressed in fashionable summer wear, drinking cocktails mixed with top-shelf liquor, engaging in sophisticated conversations sprinkled with words like "the Hamptons," "trust fund," "Hermes," "alimony," "San Moritz," and "Davos."

And yes, there is that Palm Beach. But Palm Beach County is a lot more. In 2022 population of 1.5 million people, a large city (West Palm Beach 2022 population 118,000), thousands of acres of sugarcane farmed by Haitian farmworkers, a large fine arts center hosting operas, symphonies, and Broadway shows, and a lot of bars and clubs. In contrast to other South Florida counties, its core business is not tourism, but real estate development and agriculture. The county is divided between North and South Counties. South County (Boca Raton and Delray) has more in common vibe, beach-wise, and weather-wise, with Fort Lauderdale; while North County leans towards central Florida.

Palm Beach was the first developed area in South Florida when Henry Flagler built a luxury hotel on the barrier island Palm Beach and a railroad to connect it to his hotels farther north and later to Miami. Across from the hotel on the mainland, he built housing for the staff who serviced the small wealthy Palm Beach population. However, that area quickly grew to become West Palm Beach. And for those people not on the triple-A list, that is where most of the action is.

Several things make Palm Beach County distinctive. It was the first county after the 1977 Anita Bryant campaign in Miami to pass a law protecting lesbians and gay men from discrimination (1990). It was the first county in South Florida to elect a gay Republican (Mark Foley) to Congress (although he didn't last long after word got out). In 2023 Lake Worth Beach was the first city in the state to become an LGBTQ "sanctuary city." It is one of the few places to hold an International Gay Polo Tournament and where a lesbian mayor owned a bar. No matter where you are, it is not uncommon to run into various celebrities. Previously many of the performers at the Burt Reynolds Theater, including Carol Burnett, Charles Nelson Reilly, Farrah Fawcett, Eartha Kitt, Shelley Berman, Ned Beatty, Vincent Gardenia, Kirstie Alley, Elliott Gould, Robert Hays, Marilu Henner, Alice Ghostley, Ossie Davis, and Robert Urich could be seen in many of the elegant restaurants and bars in Palm Beach and West Palm Beach.

In contrast to the two other South Florida major counties, Palm Beach County was slow in developing a visible LGBTQ presence. No doubt several wealthy older men in Palm Beach, many of whom gathered on Thursday evenings in the bar at the Colony Hotel, an elegant pink edifice built in 1947, had healthy, attractive, young male wards. In the 1960s and 1970s, when the county's population doubled, bars started to appear for people "in the know."

Compared to Dade and Broward, the bar culture in Palm Beach progressed slowly and was further hampered with the completion of I-95 which drew a lot of the bar business down to Fort Lauderdale. However, one bar, HG Rooster's, stands as a model of the role bars play in the queer community. HG Rooster's was opened in Southwest Palm Beach in 1984 on the site of Turf West, a gay bar dating back to the 1950s. Aside from quickly establishing itself as a popular gathering place for gay men in Palm Beach County, many of the Palm Beach County efforts to confront the AIDS epidemic had their origins in the bar. The bar hosted fundraisers for people with AIDS and various AIDS community organizations. It also raised money for Toys for Tots and campaigns against breast cancer. Its staff helped organize Palm Beach County's first Pride Celebration in 1992. Because of the COVID epidemic, the bar was closed in March 2020, but the owner, AJ Wesson kept the staff on the payroll to do cleaning and repairs. The owner used the $50,000 earmarked for the insurance to pay the employees. Unfortunately, a pile of rags with linseed oil combusted, and started a fire that burned the entire building down. Rebuilding was going to cost $500,000-$750,000 which Wesson did not have.

Because of the bar's cherished place in the community's heart, a GoFundMe campaign raised more than $70,000. The West Palm Beach Firefighters Union donated $9,100. Then, completing an effort it started before the fire, the West Palm Beach City Council voted to designate the bar a "Historical Site" because of its role in the development of the LGBTQ community. It is only the third gay bar so designated in the nation.

Wesson said, "The silver lining in all of this is we knew how much we loved our community, but until the fire we never knew or fully understood how much our community loved us."

At the time this book went to press there were still no definitive plans to reopen the bar, although the building remains standing.

502 (see Club 502)

824 Lake
824 Lake, Lake Worth
Circa: 1990

A short-lived bar and restaurant. The piano bar, known as the Back Door Pub, behind the dining room, had a strong gay following.

2730 Martini Bar
2730 S. Dixie Hwy., West Palm Beach
Circa: 2004

Thursday "Carnival Nights" was a popular event, featuring the Blind Date Game and an amateur strip contest. Sunday tea dance was also a draw. Sushi Groove (see listing) would later operate out of this same location.

5101
5101 N. Dixie Hwy., West Palm Beach
Circa: 1985-2004

This neighborhood gay bar was owned and operated by the same proprietor, Doris Saferight, for more than 15 years. The longest-serving bartender, Raelynn Dawson, poured draft beers and whiskey shots for more than 14 years. All this made 5101 something of an institution. The doors opened daily at 7 a.m. and didn't close until 3 a.m.

Adam's Attic
3635 S. Dixie Hwy., West Palm Beach
Circa: 1982-1989

A neighborhood bar owned by Betty James, mayor of Cloud Lake, Palm Beach County's first openly lesbian mayor. On February 13, 1986, Ronald Dailey was stabbed in a robbery attempt as he was entering the bar. The space was also home to Orion (see listing).

Alibi
255 Worth Ave., Palm Beach
Circa: 1965

The bar dates back to WWII but became a gay hangout as Worth Ave. declined in popularity in the 1960s.

Amore
Dixie Hwy., Lake Worth
Circa: 2000-2002

It was a women's hangout with a pool table or two, a bar, and tables along one wall. Judy Ireland remembers it as being "fun and casual."

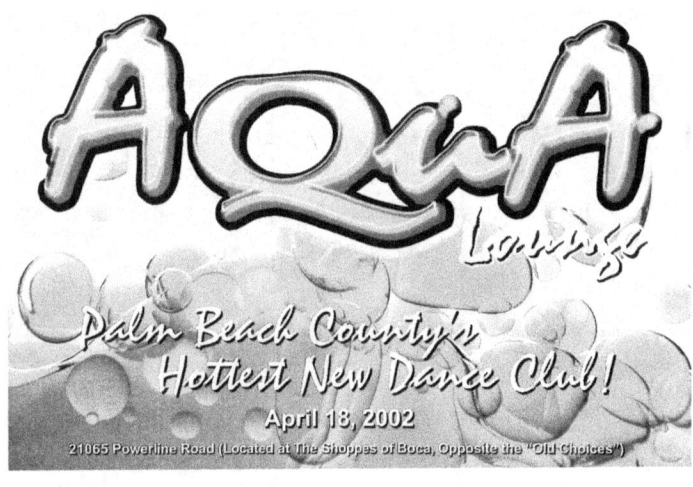

Aqua Lounge
21065 Powerline Rd., Boca Raton
Circa: 2000–2003

Thursday's "Malebox" party was the gay night at this mostly straight club.

Artie's North
5004 S. Dixie Hwy., West Palm Beach
Circa: 1989–1991

A women's bar, it was an offshoot of Artie's South. This space was also home to Crane's Nest, Leather & Spurs, and Ms. Behavin' (see listings).

Artie's South
5700 S. Dixie Hwy., West Palm Beach
Circa: 1987–1995

A men's neighborhood bar.

Bacchus
502 Lucerne Ave., Lake Worth
Circa: 1999

A dance and piano bar, it was renamed the Birdcage Cabaret in 1999 before closing in 2000 and reopening as NuBar. It was also home to Club 502 (see listing).

Bar
2211 N. Dixie Hwy., Lake Worth
Circa: 2008–2013

Owned by Penny Johnson, of Penny's at the Duke. Johnson was a bartender at Carol Moran's New Moon and Kicks in Broward County (see listings) and credits Moran with teaching her everything she knows. Johnson describes the Bar: "It was a very small bar. We had a pool table and a tiny dance floor. It was a very welcoming place."

Barracks
5907 N. Broadway, West Palm Beach
Circa: 1981

Previously Citadel, prior changing it's name in 1981.

BG's Bar
2700 S. Dixie Hwy., West Palm Beach
Circa: 1997–2002

Men's neighborhood hangout. In April 1997, two men wearing ski masks and brandishing guns robbed the bar late at night. It appeared to be part of a string of robberies of area bars and pool halls.

Birdcage Cabaret
502 Lucerne Ave., Lake Worth
Circa: 1998–1999

Club 502 was owned by Marvin Nathan, who performed at La Cage at the Riviera Hotel in Las Vegas. Nathan tried to transform the bar into a female impersonation show lounge and cabaret, but the concept never took off. The bar changed its name to Bacchus in 1999 before closing in 2000 and reopening as NuBar. It was also home to Club 502 (see listing).

Bleachers
501 Village Blvd., West Palm Beach
Circa: 1990

A cruising bar.

Blondie's
1929 N. Federal Hwy., Boca Raton
Circa: 1989–1992

Pool tournaments were popular at this neighborhood hangout.

Boss
1900 Okeechobee Rd., West Palm Beach
Circa: 2001–2002

It was popular with a Latin crowd and male strippers. Scandal Dance Club (see listing) was also located there.

Bourbon Street
1201 N. Dixie Hwy., West Palm Beach
Circa: 1984–1989

Opened as Bourbon Street (1984-1988), a dance club and piano bar featured the "best light show in the Palm Beaches." In 1989 the bar closed for remodeling and re-opened as Decadence (see listing), which would have drag shows.

Café Prospect
3111 S. Dixie Hwy., West Palm Beach
Circa: 1998

It was more of a restaurant than a bar, but in the '80s and early '90s, it hosted many AIDS fundraisers and held a drag brunch.

Carnival Bar
137 NE. 3rd Ave., West Palm Beach
Circa: 1960

A satellite of the Miami club. Dale Carter was a popular female impersonator who appeared at the club. He was killed in a car accident in 1970 and entertainers from around the area held a benefit to help support Carter's mother.

Casbar
4619 Okeechobee Rd., West Palm
Circa: 1991–1994

A men's dance, video, and cruise bar, some leather.

Chez 421
421 Lake Blvd., West Palm Beach
Circa: 1996–1998

Restaurant, bar, dancing, and entertainment mixed—men and women.

Choices
21073 Powerline Rd., Boca Raton
Circa: 1990–1998

Neighborhood spot with a small dance floor, cabaret, and karaoke.

Citadel
5907 N. Broadway, West Palm Beach
Circa: 1977–1980

Graham Brunk wrote in *South Florida Gay News*, "Palm Beach's only gay owned and operated discotheque. Remembered for its "earthquake-like" speakers with tunes spun by DJ Richard. The club, being within walking distance of the Port of Palm Beach, was frequented by sailors coming into port. By the time disco died, so did this place." It changed its name to Barracks in 1981, shortly before closing.

Club 502
502 Lucerne Ave., Lake Worth
Circa: 1996–2001

This bar featured a large dance floor. It changed its name numerous times, trying Club Betamax for a few months, then reverting to Club 502, then Bacchus, then the Birdcage, home of the Birdcage Cabaret and Birdcage Review with female impersonators in 1999. In 2001 it hosted a production of "Grease With A Twist" by Parrot Cove Productions. It closed

soon afterward with plans to open as NuBar, but there is no evidence it ever did.

Club AJ's
6 S. J St., Lake Worth
Circa: 2006–2008

Danny remembers it as, "a cruisy bar, lots of bathroom action." That is backed up by this comment from Bud. "The lights are dark, the boys are hot, the bartenders are half naked, the bathroom is a jackoff fest, and the bar is all about touching and playing." This location also housed Dug Rocks, Inn Exile, Mister Sisters, and Silver Dollar (see listings).

Club Malibu aka Club Metropolis
Polo Grounds Mall at Summit Blvd and Military Trail, West Palm Beach
Circa: 1985–1992

It originally opened as an alcohol-free teen club open three nights a week, according to an article in *The Palm Beach Post* in 1986. Graham Brunk remembers, "...it not only occupied a huge space but had some groundbreaking performances, one being a chart-topping European Group—Baltimora performed its hit 1985 song 'Tarzan Boy' in this club one night in April 1986."

At some point, it transitioned to an adult club. *The Miami Sun-Sentinel* described the bar in an article in 1992: "The mirror-laden, chalk-white interior of Club Malibu beckons a lively, well-manicured 25-to-45 crowd gyrating to a familiar hodgepodge of Top-40 and dance hits."

Club San Francisco
2209 Belvedere Rd., West Palm Beach
Circa: 1983-1984

"William H. Craton changed his bar from a redneck country bar overnight. He hired two gay male bartenders. After a couple of years, he turned it back again," remembers Pam Folsom. "It sat just outside the city limits and across the street from Palm Beach International Airport. At this time being outside the city meant they could stay open longer."

It had a very successful first few months as Palm Beach's primary gay dance venue in early 1983.

Colony Hotel (Polo bar)
736 Ocean Dr., Palm Beach
Circa: 1947-2020

The hotel bar was a gathering for dressy, upper-class, Palm Beach gays on Thursdays from 5-8 p.m. In Palm Beach society, older wealthy gay men would introduce their current young love interest as their "nephews." But, at the Colony, all pretenses were dropped. That lasted until March 2008, when, according to an article in the March 23 edition of *The Palm Beach Post*, the new general manager Roger Everingham, began to make the older gentleman and their "companions" feel not so welcome. First by roping off a section of the bar that they were confined to, and then by enforcing dress codes, once turning away an extremely wealthy patron for wearing a cashmere V-neck sweater instead of a shirt with a collar. It took several years, but by 2020, the unofficial gay night was all but a memory, and after the COVID pandemic, it disappeared altogether.

Crane's Nest
5004 S. Dixie Hwy., West Palm Beach
Circa: 1984-1987

Betty James, who also owned Adam's Attic, owned this women's bar. She was Palm Beach County's first openly lesbian elected official. This space was also home to Artie's North, Leather & Spurs, and Ms. Behavin' (see listings).

Cupid's (Cabaret)
4430 Forrest Hill Dr., West Palm Beach
Circa: 1999-2007

The only full-frontal male strip club to ever exist in the Palm Beaches. It was registered with the state as being owned by Michael Goelz and appears not to be affiliated with the Miami club of the same name. It often advertised special appearances by porn stars such as Adam Hart and Dick Masters. Its closing party ad ran in 2007. The bar dropped Cabaret from its name in 2001.

Dakota Lounge
3051 Broadway, West Palm Beach
Circa: 1995-early 2000s

A men's neighborhood bar

Decadence
1201 N. Dixie Hwy., West Palm Beach
Circa: 1989-1992

Opened as Bourbon Street (1984-1988, see listing), a dance club and piano bar featured the "best light show in the Palm Beaches." In 1989 it closed for remodeling and re-opened as Decadence, which would have drag shows.

Dillons
5509 W. Broadway, West Palm Beach
Circa: 1983-1988

The bar was slated to be a bathhouse called Studds. After community complaints, the city refused to grant a certificate of occupancy. The owners opened a "straight" club (Club 5509). As soon as it opened, it changed to a gay bar and was renamed Dillons.

Dolce
3097 Forest Hill Blvd., West Palm Beach
Circa: 2009

It was mixed, men and women, and featured dancing and drag shows. In 2008, *The Sun-Sentinel* described it as a "High-energy gay dance club that caters to hot men and sexy ladies. Wednesday is ladies' night. Thursday is Latin night, and Sunday features hip-hop." Dolce later opened as Karma (see listing).

Dude County
520 Forest Hill Blvd., West Palm Beach
Circa: 1976-1978

A hole-in-the-wall bar in an octagonal-shaped building.

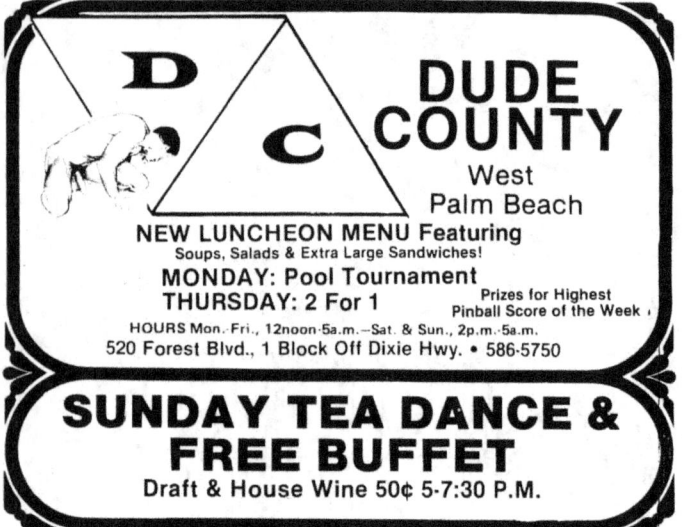

D C DUDE COUNTY
West Palm Beach
NEW LUNCHEON MENU Featuring
Soups, Salads & Extra Large Sandwiches!
MONDAY: Pool Tournament
THURSDAY: 2 For 1 Prizes for Highest Pinball Score of the Week
HOURS Mon.-Fri., 12noon-5a.m.-Sat. & Sun., 2p.m.-5a.m.
520 Forest Blvd., 1 Block Off Dixie Hwy. • 586-5750

SUNDAY TEA DANCE & FREE BUFFET
Draft & House Wine 50¢ 5-7:30 P.M.

Dug Rocks
6 S. J St., Lake Worth
Circa: 2001-2005

Doug Tesoro owned this location, which was also home to Club AJ's, Inn Exile, Mister Sisters, and Silver Dollar (see listings). The space is now home to the straight club Propaganda, which occasionally hosts drag shows.

Enigma
109 N. Olive Ave., West Palm Beach
Circa: 1994-2001

A dance club run by Carlos Garcia, Vinny Decaprio and Jack Montalbano. The upstairs was described as an S&M biker bar, with another room as Louis the XIV dripping in purple velvet. In April 1996, the club held a "Disco Inferno—A Return to the '70s" party as a benefit for the Comprehensive AIDS Project of Palm Beach County. The house DJs were David Knapp and David Padilla. This space was home to LGBTQ clubs since the 1980s, including Krome, and PB's (see listings).

ENIGMA
WORLD CLASS NIGHT CLUB
WHITE DREAMS
THE AFTER PARTY
July 29, 1995
Doors Open 9 PM
HITE H4T
THE PARTY OF PARTIES
join
ADORA
BRUCE SUTKA STAFF
And all the White Hot Dancers & Entertainers!!!
THE AFTER PARTY...DON'T MISS IT!!!
ENIGMA · 109 North Olive Avenue · 3/4 Mile North of Okeechobee Blvd.
832-5040
FREE ADMISSION WITH WHITE HOT TICKET

Fantasies
1935 NE 20th St., Boca Raton
Circa: 1986-1989

OPEN SEVEN DAYS
3 PM to 2 AM
FANTASIES'
... the friendliest bar around...
MONDAY
Pool Tournament
TUESDAY
BEST 2-4-1 Around Dancing 10-2
WEDNESDAY
F.A.U. Night
THURSDAY
Corona Bust
FRIDAY
Wheel of Fortune 5 p.m. Dancing 10-2
SATURDAY
Dancing 10-2
DAILY HAPPY HOUR
3 p.m. to 9 p.m.
495 N.E. 20th STREET   BOCA RATON
(Northwest corner of Federal Highway and 20th Street)
395-0303

Disco, mixed men/women. It was a popular bar with Florida Atlantic University faculty and staff, particularly on Tuesday nights.

Flamingo Club
Flamingo Dr., West Palm Beach
Circa: 1945

It was known for drag shows, mostly straight clientele. On September 16, 1946, *The Palm Beach Post* raved, "There has never been an audience reaction as emphatic as the one last night, at the gay Flamingo Club, which welcomed it as a 'in-demand' show..."

FRI
SAT
SUN

10 PM
TIL
5 AM

JOIN THE PARTY
ALL WEEKEND LONG
FRIDAY & SATURDAY
Sounds: Jim Horne
Sights: Kenny & Joey

SUNDAY
MADNESS TURNS TO CRAZE
BAD BOYS NIGHT OUT
WITH THE MEN OF MANPOWER
$1.75 WELL DRINKS

THE FLAMINGO CLUB • EIGHT SIXTEEN MILITARY TRAIL • CORNER OF SUMMIT BLVD. POLO GROUNDS SHOPPING MALL • WEST PALM BEACH • 471-7640

Flip for It
317 Clematis Ave., West Palm Beach
Circa: 2009

Gay on Wednesdays only, men, dancing

Forest Disco
3745 S. Military Trail, Lake Worth
Circa: 1977-1979

It was mostly a young crowd. Historian Graham Brunk said, "As disco died, their business did too. They started offering drag shows to attract LGBTQ clientele."

Fort Dix
6205 Georgia Ave., West Palm Beach
Circa: 2007-2019

Mostly a men's bar with weekly leather nights and underwear parties. It had pool tables and would host the occasional drag show. The bar held community fundraisers for children's

charities, especially around the holidays. Formerly the site of Kozlow's (see listing).

Forum Bar & Grille
1649 Forum Pl., West Palm Beach
Circa: 1990

Fuel
708 Datura, West Palm Beach
Circa: 2004

Bob Cole and Carlos Garcia opened the bar on July 16, 2004. Wednesdays were women's night, Thursday drag queens, Friday "Latin Fever" and Sunday tea dance.

Garbo's
320 W. Federal Hwy., West Palm Beach
Circa: 1997

Heartbreaker's
2677 Forest Hill Blvd., West Palm Beach
Circa: 1991-1999

Originally a straight bar, the club's owners, Danny and Marlane Cardona, realized that going gay was profitable. The club occupied a gigantic space with a huge dance floor and a memorable sound system.

For much of the late 1990s, this was the place to go for a night out of cruising and dancing. In 1993, the bar set up a cocktail lounge, it was called Chatters. The bar achieved notoriety when two hustlers lured a man from the bar and robbed and killed him in 1995. After it closed, Throb (see listing) moved into its space.

Nikki Adams remembers that it was a wonderful place to do shows, "A very appreciative crowd."

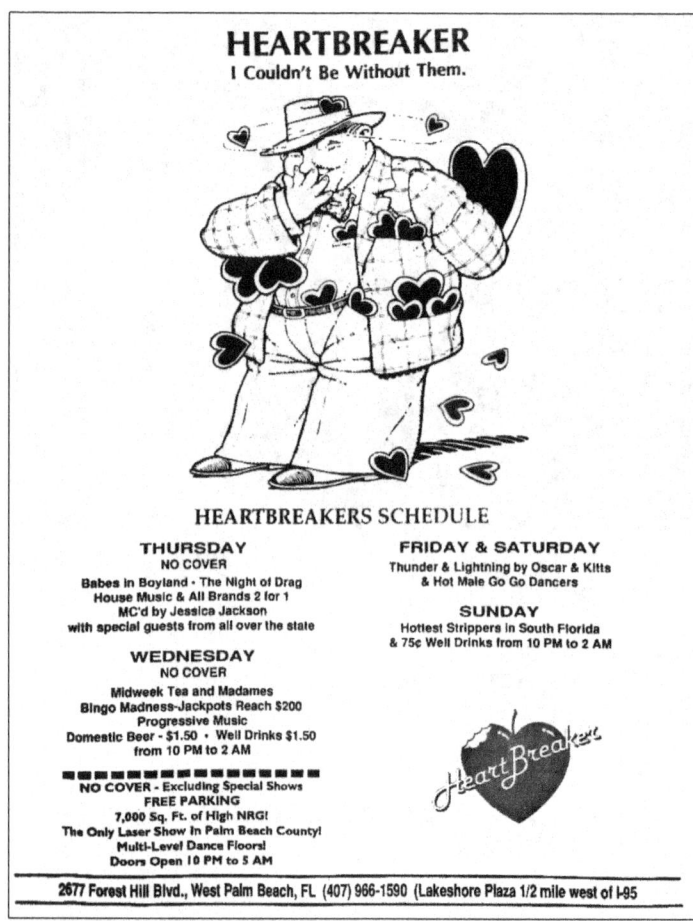

HG Rooster's
823 Belvedere Rd., West Palm Beach
Circa: 1984–2020

It was the site of gay bars going as far back as the mid-1960s. It was previously Turf West (see listing), then, for a brief time, a straight bar. Bill Capozzi and his business partner, Tom McKenzie, took over with plans for a gay bar. In 1984, HG Roosters opened. (The HG stands for Heidi and Greta, the two men's nicknames). Before Capozzi died in 2006 of pancreatic cancer, he sold the building and half the business to AJ Wasson and willed the other half to longtime manager Michael Brown. Rooster's was a cruisy bar and the site of one of the last known police raids of gay bars. The raid came after a tip from a competing bar owner that lewd behavior was taking place. Lack of evidence led to an end to police raids.

In 2008 Brown died violently when he was beaten and stabbed at his Flagler Drive condominium by a former boyfriend, according to police reports. Wasson was traveling around the country as a promoter for Live Nation and Clear Channel. And he did his best to keep the bar going without his two partners. Then COVID hit. He kept his employees on payroll cleaning and painting the bar, but when he got an insurance bill for $50,000, he had to choose between paying the bill or his employees. He let his insurance lapse. The building caught fire and burned down.

The community rallied and raised funds to help rebuild the bar—though not enough to rebuild it. In April 2021, the West Palm Beach City Commission granted Roosters a historic designation. "Roosters is far more than a bar that has catered to an LGBTQ clientele," Rand Hoch, president of the Palm Beach County Human Rights Council, said in a letter urging the city to support the designation. A plan to reopen the bar was underway as we went to press. This was also the location for My Apartment (see listing).

Hullabaloo
517 Clematis St., West Palm Beach
Circa: 2012–present

A gastropub that's so LGBTQ+ friendly that it states it right on its Facebook page. Drag shows are held every Friday after dinner service is completed. The Lounge (see listing) was previously open at this location.

Hurricane Bar
425 25th St., West Palm Beach
Circa: 1992–1993

An ad boasted, "Lyme, Richard, Gene, Jazz, and Bobby, open daily at 1 p.m."

Illusion
4340 Forest Hill Dr., West Palm Beach
Circa: 1993–1994

A women's club.

Inn Exile
6 S. J St., Lake Worth
Circa: 1989–2000

Palm Beach's first "video nightclub" featured male dancers. It was an outpost of one of Chicago's longest-running gay bars (the Chicago location closed at the beginning of the COVID pandemic of 2019-2020). Bass, now located in Washington, DC, remembers visiting Inn Exile, his first gay bar, "I was 17 and went in, had a Coke, and left. I was there all of 15 minutes, but I left shaking and screaming in my car because I did it and couldn't wait to go back!" This location also housed Club AJ's, Dug Rocks, Mister Sisters, and Silver Dollar (see listings).

Jackson Hart's Bar & Grille
2930 Military Trail, West Palm Beach
Circa: 2009–2010

Jeffrey's
29 S. Dixie Hwy., Lake Worth
Circa: 1998–2003

Jeffrey's was started by a bartender at Kathy's, who kept the bar after Kathy opened her new bar, K&E's (see listing), two doors away. The bars' openings overlapped.

Joe and Craig's Place
6898 Powerline Rd., Boca Raton
Circa: 2007-2010

A men's bar with country dancing.

K&E's
29 S. Dixie Hwy., Lake Worth
Circa: 1994-2001

Mostly women, sometimes called II Doors Down or II Doors South. K&E were Kathy & Elaine. Kathy had owned Kathy's Place (see listing), and they moved the bar to a new location two doors down from her place to open their joint venture.

Pam Folsom recalls, "There was a big women's music scene, and we would have people play there."

Karma
3097 Forest Hill Blvd., West Palm Beach
Circa: 2011

Dolce was also listed at this address (see listing).

Kashmir
1651 S. Congress Ave., West Palm Beach
Circa: 2000-2018

In its prime, it was Palm Beach County's premier gay dance venue and probably the last major successful one to exist. Previously home to SIN (see listing).

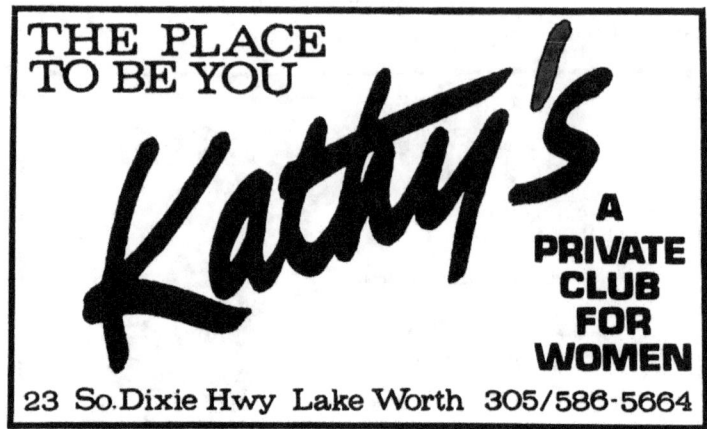

Kathy's (Place)
23 S. Dixie Hwy., Lake Worth
Circa: 1977-1989

Listed as both Kathy's and Kathy's Place, it was a women's bar, "Built by wimmin for wimmin," Kathy was a popular bartender at the Tap Room (see listing) before she opened her own place. Pam Folsom remembers that Kathy was always ready to help women in need, especially younger women, who had been thrown out of their homes. Kathy would later partner with Elaine to open K&E's (see listing), sometimes listed as II Doors Down (see listing) because it was two doors away from her old bar.

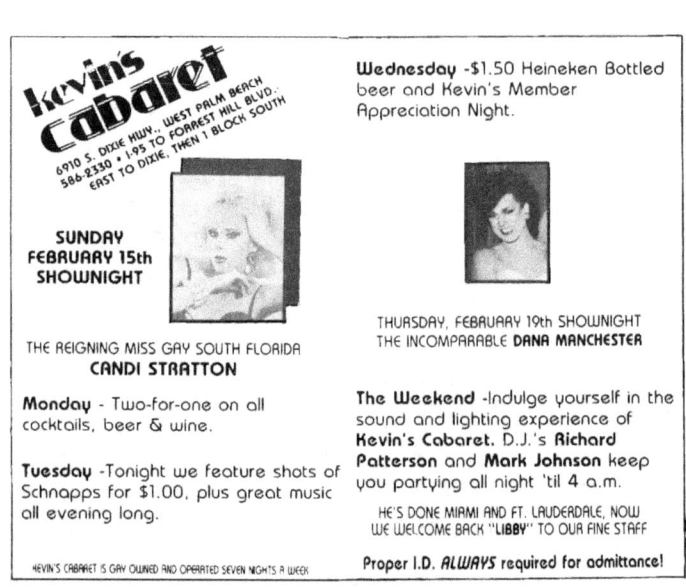

Kevin's Cabaret
6910 S. Dixie Hwy., West Palm Beach
Circa: 1983-1992

It was originally named Le Cabaret (see listing) and then went straight for a while before reopening as Kevin's Cabaret. Kevin's is remembered for its midnight drag shows featuring performers such as Melissa St. John, Dana Manchester, and Brandie McDaniels and the sounds of DJ Mark Johnson.

Kismet South
1412 Southern Blvd., West Palm Beach
Circa: 1978-1987

The Florida outpost of Columbus Ohio's Kismet. Mirrors, funky wall patterns, and dice hanging from the ceiling made it the ultimate '80s-era late-night spot. Alice, just billed as Alice, was a popular drag performer there. Pam Folsom recalls, "There were a lot of swingers that would come to the bar, a well-known socialite would come in looking for a girl for three ways."

Kozlow's
6205 Georgia Ave., West Palm Beach
Circa: 1988-2003

KOZLOW'S

A Favorite Neighborhood Club
and Patio Bar

**Proudly Entering Our
5th Successful Season!**

"Where Friends Meet"

**6205 Georgia Ave.
West Palm Beach
(407) 533-5355**

Country and western themed, later site of Fort Dix (see listing). In 1998 *The Sun-Sentinel* reported that "Bradford Lemire of Lake Worth, was found in his 1993 Mercury in the parking lot outside Kozlow's Bar. Patrons in the bar, responding to gunshots, found Lemire shot several times in the mid-section. He was rushed to St. Mary's Hospital where he later died. Patrons told police they saw two young men, thought to be in their teens or early 20s running from the scene."

Owner Mark Kozlowski was willing to cooperate with the FBI and police when they were searching for Versace's killer, Andrew Cunanan, in Palm Beach, but said, "We haven't heard anything and haven't seen posters anywhere," when interviewed by *The Palm Beach Post*.

Krome
109 Olive Ave., West Palm Beach
Circa: 1999-2001

Perhaps giving your club the same name as one of the most notorious detention centers in South Florida isn't the best business decision, even if it sounds like a cool way to spell chrome. The first floor featured techno music on a large dance floor, black lights, and a smoke machine with a large bar. There was also a piercing station. Upstairs a central catwalk allowed folks to look down on the dance floor or head into two smaller bars—one featured hip-hop and the other retro dance music.

This space was also home to Enigma and PB's (see listings).

Leather & Spurs
5004 S. Dixie Hwy., West Palm Beach
Circa: 1997-2001

A leather bar. This was also home to Artie's North, Crane's Nest, and Ms. Behavin' (see listing).

LIFE IS

Le **CABARET**

THE SOUTH'S NEWEST AND BEST SHOWBAR AND DISCOTHEQUE

"Here Life is Beautiful"

BECAUSE

* 500 sq. ft. lighted dance floor!

* Fantastic neon pinwheels & strobes!

* THE BEST SOUND SYSTEM IN FLORIDA!

* 3 full service bars!

* Ample lighted parking!

* Silver lame show stage!

* Upper level lounge & game room!

DANCE DANCE DANCE

TIL 5:00 A.M. 7 DAYS!

Come to *Le Cabaret* in

WEST PALM BEACH

6910 So. Dixie (U.S. 1)   305-588-3751

Leather & Spurs
5812 S. Dixie Hwy., West Palm Beach
Circa: 2002-2004

The leather bar moved a few blocks down the street, James Rosa owned both.

Le Cabaret
6910 S. Dixie Hwy., West Palm Beach
Circa: 1975-1981

An ad in *David Magazine* from 1975 read, "Le Cabaret is a GAY discotheque and show bar operated for the GAY people of South Florida and their friends." In May 1976, Cruella DeVille hosted the Mr. Sweet Cheeks Contest. According to *The Palm Beach Post* of Aug. 7, 1975, "Le Cabaret cannot be described as sophisticated. It does, however, have...the most comprehensive sound and lighting system and is according to one of its owners, Christian Gonyea, 75% gay and 25% straight. ...Le Cabaret also has the most equal number of blacks and whites..."

Six weeks after it opened the bar was attacked by an arsonist who poured gasoline down an air duct and then set it aflame. It ignited immediately using up all the oxygen before it could do much damage. Later home to Kevin's Cabaret (see listing)

Le Club
1900 Broadway, Riviera Beach
Circa: 1980

Previously home to a popular straight bar, Captain Alex's Lounge. New owners reopened it as a gay bar, featuring a piano bar and cabaret, but it did not last long.

Lido
420 Ocean Blvd., Palm Beach
Circa: 1964-1965

Lifestylez
4430 Forest Hill Blvd., West Palm Beach
Circa: 2007

A "watch for opening" ad ran in a 2007 *Buzz Magazine*. There is no evidence that it ever opened. This was the former location of Cupid's Cabaret (see listing).

Lilo's
701 Lake Ave., Lake Worth
Circa: 2017-present

While Lilo's is primarily a restaurant, the Library is a section in the back that provides a much different, speakeasy-style environment for people to enjoy special craft drinks. While not exclusively LGBTQ, Lilo's is a longstanding and steadfast ally of the LGBTQ community, hosting regular fundraisers for groups such as Compass Community Center and the Imperial Sun Court of All Florida. Lindsay Lipovich is the co-owner and general manager.

Lounge
517 Clematis Ave., West Palm Beach
Circa: 2008-2010

Hullabaloo (see listing) would later open at this location.

Lou's Pub
4316 Parker Ave., West Palm Beach
Circa: 1981

Lulu's Place
640 Atlantic Ave., Delray Beach
Circa: 1999-2020

Owned by real estate broker Terry Eichas, it was a piano bar, that served food and specialized in martinis. It closed during the COVID pandemic.

Mad Hatter
1532 N. Dixie Hwy., Lake Worth
Circa: 1999-present

The bar was known for cheap drinks and offered free pool. It did not originally open as a gay bar, but when Ron Amodo became owner in 1999, he reached out to a gay clientele. It featured a mixed crowd of gay men and lesbians. One of the patrons says, "Jimmy Z is a top-tier bartender. He has shown dedication to the bar by being dunked in a water booth, participating in several Pride Parades, raising money for several causes, and treating everyone like family."

Gay Travel reported, "It's all about happy hour drinks and bar games at this laid-back dive joint with friendly locals to chat up."

Matthew S. described why he enjoys the bar as a "super low-key and super fun gay bar in Lake Worth. Friendly crowd and a busy place full of friendly gay men."

Malibu's
750 Military Trail Rd., Delray Beach
Circa: 1990-1993

A young crowd favored this after-hours club.

Man's Country/Man's Land
508 W. 25th St., West Palm Beach
Circa: 1976-1979/1979-1994

The bar featured go-go boys and was popular. It had to change its name after a lawsuit by a similarly named California bar. It was open until 6 a.m. daily, and it had leather nights, roller skating tournaments, and the Mr. West Palm Beach contest. It had a backyard with trees that had slings for sex. Lisa Caprice hosted the Mr. Man's Country contest in June of 1976.

In 1994, shortly after a shooting at the bar, it lost its liquor license. The business went downhill, and it tried running as a "dry" bar. It closed shortly thereafter.

Mata Hari's
630 Okeechobee Rd., West Palm Beach
Circa: 1987-1988

Although it ended up as a women's bar, it was previously home to the Okeechobee Bar in the '70s (see listing).

Melody Club
318 1st St., West Palm Beach
Circa: 1947–1955

The club featured drag shows for a mostly straight clientele. One ad read, "Direct from Pinnochio's (sic) in 'Frisco...the zaniest, the funniest and the most exotic show in Palm Beach County."

Mister Sisters (aka Myster Sisters)
6 S. J St., Lake Worth
Circa: 1985–1989

This was a women's bar. The location also housed AJ's, Dug Rocks, Inn Exile, and Silver Dollar (see listings).

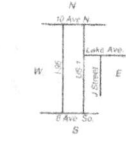

Mojito's/Revolution
129 N. Federal Hwy., Lake Worth
Circa: 2011–2012

Mostly straight, Friday was gay night.

Monarchy
221 Clematis Rd., Lake Worth
Circa: 2011–2012

Still open, but no longer a gay bar.

Ms. Behavin'
5004 S. Dixie Hwy., West Palm Beach
Circa: 1992

A neighborhood bar, the tagline was "Your women's club in the Palm Beaches." It sponsored softball games and pool tournaments. Also listed at this address were Artie's North, Crane's Nest, and Leather & Spurs (see listings).

Music Box Lounge (Bill's)
628 Lake Ave., Lake Worth
Circa: 1968–1984

The neighborhood bar had an easy and relaxed atmosphere. In the '70s it was popular with a young crowd. Piano background music and a pool table were the usual entertainment, plus the occasional amateur drag show. The bar closed soon after owner Bill Brunet passed away in 1983.

MY APARTMENT

KEY CLUB

823 BELVEDERE ROAD, WEST PALM BEACH

FLORIDA'S MOST UNIQUE KEY CLUB

My Apartment
823 Belvedere Rd., West Palm Beach
Circa: 1971

A private key club, it was previously home to Turf West and later to HG Rooster's (see listings).

New York Comedy Club
8221 Glades Rd., Boca Raton
Circa: 2008-2012

Nightstalker
3516 S. Dixie Hwy., West Palm Beach
Circa: 1983

A cruisy bar that attracted a young crowd.

Novello's Upstairs Bar
221 Datura St., West Palm Beach
Circa: 1977

Located in the Guaranty Building, it was owned by Gene Greeter, who also owned the Turf bars. Turf South (see listing) was on the first floor.

NuBar (see Club 502)

Okeechobee Bar
630 Okeechobee Rd., West Palm Beach
Circa: 1975

Mixed straight and gay. Later home to Mata Hari's (see listing).

Orion
3635 S. Dixie Hwy., West Palm Beach
Circa: 1975-1981

Described by *Cruise Magazine* as a "space age disco" in 1979. Later home to Adam's Attic (see listing).

Other Place
736 Belvedere Rd., West Palm Beach
Circa: 1973-1975

A small club with a tiny dance floor attracted a mixed crowd of women and men. Pam Folsom remembers, "A keyboard player at Burt Reynolds' theater in Jupiter brought a bunch of us up to Burt's ranch to watch them stud a bull. Dinah Shore was there, and she was kind of into the women."

Paradise Club,
1745 NW. 2nd. Ave., Boca Raton
Circa: 1993-1996

In early 1994, four members of the Boca Raton Rugby Club, including an assistant state's attorney, dressed in women's clothing and drunk, marched into the bar and began tearing it apart and throwing stuff at its patrons while screaming vulgar terms. They were arrested and it was the first time a crime against the LGBTQ community in Palm Beach County was recognized as a "hate crime" in court.

PB's
109 Olive Ave., West Palm Beach
Circa: 1979-1980

Polly (sometimes identified as Paula) Butler owned this dance club that catered to men but was women-friendly. It held a benefit for the National Lung Association during its opening

109 N. Olive Ave., West Palm Beach, Fla.
833-3731   833-3732
COMING ATTRACTIONS

PB's

THIS SUNDAY JULY 27th 12:30 A.M.

PLAYBOY OF THE MONTH
Trophy and Cash Prizes

THURSDAY, JULY 31st
NEW YEAR'S EVE PARTY
With PB's own
ESME TORRES
KIM CORRELL &
MICHELLE DEE
12:30 Show

Coming July 22nd
ALL NEW SUPPER MENU

SPOTLIGHT RESTAURANT
OPEN 9 P.M. - 4 A.M.
Serving Supper and an early breakfast from midnight til 4 A M

NO COVER
FREE PARKING
CLOSED MONDAY

week in May 1979. It had live shows on Sundays, and DJs five nights a week. The décor was described in *The Palm Beach Post* as "Basic black and red wall under high warehouse ceilings." Charles Nelson Reilly used to hang out here when he worked at

Burt Reynolds' Theater in Jupiter. This space was also home to Enigma and Krome (see listings).

Penny's at the Duke
902 Dixie Hwy., Lantana
Circa: 2013–2021

The Duke has been a bar since the 1940s, each owner retaining the name. When Penny Johnson bought it, she was asked to keep the name, but she wanted to personalize it, hence "Penny's at the Duke." Johnson describes it as "a place for everyone. Some may think of it as a women's bar, but we welcomed everyone, men, women, gay and straight. We had a group of

The Duke bar, circa 1940s

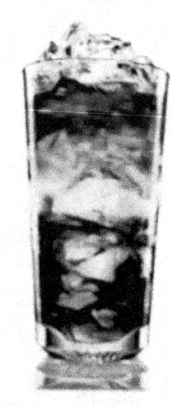

at the Duke

A Place Where Everyone is Family
902 North Dixie Highway
Lantana, FL 33462
find us on facebook @PennysAtTheDuke

leather guys that hosted a leather night once a month. And when HG Rooster's had a fire and had to close, we hired some of their bartenders for a weekly Rooster's party."

When Penny Johnson bought the bar she decorated it with pennies, using them as floor tile and to cover the bar and front

of the stage. Johnson sold it when her rent increased and a California company, wanting her liquor license, made her, as she put it, "An offer she couldn't refuse."

Platforms
99 SE. 1st Ave., Boca Raton
Circa: 2010–2020

Mostly straight, but LGBTQ-friendly, it featured music of '70s-'90s.

Players
2000 S. Dixie Hwy., West Palm Beach
Circa: 1997–1998

Pub
1927 N. Federal Hwy., Boca Raton
Circa: 2008

Mostly men, a dance bar.

GRAND OPENING
Announcing the Grand Opening of
Respectable Street Cafe,
A Restaurant and Night Club,
Featuring Progressive Music,
in the Heart of Downtown
West Palm Beach
FRIDAY, JUNE 5, 1987
From 9:00 p.m. until 4:00 a.m.

Respectable Street Café
518 Clematis St., West Palm Beach
Circa: 1987–present

Opened in 1987, the first location was in an old 1920s Salvation Army building. It hosts bands, and how gay it is, depends upon the entertainment. Despite the name, it is primarily a bar. Since its opening, this South Florida institution has hosted more than 1000 live acts including the Red Hot Chili Peppers, The Damned, and The Misfits. While not LGBTQ, it is all-welcoming, all the time.

Ricky's Place
3240 S. Dixie Hwy., West Palm Beach
Circa: 1975–1984

A cruisy disco, mixed gay and straight.

Scandal Dance Club
1900 Okeechobee Blvd., West Palm Beach
Circa: 2002–2007

A late-night/after-hours club, formerly home to Boss (see listing).

Silver Dollar Lounge
6 S. J St., West Palm Beach
Circa: 1984

Most notable for having a customer bring home a trick who murdered him by stabbing him multiple times on his waterbed. This location was also home to Club AJ's, Dug Rocks, Inn Exile, and Mister Sisters.

SIN
1651 Congress Ave., West Palm Beach
Circa: 1999-2000

A short-lived dance club, later home to Kashmir (see listing). This is now the location of a Conviva Care Center.

Sneakers
331 N. Dixie Hwy., Lake Worth
Circa: 2015-2017

Neighborhood bar, gay friendly.

Spanky's
320 N. Federal Hwy., Delray Beach
Circa: 1993-1995

A neighborhood hang-out.

Sushi Groove
2730 S. Dixie Hwy., West Palm Beach
Circa: 2009

Mostly straight dance club, but Sunday was gay night. Martini Bar (see listing) operated at this location at an earlier date.

Ta-Boo
221 Worth Ave., Palm Beach
Circa: 1959-1970

Owned by Jim Peterson, it was a society hangout in the early evening, but "turned gay" as the night wore on.

Tag Bar
25 NE. 2nd Ave., Delray Beach
Circa: 2011-2012

Billed as Delray Beach's only gay bar. It featured a dance floor, video bar, piano/cabaret, and drag stage. Owned by a straight man who wanted more business. He hired Slaton Wilson, who managed Lulu's, formerly Delray's oldest and only gay bar which had closed a few years before. "We've needed a gay place in Delray since Lulu's. My Lulu's regulars are starting to come in and are becoming regulars again. It's wonderful. Happy hour is filling up and the place hits capacity practically every Thursday, Friday, and Saturday."

Tag bar had been straight before it turned gay. Some of the previous customers kept coming in and treating the gay customers rudely, so the bar never took off as a gay bar.

Tap Room Lounge
3625 Dixie Hwy., West Palm Beach
Circa: 1975-1979

It was the main women's bar when it first opened. Kathy from K&E bartended here before she opened her bar, Kathy's.

THREE O'CLOCK CLUB
Proudly Presents
HOLLYWOOD'S FAVORITE FEMALE IMPERSONATOR
MOVIELAND'S DELINEATOR OF SONG AND FASHION
The Fabulous—
MR. ADRIAN AMES
FEATURING AN ALL-STAR GIRLIE REVUE
MISS ARLETTE MOREAU
The Favorite of New Orleans French Quarter
Plus HAL HEENEY, M.C. and
MISS DUSTY CLARK — 6 ft. 4" of Loveliness
Plus Big 6 and His Orchestra For Your Dancing Music
The Greatest and Top Show Ever To Play West Palm Beach
3—Thrilling Shows Nitely—3 . . . 10:30 -- 12:00 -- 2:00
YOU'VE SEEN THE REST — NOW SEE THE BEST
MR. ADRIAN AMES   1901 No. Dixie   Phone 9193 for Reservations

Three O'clock Club
1901 N. Dixie, Lake Worth
Circa: 1949

A drag bar.

Throb
2677 Forest Hill Blvd., West Palm Beach
Circa: 1999-2001

A late-night dance club. In September 1999, it hosted the White Ball to benefit the Comprehensive AIDS Program of Palm Beach County. It was formerly home to Heartbreakers (see listing).

Town Pump
205 Datura Blvd., West Palm Beach
Circa: 1979

Attracted an older crowd, some leather. The bar was short-lived after a shooting and stabbing incident.

Turf North
1901 N. Dixie Hwy., West Palm Beach
Circa: late 1950s-1978

A neighborhood hang-out. It was owned by Gene Greeter, as were the other Turf bars. (See Turf South for more information). In 1974, a fire damaged the interior of the bar causing it to be shuttered for repairs, but it did reopen and remained in business for a few more years. From the gossip column in *David Magazine* of January 18, 1976, "The Miss

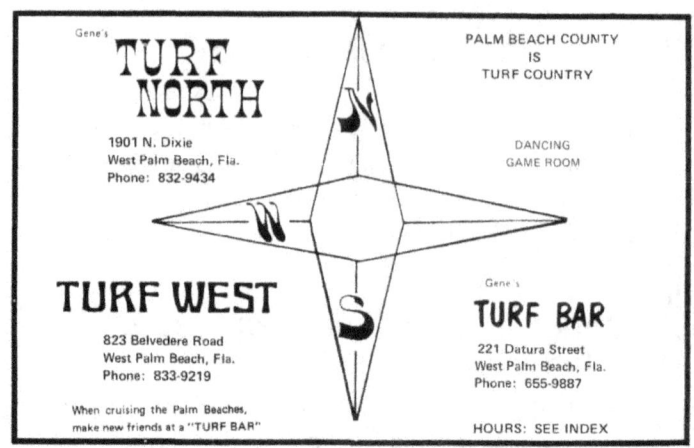

Gene's
TURF NORTH
1901 N. Dixie
West Palm Beach, Fla.
Phone: 832-9434

PALM BEACH COUNTY
IS
TURF COUNTRY

DANCING
GAME ROOM

TURF WEST
823 Belvedere Road
West Palm Beach, Fla.
Phone: 833-9219

Gene's
TURF BAR
221 Datura Street
West Palm Beach, Fla.
Phone: 655-9887

When cruising the Palm Beaches, make new friends at a "TURF BAR"

HOURS: SEE INDEX

Palm Beach contest got underweigh (sic). The crowded bar cheered for their favorite contestants, but the packed crowd chose Chi-Chi as the winner."

Turf South
221 Datura Ave., West Palm Beach
Circa: 1953-1978

Turf South was the main bar owned by Gene Greeter. It is reported that he was straight, and became an ally to the community, but an article in the February 1973 issue of *David Magazine* makes no mention of him being straight and features many pictures of him shirtless. He would be described today as a muscle bear. All three Turf bars were comfortable neighborhood hangouts. Novello's (see listing), also owned by Greeter, was located upstairs.

Turf West
823 Belvedere Rd., West Palm Beach
Circa: mid-1960s-1979

This was the last Turf location to close. My Apartment (see listing) was a separate bar upstairs of Turf West. This location became HG Roosters (see listing).

Vic & Iggy's
2258 N. Congress, Boynton Beach
Circa: 1994

Although primarily a restaurant, the cocktail lounge was a popular cruising spot, no doubt because of the two-for-one well drinks during happy hour. An ad in the July 1992 issue of

David Magazine touts "another alternative in Palm Beach County. Try Us!"

Wheel of Fortune
1330 S. Military Trail, West Palm Beach
Circa: 1989

A late-night bar, open until 5 a.m.

Woody's
208 Dixie Hwy., Lantana
Circa: 1993-1994

Zippers
308 Dixie Hwy., Lantana
Circa: 1994-1996

In 1994 an AIDS fundraiser was held at the bar. The country dance event was titled "Stompin' Out AIDS." By 1995, the owners were running classified ads to sell the bar, and by 1996 it closed.

Fred Fejes & Rick Karlin

THE GAY DECEIVERS

HIT THE GOLD COAST

Pryse Williams

Frost Martin

To many, Sunday May 9th may not be a historic date to remember. However, to those fortunate enough to be at KEITH'S CRUISE ROOM in Hallandale on this date they will long remember that evening. For this is when the great "Gay Deceivers" put on their first show in our area.

Fortunately, for us, Mr. Pryse Williams and Mr. Frost Martin, the two performers, were on vacation in Miami after completing an engagement at The International Hotel in Las Vegas, where they appeared along with Tom Jones.

Their act is strictly top show biz performance. From their Las Vegas type gowns to their unbelievable voices, when they sing their many songs.

A bit unusual is the fact that they use no recordings. Their complete show is done with only a three piece band.

Mr. Pryse Williams, who has been billed as "The Toast of Europe and U.S.A." is undoubtly now the "Double Toast of the Gold Coast."

Opening with "Hello Dolly" and "Stranger in the Night", each song takes on a suggestive meaning within the lyrical turns. In his rendition of "My Man", "If it's one thing I'm not it's a man". Then Mr. Williams goes even further to prove his point to everyone's amazement.

The wild and wacky Mr. Frost Martin does comedy routines as many have never attempted. When you hear him say "If you think the face is bad, wait till you see the body" just sit back and brace yourself for that is coming next. When Mr. Martin gets down to his bare essentials, a bra and a G–String, he still manages to produce a lolipop, a banana, and a feather duster for his admiring fans.

Keith has promised us that with the help of Mr. Tubby Boots he will have the Gay Deceiver's back in the CRUISE ROOM after their engagement in Las Vegas in approximatly six months.

For those who were not fortunate enough to see last month's show be looking for their return engagment. This show is a must to see for anyone who enjoys a professional female impersonation performance.

Article about a show at Keith's Cruise Room, Hallandale, David, June 1971

BROWARD COUNTY
LESS IS MORE

Fort Lauderdale and Broward County developed in the shadow of Miami and Palm Beach. While those cities attracted wealthy tourists who rode Flagler's railroad and stayed in his luxury hotels, Fort Lauderdale had more modest beginnings. In the 1830s it started as a short-lived fort, named after Major William Lauderdale, who led a detachment of Tennessee Volunteers in the first Seminole War.

In the 1890s it became a stop on Flagler's railroad between Miami and Palm Beach, where produce from Broward County's growing number of farms producing tomatoes, green beans, and pineapples were loaded.

Starting in the 1920s the picture changed as the newly built Dixie Highway brought a new type of tourist. Driving their new Model T automobiles, more common folk from the Midwest and Northeast began to make the trek to South Florida to enjoy the warm winter weather. Rather than staying in luxury hotels (Fort Lauderdale had none) they parked on the side of the road and set up camp. These "Tin Can Tourists," quickly created a lively scene with all-night parties in the camp. The tourist potential of Fort Lauderdale quickly became evident.

The 1920s saw a building boom, with new construction throughout South Florida. In Broward, the town of Hollywood was built, modeled after the new communities then being built in Dade. Although central and north Broward County were mainly agricultural areas, south Broward County, particularly the cities of Hallandale and Hollywood, were developing more as satellite areas of Dade County. It was there that the first signs of an LGBTQ presence were seen.

The first club featuring female impersonators, Club Ha Ha, opened in Hallandale in 1938. There one could dance with "gentle entertainers in ladies' dinner frocks and get them to stand by your table...and sing hair-raising pornographic ballads." By 1946, Club Ha Ha attracted the attention of the editor of the *Fort Lauderdale News*, which called for its closing. In 1947, the county ordered its closing because of the homosexuals in the audience. The owner took the case to the Florida Supreme Court but lost. The club then moved down to Miami. Nonetheless, another popular place, Club Aloha, offering female impersonators opened just south of Fort Lauderdale.

There was a population explosion in Broward post-WWII. The population in 1940 was 39,000; by 1970 it was 620,000. The national success of the 1960 movie *Where the Boys Are* helped to establish Fort Lauderdale as the sun and fun capital for the upcoming younger generation. The queer presence began to emerge with the population boom. In the 1960s, newspaper stories about gay bars in Broward began to appear. When members of the county PTA called for the shutting down of the bars, the county Sheriff responded, "You can't arrest a fag just for sitting in a bar having a drink."

In 1970 the nation's first all-gay winter resort hotel, The Marlin Beach, opened and quickly became the epicenter of gay life in Fort Lauderdale. In 1974 the first all-gay Caribbean cruise set sail from the city's Port Everglades. Throughout the 1970s gay bars, clubs, guest houses, motels, and restaurants were opening throughout the county. All of this was happening under the radar of Fort Lauderdale's establishment.

In 1977, perhaps emboldened by Anita Bryant's campaign in neighboring Dade County, Fort Lauderdale's mayor Clay Shaw proclaimed that "The city's gays must go," and tried to shut down the Marlin Beach Resort complex, saying, "If a family from the Midwest comes to Fort Lauderdale and sees men making love on the beach, what would they think?"

For the first time in Broward history, the queer community protested in front of the mayor's office and called for his resignation. Even the local newspaper The *Fort Lauderdale News* now recognized the importance of the gay community for tourism and criticized the mayor for "Hip-shooting on homosexuals." The Marlin Beach remained open and its Sunday afternoon tea dance by the pool remained the center of social life for the LGBTQ community.

No Invasion Here By Homosexuals

Although Ft. Lauderdale police have received several complaints concerning allegedly homosexual persons during the last few days, this city is not being invaded by individuals of questionable character who have been made unwelcome in Miami, Police Chief Roland R. Kelley said today.

"We will not tolerate the presence of those characters in Ft. Lauderdale," Kelley declared. "We will appreciate any information on the appearance of homosexuals here that we can receive."

Miami recently cracked down on the characters with police ordering scores of them out of town.

Fort Lauderdale Daily News, 1954

11 Nightclub
1116 W. Broward Blvd., Fort Lauderdale
Circa: 2011-2012

A neighborhood bar next to a police station, this space also home to Bottom's Up, GLOW Lounge, and Johnny's (see listings).

13 Buttons
1440 SE 17th St., Fort Lauderdale
Circa: 1977-1984

Named after the 13 buttons on sailor pants, it attracted a young crowd and was known for its "wild" back room. Its location near the port made it popular with sailors.

According to an article in the *Fort Lauderdale News* on Apr. 1, 1980, Brian Patler, the bar's manager, was elected a Ted Kennedy delegate to the 1980 Democratic National Convention.

13/Even
2037 Wilton Dr., Wilton Manors
Circa: 2014-2018

An upscale wine bar with food, owned by Carol Moran, who has a long history of running women's bars in Wilton Manors with her partner, Nancy Godwin. Tony Dee (see Chardee's listings) owned the building at the time. Many years earlier, Gelati Martini Bar was open in this location (see listing).

21 (see Club 21)

22
26th St. & N. Federal Hwy., Fort Lauderdale
Circa: 1980s

501 Club
501 N. Federal Hwy., Hallandale
Circa: 1975

An ad in a January 1975 *David Magazine* advertised The Femme Jesters and boasted "The only club in town with a show every night."

825
825 E. Sunrise Blvd., Fort Lauderdale
Circa: 1989-1993

A piano bar in one room, with strippers and a dance floor in another. It was sometimes listed as Club 825. An ad in a 1989 issue of *David Magazine*, read, "Watch for our opening."

The building has since been demolished. It was among the male strip clubs cited in a surprisingly positive 1997 article in the *Sun-Sentinel* newspaper.

Tim Miller remembers, "That was mostly a stripper bar. I remember they used to have a glass shower and the boys would dance on stage in the shower."

Electra remembers, "I hosted the Monday amateur strip contest. Ed Cossman bought the club from Paul Hugo, who used to own the Coliseum and is now part owner of The Manor, and Scott Holland, who runs *Hot Shots* now, was the manager."

1800 East
1800 E. Sunrise Blvd., Fort Lauderdale
Circa: 1985

It was also known as the Embassy Club. It tried to be a gay bar/restaurant, retaining the clientele from when it had been known as Together (see listing) under a previous owner.

2440
2440 Wilton Dr., Wilton Manors
Circa: 2005

After buying the building and doing some cosmetic makeovers, Carol Moran called her bar 2440 for a few months while waiting for the paperwork for New Moon (see listing) to come through. This bar was later home to Progress, Chardee's Lounge, Listen, and now, Lit (see listings).

2509 West
2509 W. Broward Blvd., Fort Lauderdale
Circa: 1998–1999

A bar with a patio. Earlier this space was home to Tacky's (see listing).

Adventures
303 SW 6th St., Pompano Beach
Circa: 1996–2002

A country and western bar.

Alibi (Alibi/Monkey Bar)
2266 Wilton Dr., Wilton Manors
Circa: 1997–present

Often credited with establishing Wilton Manors as a gay destination/community. It was not the first bar to open in the area, but it did function as a co-anchor alongside the previously established Chardee's and The Otherside (see listings) across the street. Opened as Georgie's Alibi by George Kessinger, who previously owned Georgie's on Sunrise (see listing) and managed The Stud (see listing), both in Fort Lauderdale, He'd decided to open his bar and hadn't thought of Wilton Manors, but when he saw the large, empty parking lot and an empty storefront across the street from two popular bars, he knew he had the right location. The bar now features multiple rooms: a piano/cabaret bar, dance floor, main bar with male dancers, and an outdoor dining patio, and overflows into the parking lot on weekends.

The restaurant is not just an afterthought; it has won the *Fort Lauderdale Sun-Sentinel's* "Best Burger" award numerous times, beating out such competitors as Capital Grille and Morton's Steakhouse.

Under Kessinger's management, the bar also hosted many benefits for the LGBT community and AIDS/HIV service agencies.

Kessinger sold it to Jackson Padgett and Mark Negrete around 2007. During their ownership, many of their employees were disgruntled and left to work at The Village Pub (see listing). Padgett and Negrete sold the bar to Johnny YK Pak, the owner of Provincetown's Monkey Bar in 2012. He dropped Georgie's and renamed it Alibi/Monkey Bar. Drag brunch on Sundays is a draw. Randy Clark recalls, "I used to go to Alibi to see Jennifer McClain at their cabaret Monkey Bar. It was every Saturday night, and she would pack the room. She sang like a songbird."

Entertainer Shaun Palacious, aka Kitty Meow, explains the difference between Miami's bar scene and Broward County, "I never fit into those specific genres (of drag), so I just let my freak flag fly. In Miami, the bars were all filled with muscle boys, in Fort Lauderdale, and even more so in Wilton Manors, it's more diverse. They are so supportive, and really give you the opportunity to come and just display your talent."

Andrews Extension
1753 N. Andrews Ext., Fort Lauderdale
Circa: 1993

Advertised as a "lifestyle club" on an undated flier. The space was also home to Anywayz, Gaylord's, and Side Street (see listings).

Andy's Lounge
12450 W. St. Rd. 84, Davie
Circa: 1996-2015

It was primarily straight but gay-friendly. It was a neighborhood spot that was open until 8 a.m. Steve C. described it as having "Dark leather sofas, a stripper pole, and walls that don't talk! It was tucked away at the end of a tiny little strip mall facing the I-595 highway, adjacent to a gas station."

Annex
Moffet St., Hollywood
Circa: 1964-1968

In 1967 there was a county campaign against the "homosexual menace" led by the State's Attorney Roger Harper that targeted

this bar. It didn't go anywhere as Harper was fired that year by the governor after it was discovered that, although married with ten children, he had a mistress and was using the state's money to pay for her housing.

Anywayz
1753 N. Andrews Ext., Fort Lauderdale
Circa: 2003-2005

Mixed men and women, it offered entertainment. This space was also home to Andrews Extension, Gaylord's, and Side Street (see listings).

Apt. 9F
2163 Wilton Dr., Wilton Manors
Circa: 2021-present

It was run by Nancy Godwin and Carol Moran who have a long history with lesbian bars in Wilton Manors. Apt. 9F is a women-run, male-friendly restaurant, and bar. Earlier this was home to The Naked Grape (see listing).

Art Bar
300 SW 1st Ave., Fort Lauderdale
Circa: 2008-2009

This was primarily straight, but gay-friendly. Michael Randhona owned it. *Inside Fort Lauderdale* wrote, "It just reminds me of the kind of place I went to in college when I didn't have any money and I went wherever there were girls and cheap drinks." This part of the Riverfront Complex was also home to Zu Bar and The Living Room (see listings).

B's (See Bill's Filling Station)

Bacchus
4050 N. Powerline Rd., Oakland Park
Circa: 1978-1983

A dance club, also known as Zelda's Bacchus, then just Zelda's (see listing).

Backroom
800 N. Federal Hwy., Hallandale
Circa: 1979-1981

A women's dance bar, it was listed in *The Damron Guide* from 1977-1981, although this conflicts with the years that Ladies' Choice (see listing) was advertising at this location (1978). This space was also home to Lou's (see listing).

Backroom
800 N. Federal Hwy., Hallandale
Circa: 1979-1981

A women's dance bar, it was listed in *The Damron Guide* from 1977-1981, although this conflicts with the years that Ladies' Choice (see listing) was advertising at this location (1978). This space was also home to Lou's (see listing).

MEN AT PLAY!

MONDAY
Chicken of the Week
$50 Prize
50¢ Bar Drinks 9-11
TUESDAY
The Original Gay Gong
$50 Prize
50¢ Bar Drinks 9-11
WEDNESDAY
Dance Contest
$50 Prize
50¢ Bar Drinks 9-11
THURSDAY
JULY 31st
ALL GIRLS IN CONCERT
FREDA, MAXINE,
ROXANNE
FRI. & SAT.
HOT MACHO DISCO
50¢ Bar Drinks 9-11
SUNDAY
July 27th
Roxanne & Special
Guest Star
50¢ Bar Drinks 9-11
No Cover

DANCE TO SOUTH FLORIDA'S
HOTTEST D.J.
"The Player,"
DEAN FERGUSON!!

Bacchus

4050 N.W. 9th Ave. (Powerline Rd.), Ft. Lauderdale
Between Oakland Park Blvd. & Commercial 563-8900

OPEN TILL 4 A.M.

Backstage Lounge
2209 Wilton Dr., Wilton Manors
Circa: 1992

Advertised as "for the Young at Heart," it featured "Laser Karaoke." This space was home to many LGBTQ bars including Bill's Filling Station/Bill's/B's, The Blue Parrot Lounge, Chardee's, Club Silver, The Eagle, The Palms, Southern Nights, and Wolf (see listings).

Backstreet
200 W. Broward Blvd., Fort Lauderdale
Circa: 1981-1988

The South Florida outpost of the popular Atlanta club, owned by Frank A. Cashman. Opened February 14, 1981, as a disco in a multi-room complex. It was a large building, taking up an entire city block with another entrance at 101 SW 2nd Ave. Multiple storefronts housed other LGBTQ businesses in a complex called Village Mall, including Storm, Club Q, and Good Timers (see listings) in the Himarshee Village neighborhood, near Johnny's (see listing). In 1985, the owners led a movement to start a Pride Parade.

Cynthia Lopez remembers, "I met Lenny Kravitz's mom, Roxy (Roker), at Backstreet. She was sitting at the front bar having a drink."

Deborah DeMola recalls, "On Sunday afternoon tea dance at Backstreet they had a hot air balloon ride in the parking lot. It didn't go high up in the sky. I believe it was tied but did go off the ground."

Tim Miller calls it, "The best gay bar Fort Lauderdale ever had. It was two levels with an upper level that went all the way around the bar where you could look down on the dance floor. Belle Kinkaid was this enormous Black drag queen, she had to be six and a half feet tall, and she ruled that place. They'd play clips from *Dynasty* every Sunday night at midnight. And Belle

would narrate all the dialogue. She'd have Crystal Carrington say, 'Oh Blake, you eat out pussy so well.' She'd have the club roaring. One New Year's Eve, she was being lowered from the rafters and she fell about 15 feet and was knocked out. They called an ambulance and everything. Everyone thought it was part of the act, but she was really hurt.

"Bob Mero was a straight guy that DJ'd there. He was close to the community. God, I had good times at that bar. And if you didn't get laid at Backstreet, you went across the street to the bathhouse."

Badd Boys
321 W. Sunrise Blvd., Fort Lauderdale
Circa: 1993–1995

A piano bar in a space that has housed numerous gay clubs since the 1970s including Georgie's, The Fireside, Impulse, and most recently Slammer 321 (see listings).

Ballz
2031 Wilton Dr., Wilton Manors
Circa: 2015–2016

Supposedly a sports bar, according to owner Sean David (also former owner of LeBoy). Let's reword it to: His attempts to open the bar were blocked by Wilton Manors because the city did not want a stripper bar on Wilton Drive. They cited the fact that he installed stages and stripper poles in the bar. He sued the city but ultimately was denied a hearing. Open from December–March, many of those months under the name Pint. (see listing). This space has been home to other clubs, including Circuit, Club 2031, G Spot, and Sidelines (see listings).

Bam
2829 W. Broward Blvd., Fort Lauderdale
Circa: 2015–2017

Ty L said, "A very eclectic group of men and drag queens. You can source just about anything you can think of here."

In 2017, Broward Sheriff's officers responded to the scene near Bam around 5 a.m.—one person was dead, and two others were hospitalized after an early morning shooting. The club closed shortly afterward. Other clubs at this location include Torpedo Bar and Phases (see listings).

Bar Amici
1301 E. Las Olas Blvd., Fort Lauderdale
Circa: 2003

Owned by the late philanthropist Richard Fasenmeyer, who also owned Cathode Ray. He expanded it to include Bar Amici, more of a restaurant than a bar. Under Fasenmeyer's stewardship, Bar Amici grew to prominence as 'the place to be,' from monthly luncheons for Gamma Mu to daily and weekly business meetings for LGBTQ groups and associations.

After Fasenmeyer passed away, Larry Wald took over and continued the tradition of hosting community groups and sponsoring neighborhood functions. However, few men had the deep pockets of Fasenmeyer, a wealthy Republican who had been one of President George Bush's top 200 donors.

Walter Silverman remembers, "It had a nice restaurant, and the food was very good. Then the original owner died, and it all went downhill pretty quick."

Bay City Station (see Flamingo Bay)

Beach Betty's
625 E. Dania Beach Blvd., Dania Beach
Circa: 2004–2015

A women's bar often described as a lesbian version of *Cheers*, it was a neighborhood pub that occasionally hosted rock and roll bands. It also had a pool table, darts board, and drink specials served by friendly bartenders.

The patrons at Beach Betty's were mostly women who love women, with a few straights and gay guys thrown in for good measure. The bar, located in a strip mall, was cozy and quaint, with a beachy-themed mural adorning its walls.

"I opened the bar because there was no place for women who liked women to go," said owner Karen Guethle. The bar celebrated its 6th anniversary in 2010 and only closed in 2015 because a developer razed the building. Partners, Champagne Taste, and Second Time Around (see listings) were also at this location.

Bear Cage
Address Unknown
Circa: 1991

A "coming soon" ad appeared in the February 24, 2011, issue of *Hot Shots*, but no information on the bar ever appeared in print.

Berlin Bear
2922 SE Cortez St., Fort Lauderdale
Circa: 1983

A listing in the 1983 *Damron Guide* said, "Looks Promising." There was no other mention in any press, and it never appeared in the *Damron Guide* again, although there was a motel (since demolished) by that name at the address.

Big Bill's
2889 W. Broward Blvd., Fort Lauderdale
Circa: 1974-1975

It opened as Gallery (see listing), a late-night bar offering male strippers. Near the end of its run, it briefly changed its name to Big Bill's but had the same owners and management. Good Times (see listing) later occupied this space.

Bill's (aka Bill's Filling Station, aka B's)
2209 Wilton Dr., Wilton Manors
Circa: 2010-2015

Bill's Filling Station moved from its original location on NE 11th Ave and 13th St. to Wilton Dr. Soon after moving to the new location, it dropped Filling Station and went by Bill's. "Growl Fridays," a bear party, was a popular event. In 2014, Jackson Padgett and his husband, Mark, purchased the bar and changed its name to B's. The bar closed shortly thereafter. Other clubs at this location include Backstage Lounge, Blue

Parrot Lounge, Chardee's, Club Silver, The Eagle, The Palms, Southern Nights, and Wolf (see listings).

Bill's Filling Station
1243 NE 11ᵗʰ Ave., Fort Lauderdale
Circa: 1996-2009

Initially was named Bill & Jerry's Filling Station. It dropped Jerry's in 2000. Ricardo B remembers it, "Friendly bartenders, good drinks, good video music. Excellent choice for the bear/admirer crowd...not enough parking but hey..."

In 2008, a then-unknown singer, Stefani Germanotta, debuted her first single recording, "Just Dance" at Bill's Filling Station while in Miami for the Winter Music Conference, using the stage name Lady Gaga. Other bars at this location include Two on a Match, Depot, Hector's, and Le Boy (see listings).

Birdcage
3917 S. State Rd. 7, Fort Lauderdale
Circa: 1965

A drag bar, not to be confused with the short-lived cabaret room of the same name at Boardwalk (see listing).

Bishop's (Tony)
1313 E. Las Olas Blvd., Fort Lauderdale
Circa: 1998

A jazz club and restaurant. The female jazz singer was known for her ability to mimic animal sounds.

The bar's name appears to be no relation to the similarly named gay porn star, Tony Bishop.

Black Banana
6890 N. Powerline Rd., Fort Lauderdale
Circa: 2009-2010

A men's dance club with a mostly Black clientele was in a large warehouse with two bars, a lush VIP lounge, and a small dance floor. The building was demolished. This was previously the location of Manhattan South (see listing).

Blue Parrot Lounge
2209 Wilton Dr., Wilton Manors
Circa: 1989

It was a women's bar adjacent to the Palms restaurant. It didn't last long and soon became the Palms' cabaret room (see listing). Other clubs at this location include several LGBTQ bars including The Backstage Lounge, Bill's Filling Station/Bill's/B's, Chardee's, Club Silver, Eagle, Southern Nights, and Wolf (see listings).

Boardwalk
1721 N. Andrews Ave., Fort Lauderdale
Circa: 2002-present

After closing in Miami, Boardwalk owner Victor Zepka moved his all-male strip club to Fort Lauderdale, just across the river from Wilton Manors. Originally Zepka envisioned a cabaret restaurant attached to the strip club, but with a separate entrance. It was to be named The Birdcage. Those plans fell through, so he opened the room up as a patio bar and restaurant. The focus on the restaurant varies. It has gone by several names and has brought in several chefs. Most recently it has been named Gussy's Café and the bill of fare consists of chicken wings and tenders, shrimp cocktail and tempura, chili, quesadillas, loaded tater tots and spring rolls, as well as burgers, sandwiches, salads, and entrees such as pasta, ribs, and steak.

Electra remembers, "Victor always loved food and cooking. The building was originally Flannigan's (a chain of Florida restaurants). Since it had a restaurant, Victor decided to have a restaurant cabaret, where the queens would perform and serve the customers, kind of like Lips."

It is now only young, skinny, male strippers and the restaurant. Vicki is a popular bartender on the outside patio.

Bobby Winn's
201 SW 2nd St., Fort Lauderdale
Circa: late 1980s

An Italian restaurant and bar. Bobby hosted while his mother cooked. This space was also home to two short-lived bars, Hannibal's, and Regatta (see listings).

Boom
2708 SW Powerline Rd., Fort Lauderdale
Circa: 1986–1995

Adjoined the Club Ft. Lauderdale bathhouse. Boots was also a bar attached to the bathhouse (see listing). Both were preceded at this site by a bar called Helen's Hole (see listing). They had different addresses but were in the same building with separate entrances.

Boom (Atomic)
2232 Wilton Dr., Wilton Manors
Circa: 2003–2013

At first, the dance club was quite popular, but when other clubs opened, it lost much of its following and struggled during its last few years (its nickname near the end was Doom). For a while, it was the home of Rising Action Theater, Wilton Manors' first LGBT Theater Company.

The owners tried merging with other clubs, bringing in new owners, who changed the bar's name to Atomic Boom and then back to just Boom shortly before closing.

In 2011, David K wrote in a gay publication, "If a club goes boom and no one is there to hear it, does it actually make a sound? The answer is probably yes, but what's the point?"

Electra remembers, "I hosted the opening of the bar. It had an airplane wing that hung from the ceiling."

Hunter's (see listing) later opened in this location.

Boots
2708 SW Powerline Rd., Fort Lauderdale
Circa: 1983–1986

This was originally Helen's Hole (see listing) and was adjoined to Club Fort Lauderdale bathhouse. The name was changed to Boots, a western/leather bar—they had different addresses, but were in the same building, using different mailing addresses. Eventually, the bathhouse closed, and Boots took over the

entire space. John Asbury owned the bar. Dale Murphy, Asbury's lover, took over the bar after Asbury died in 1996. He had previously owned Camp-It, a gay campground in Michigan.

Tim Miller recalls, "They had hundreds of boots hanging from the ceiling and there was a door that led to a small bathhouse next door, and you could go back and forth between the two in your towel."

According to Jesse Monteagudo, "Many of the boots, which covered the ceiling, belonged to patrons of the bar lost to AIDS."

Boom (see listing) was also at this address.

Bottom's Up
1116 W. Broward Blvd., Fort Lauderdale
Circa: 1993–1994

A neighborhood bar next to a police station. This was also home to GLOW Lounge, Johnny's, and 11 Nightclub (see listings).

Buddy's
2312 NE 26th St., Fort Lauderdale
Circa: 1983–1987

The grand opening was held in June 1983. Karaoke, bingo, and male strippers were attractions at this neighborhood bar. "It was an old men's bar, and it had the same owner as Juno's,"

according to Lori Tanner. Robert Fonner recalls, "It had a pool table. Once I ran into a friend of my stepbrother there. I had a crush on him when I was about ten years younger."

This was also the site of Lefty's II, Juno's, and Phoenix (see listings).

Bushes
2400 E. Oakland Park Blvd., Fort Lauderdale
Circa: 1993–2004

A piano bar, formerly the location of Little Jim's and Simba's, now the location of Smarty Pants (see listings).

Bus Stop
2203 S. Federal Hwy., Fort Lauderdale
Circa: 1989–1998

It was a men's bar owned by Arthur Smith, an attorney. It was popular with sailors from nearby Port Everglades. Tim Miller remembers it as a hustler bar.

Cabaret/After Dark
124 S. Federal Hwy., Hallandale
Circa: 1977

Cabaret Carousel and Lounge
Location unknown
Circa: 1980s

Advertised as a "show lounge." Cabaret offered a dinner theater, combining both fine dining and musical acts ranging from dancing go-go boys to drag queens and singers.

Camp David
5375 N. Dixie Hwy., Fort Lauderdale
Circa: 1983

A disco, not to be confused with the clothing-optional, gay, RV park of the same name.

Cape
2004 Wilton Dr., Wilton Manors
Circa: 1991

Opened in December 1991, short-lived, it was followed by Club Classics and later home to Tropics (see listings).

Castle Lounge
2674 E. Oakland Park Blvd., Oakland Park
Circa: 2011–2012

A short-lived club. Previously, it was the location of Cozmo's Lounge (see listing).

Castle Lounge
1322 N. Dixie Hwy, Hollywood
Circa: 2013–2020

Originally opened as Trixie's with the ad, "Enjoy nightly shows, drag queens, transgenders, cross-dressers, and the men who love them." Dean Gramenidis owned the Castle. Near the end of its run, it was more of a straight, rock club.

Cathode Ray
1105 E. Las Olas Blvd., Fort Lauderdale
Circa: 1985-2000

Fort Lauderdale's first video bar attracted a young crowd. For many years, it was the bar to be at on Monday nights. It overlooked a small river and was about a half mile from the popular Marlin Beach Hotel. Originally owned by Wayne Gibson. Sold in 1991 to John Manzi, then Larry Wald and Scott Beldin. Sometimes listed as Club Cathode Ray. Tim Miller recalls, "The original Cathode Ray was the best. Monday was a beer bust. It was something like $6 to get in and all the draft beer you wanted. Everybody went there on Monday night. Kenny Poole was the VJ."

Cathode Ray
1307 E. Las Olas Blvd., Fort Lauderdale
Circa: 2000-2006

The original bar was sold to Dick Fasenmeyer, a wealthy Republican, who moved the bar a few blocks east to a larger space. He also opened an adjoining restaurant, Bar Amici (see listing), and offered the use of the club for meetings of various community groups. While popular, it never achieved the success of the previous incarnation.

Chainz
1931 S. Federal Hwy., Fort Lauderdale
Circa: 1999-2001

Tim Miller recalls, "The owner/bartender was a guy named Sterling. He took over from when it was Everglades (see listing). I think it's now a place called the Mental Ward." (It is a costume shop now operating under a different name).

Champagne Taste
625 E. Dania Beach Blvd., Dania Beach
Circa: 1984

It was a disco that also showed football games. This was also the location of Beach Betty's, Partners, and Second Time Around (see listings).

Chaps/Corral
1727 N. Andrews Ext., Fort Lauderdale
Circa: 1999-2005

A leather and country and western bar. It was first named Chaps. Beginning in 2000 the name was changed to Chaps@Corral, then in 2003 solely as Corral. "It was one of the first bars with a back room," recalls Tim Miller.

In 2002, the bar was raided, and ten people, including the bar's owner, were arrested. Among those arrested was a Coral Springs teacher who was charged with lewd behavior for having oral sex in public. *The Sun-Sentinel* reported that he decided to

Raid revives penalty issue for teachers

Man's arrest at club raises moral debate

BY BILL HIRSCHMAN
EDUCATION WRITER

A Broward teacher was arrested in a raid at a gay club Tuesday, mirroring circumstances that ignited a 1999 firestorm over whether educators can be punished for what they do in their private lives.

An internal school investigation began Wednesday after Fort Lauderdale police told district officials they had arrested a Ramblewood Middle School teacher, according to Joe Melita, chief of the school's Special Investigative Unit.

Mark Raskind, 52, was charged with one misdemeanor count of lewd behavior at Chaps lounge at 1727 N. Andrews Ave., allegedly for having oral sex in the bar, police reported. Ten others, including the bar owner, were arrested.

Raskind, a 30-year educator, has worked for the school district since 1986, much of it at the Coral Springs school where his wife also is a teacher. He has been reassigned to administrative duties off-campus while the investigation continues, Melita said.

If Raskind is convicted, the Broward School Board will find itself dealing once again with an issue that has divided the board and the community.

"This will resurrect it," Board Chairman Bob Parks said. "But this time we'll have a clearer understanding of what questions need to be asked before we make a decision."

In 1999, sheriff's officers sent undercover agents into Athena's Forum, a swingers' club in Pompano Beach. Several people were arrested on sex-related charges, including two Broward teachers.

A passionate debate raged over whether their actions in a private club should have any impact on their employment as teachers. After the board launched the process to fire them, one resigned and the other cut a deal in which he gave up his tenure and was reassigned to teach adult-education classes while on two years' probation.

In this new case, Parks thinks the board needs to consider these issues: was the raid legal, did the teacher violate the state code of ethics, did the teacher violate his contract with the district and what is the definition of moral turpitude — the key question in the 1999 debate.

Board member Lois Wexler also expects that newer policy changes and clarifications will make the discussion smoother. "Yes, here we go again, but this time we have more protocol and more rules," she said.

Conviction of sexual battery or inappropriate sexual conduct could result in anything from a suspension to a dismissal.

challenge his dismissal from the school, where he taught with his wife.

Chardee's
2209 Wilton Dr., Wilton Manors
Circa: 1990–2007

One of the earliest businesses, along with Georgie's Alibi and The Otherside, that helped make Wilton Manors a gay mecca. Tony Dee and his partner in life and business, Charles Mielke, a strip mall developer, took over the Palms from the straight woman who owned it and turned it into an upscale supper club and combined their names to dub it Chardee's. After being open for a few months, Tony Dee saw that the place was going to be a success, and in October 1990, he purchased the entire building. It was one of the first openly gay restaurants in Broward County.

According to an extensive 2005 *New Times* article, it was "aimed specifically at silver foxes and their admirers. It's a glittering gay mirage in a desert of boarded-up strip malls, trailer parks, crack houses, and abandoned buildings strewn with garbage."

Electra echoes that, "There was nothing else around, it was just a slum, termite-ridden dump. You entered from the parking lot on the other side. Tony Dee bought every building between 21st St. and 6th Ave. Then when Alibi moved in, it started clicking."

Chardee's featured entertainers such as Eartha Kitt, Pudgy, Jennifer Holliday, Judy Tenuta, Sam Harris, and the then-current incarnations of the Glenn Miller Orchestra and the Ink Spots.

In 1995, Dee sold the bar, but not the building, to Don Hastings, who had it for 10 years. He then sold it to Norman Arntz who had it for about a year before declaring bankruptcy and closing it.

Randy Clark says, "It always had a crowd. It was known all around the world."

Other clubs at this location include The Backstage, Bill's Filling Station/Bill's/B's, The Blue Parrot Lounge, Club Silver, Eagle, Palms, Southern Nights, and Wolf (see listings).

Chardee's Lounge
2440 Wilton Dr., Wilton Manors
Circa: 2017

In the days before Wilton Manors became a gay Mecca, this space was home to various straight bars, including The Swinging Door and Muldoon's. In 2005 Carol Moran bought it and opened 2440/New Moon (see listings). She eventually closed the bar, and the space was vacant for a brief time. Progress, a bar from Chicago, opened a short-lived outpost in the space (see listing). The space sat empty for a few more months until Tony Dee, with his new husband Andy Martin,

tried to recapture the magic of the original Chardee's by purchasing the building. Dee and Martin held a "soft" opening in December 2017. Within a few months, Martin had health problems and they sold the bar. The space was taken over by Listen and then Lit bar (see listings).

Chase
2376 N. Federal Hwy., Fort Lauderdale
Circa: 2004-2006

A video bar. Mondays were Brazilian Night.

Cheekers
1150 N. Federal Hwy., Fort Lauderdale
Circa: 1976-1978

It was a women's bar with a young crowd, owned by Sherry Robbins Valverde. It offered dinner service, theater, and shows. Nikki Adams recalls, "It had been a roller rink or something. It had these big arched ceilings, and it had these huge taxidermy animals there. It never took off—I think it was too big."

Chill Wine Bar
1828 E. Sunrise Blvd., Fort Lauderdale
Circa: 2013-2018

It was more straight than gay, but it hosted events for the Stonewall National Museum and Archives and the Fort Lauderdale LGBTQ Film Festival.

China White
109 SW 2nd St., Fort Lauderdale
Circa: 2005-2007

A short-lived Studio 54 wanna-be co-owned by John Cahalin. Sundays were the official LGBTQ Night, but it was pretty gay all the time. The music was a mix of house, hip-hop, Latin, reggaeton, retro dance, and rock, and the room was dominated by a giant elephant. This space was also home to Jet Set and Q (see listings).

Electra remembers, "It was very upscale, it had a Moulin Rouge vibe."

Circuit
2031 Wilton Dr., Wilton Manors
Circa: 2005-2006

Mostly a male crowd, it featured drag shows and male dancers. This space has been home to other clubs including Ballz, Pint, Club 2031, G Spot, and Sidelines (see listings).

Clever Bar Disco
2999 W. Broward Blvd., Fort Lauderdale
Circa: 1979-1980

A dance club, it also offered free food almost every evening and held pool tournaments.

Cloud 9
7126 Stirling Rd., Hollywood
Circa: 2004-present

We'll let *The Sun-Sentinel* description, which has run for 15 years, describe the bar, "Gay women rule here. Dance Floor, pool and beer pong tables, dart boards and drag shows, karaoke." It is primarily a Black and Latina lesbian bar but is also male and trans-friendly. It is also known for serving good chicken wings. Galit, the owner, brags, "The longest happy hour around, 7 a.m.-7 p.m. Monday through Saturday, Sunday noon-7 p.m. for half-price on all drinks." The Office (see listing) was previously at this address.

Club 21
2920 SW 30th Ave., Hallandale
Circa: 1984–1998

According to longtime Miami and Fort Lauderdale bartender Lori Tanner, "It was owned by Joel Steadman who also was part of the group who owned Twist in Miami (see listing)." It was sometimes known as Exit 21 and attracted a young disco crowd. Miss Puddin' hosted a lot of shows there. In 1987, new owners installed a new sound and light system, rebranded it as "New Club 21 Open until 6 a.m." and held a sneak preview party on November 27. An episode of *Miami Vice* was filmed in the bar.

On April 14, 1988, a special live show called "The Church Lady Part II starring Bobby Settani as the Church Lady with Hot Male Strippers. Back by popular demand."

The bar, along with the Copa bar (see listing) was raided on May 3, 1991, for drug sales and, according to the arresting

officers, two men were arrested for "...performing live sex acts on the dance floor." Following the raid, the Broward chapter of the ACLU offered to finance a class-action lawsuit against the Broward Sheriff's Office. After a protest by 60 community activists, the charges against many of those arrested were dropped. Community activist and lawyer Norm Kent won a class-action suit. In the investigation, it was revealed that all police records of the incident were destroyed under the administration of then-Sheriff Nick Navarro. The Broward Sheriff's office, as part of the settlement donated $10,000 to Center One, an AIDS Service Agency, according to a report by *The Sun-Sentinel* in November 1993.

Nikki Adams describes what happened during one of her shows. "They had a huge mirror ball with neon rings around it. I was doing a number where I had a bullwhip, and when I cracked the whip it wrapped around the neon light, and I broke it off."

Tim Miller reflects, "It was a great dance club. It was named that because it was right off exit 21 of I-95. It was the place to go on Saturday for just a few years."

Club 1951
1951 N. Powerline Rd., Fort Lauderdale
Circa: 1990

This was a women's bar. Cupcakes (also a women's bar), Eagle, Steel, and Uncle Charlie's (see listings) all occupied this space at various times. The building has since been demolished.

Club 2031
2031 Wilton Dr., Wilton Manors
Circa: 2020

This bar was open for less than three months. Ballz, Pint, G Spot, Circuit, and Sidelines (see listings) all occupied this space.

Club Aloha
3702 S. Federal Hwy., Fort Lauderdale
Circa: 1947–1963

Advertised as a "Star-Studded Show of Female Impersonators," including Don Dache, Terry Lane, and Jan Del Rio, it featured music by Skip and her boys and an "unusual gay boy revue." In 1963, owners Mable Biddle and Elizabeth Felker sued the state liquor commission, which tried to revoke their license for "permitting a lewd and lascivious show." The judge ruled in their favor.

Club Atlantis
219 N. Fort Lauderdale Beach Blvd., Fort Lauderdale
Circa: 1990–1994

A mixed straight/gay rowdy spring break haven, often shut down for serving underage patrons. They had a gay night on Sunday, but just for one season. It was described in *The Sun-Sentinel* as "... condemned by city officials as the most notorious watering hole on the beach."

Club Caribbean Resort
2851 N. Federal Hwy., Fort Lauderdale
Circa: 1989–2000

It held its grand opening on February 17, 1989, and had a huge dance floor. It was co-owned by George Kessinger (in between Georgie's and Georgie's Alibi) with Brad Casey. Casey also owned *Scoop Magazine*.

Tim Miller remembers, "When Marlin Beach started to decline, Club Caribbean opened and continued the tea dance."

A new owner took over in March of 1990. Numerous bars on the premises included Treetop Disco (which became Manatee), Garden, and Cafe Martinique, a jazz club.

Nikki Adams recalls, "I did a lot of shows with Dana Manchester by the pool."

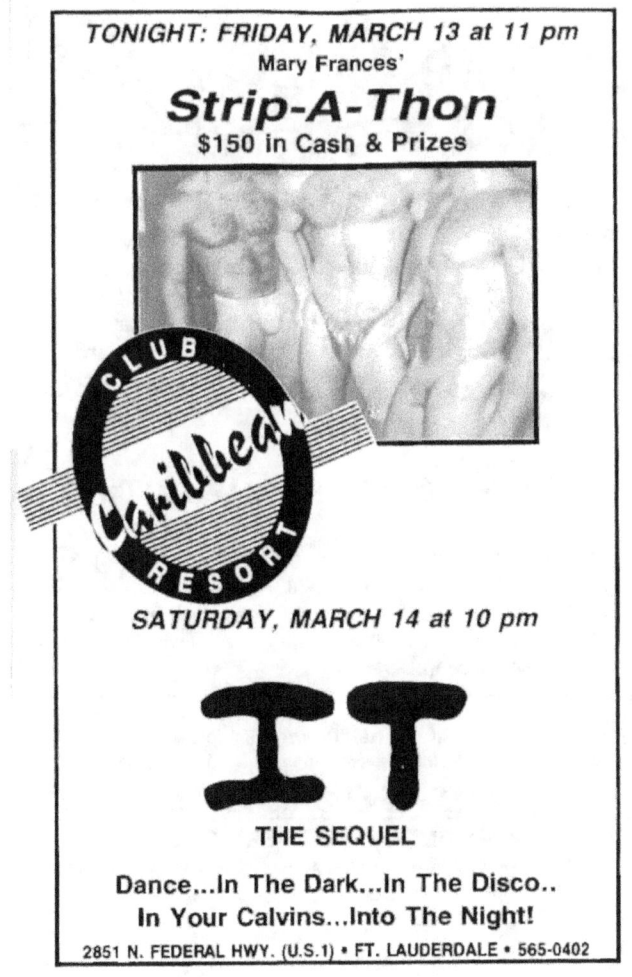

Club Classics
2004 Wilton Dr., Wilton Manors
Circa: 1991–1998

It was best known for its Sunday tea dance. Lori Tanner says, "It was owned by David Rodgers, he was also involved in the Sea Monster." Cape preceded it and Tropics now occupies this space (see listings).

Club Electra
1600 SE 15th Ave., Fort Lauderdale
Circa: 1991–1999

It featured male dancers and catered to a young crowd.

Nikki Adams recalls, "I worked there every Wednesday night, some contests with boys in their underwear. The back of the stage was covered with these huge lamps, about two inches around and very bright. You could feel the heat on your back. They'd turn them on every once in a while and it blinded the crowd. They loved it."

Club Heat
3200 N. Federal Hwy., Fort Lauderdale
Circa: 1989–1990

The top floor of a building in the Coral Ridge Mall, where a Target store stands today, was packed with a young crowd attracted to the large, upper-level deck. Police were called a few times when things got rowdy between rival street gangs. In 1989, one gang member was murdered by a rival gang member in the parking lot after an altercation that began in the bar.

Clubhouse Connection
3050 NE 26th Terr., Fort Lauderdale
Circa: 1982–1983

It was a bar attached to a bathhouse. Later New Connection (see listing) opened here.

Club Pierre
3419 N. Andrews Ave., Fort Lauderdale
Circa: 1985

The bar attracted an older crowd and featured slow dancing. It is also the location of Rustlers (see listing).

Club Q
200 W. Broward Blvd., Fort Lauderdale
Circa: 1993-1994

Sunday was the gay night at this straight club. According to Electra, Cindy Bablock oversaw gay night, "They tried to recapture the Backstreet (see listing) crowd when Backstreet closed."

Later Good Timers and Storm opened in this space. (see listings).

Club Shadows
715 S. 21st Ave., Hollywood
Circa: 1986-1992

A disco and restaurant that was often called just Shadows. It was sued in 1989 for firing an employee after finding out he was HIV positive. A jury later awarded the man $20,000 to be paid by the Department of Correction for violating his privacy.

Nikki Adams said, "I worked there a lot when I first got here. It was very neighborhoody. Everybody knew everyone."

This was previously home to the Executive Room and Hollywood Nights (see listings).

Club Silver
2209 Wilton Dr., Wilton Manors
Circa: 2019-2020

A short-lived club opened by Salvo Mule, the building's owner, and manager. It billed itself as "the largest piano bar in all of South Florida!"

Other clubs at this location include Backstage, Bill's Filling Station/Bill's/B, Chardee's, Eagle, Palms, Blue Parrot, Southern Nights, and Wolf (see listings).

Club X
1000 E. Sample Rd., Pompano
Circa: 1993

It showcased strippers and was billed as a "Continuous erotic male review."

Club Xanadu
2750 E. Oakland Park Blvd., Oakland Park
Circa: late 1990s

Advertised as female-owned and operated, it attracted a mixed crowd, many bi. For a few months, it went by the name Club

Xanadu, then reverted to Whale & Porpoise. It was also home to Gypsy's Cabaret (see listings).

Club Xtra
2245 Wilton Dr., Wilton Manors
Circa: 2022–2023

A burlesque show featuring trans performers. This space was formerly occupied by the short-lived Wilton Biergarten (see listing).

Coliseum
2520 S. Miami Rd., Fort Lauderdale
Circa: 1991–2008

Formerly a straight country bar called Desperado. The Coliseum, located near the airport, was open only on Friday and Saturday. Owned by Paul Hugo and Brett Tannenbaum (later owner of The Venue/The Manor). It was named "Best Dance Club" in 2004 by *The New Times*. A separate bar, but connected to Coliseum, Louise's Venus (see listing), was a women's club. There was also another "bar within the bar" called Jocks. It wasn't around long enough to rate a listing in the gay papers or guides of the time.

Tim Miller said, "It was right next to The Copa and you either went to one or the other. There wasn't a lot of going back and forth. I was a Copa boy. It was open a couple of years after Copa closed."

In the 1980s and 1990s, when some gay men in business or politics in Palm Beach County felt that they had to be discreet, they went to the bars and discos in Broward County. Mark Foley, a gay Republican congressman from Palm Beach, could often be seen at the Coliseum. He recalls those days and says it is where he met his life partner, a prominent Palm Beach doctor.

Nikki Adams recalls, "We filmed a pilot for a television show in that bar. It was a mix of *American Idol* and *Drag Race*. It never got picked up."

Electra concurs, "I was in the pilot too. The model Tyson hosted it. He was gorgeous!"

Cookie's Intimate Lounge
2100 Hollywood Blvd., Hollywood
Circa: 1980

A disco. This space was also home to Zelda's, Glitz, and was billed at various times as Ladies' Disco and Ladies' Loft (see listings).

Copa
2800 S. Federal Hwy., Fort Lauderdale
Circa: 1975–2005

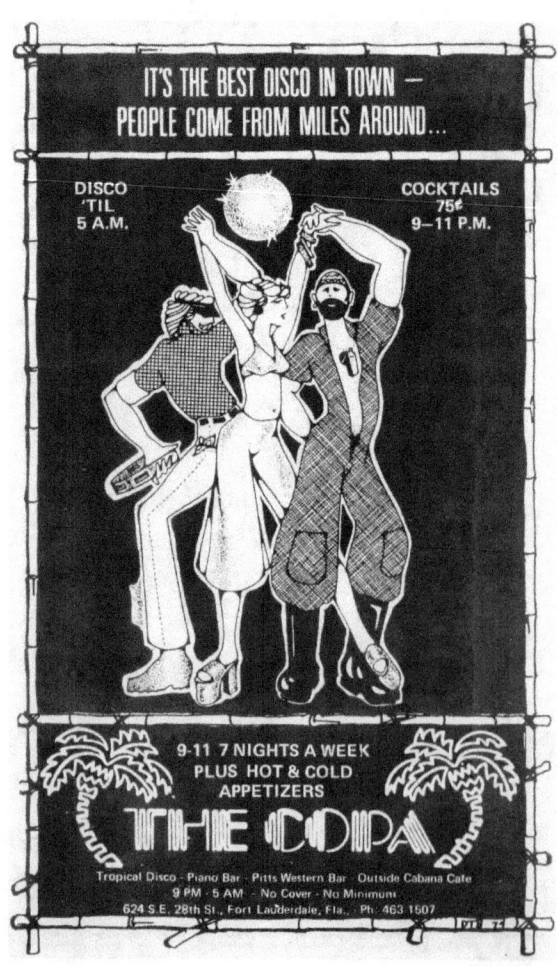

John Castelli and Bill Bastiansen originally owned the bar. It was the premiere dance club in Fort Lauderdale and encompassed more than five acres. The complex included the Tree Bar, Tropical Disco, Cabana Café, and Pitts, a Western-themed bar. On weekend nights, it attracted more than 1,500 people. On April 18, 1988, Stacey Q performed her latest release, "Don't Make a Fool of Yourself," at the Copa. Evelyn "Champagne" King sang there on April 9th, 1988.

Lori Tanner says Greg Bernard bought the club and ran it until Hurricane Wilma came and destroyed the club."

Vivian Oliva remembers that it was worth the trip up from Miami—Grace Jones appeared there, and she was very high. They had very nice outdoor areas."

Andrew Armani recalls, "I was a male stripper, and we went to the Copa religiously! I remember watching Nikki Adams and Electra and thinking this place is so fun! They had the bare buns contest. I ended up winning it once!"

Tim Miller remembers, "There was no cover if you got there before midnight, so we always tried to get there just before. Bill Bastiansen's Aunt Kathleen, a tiny old woman, was there every night to take your money. There was a blue laser that shot above the dance floor. I remember so many of the bartenders: Michael Bartlett still tends the bar at Scandals (see listing), and Bob Petty and Greg Duranga. So many of them are gone now."

Nikki Adams worked there often. "That was my home. It was so innovative. They also closed for a week every year around their anniversary and redecorated the entire place. So many famous acts performed there. You could get any drugs you wanted in an area of the bar known as the alley."

Randy Clark remembers, "It was phenomenal, we came up from Coral Gables. It was a big drug crowd."

In 2005, Hurricane Wilma badly damaged the bar, which never reopened. The building has since been demolished.

Corner Pub
1915 N. Andrews Ave., Fort Lauderdale
Circa: 2002-present

A neighborhood dive bar with a quiet, hard-drinking crowd, it first opened as Shannon & Anthony's Corner Pub. A year later, it was just listed as Shannon's Corner Pub, and a year after that, it was just Corner Pub. In August 2022, a man brought a hand grenade into the bar, apparently to confront someone he knew. The bartender quietly got everyone to leave the bar while another customer who was an ex-Marine, engaged the man in conversation, eventually getting him away from the grenade and tackling him. He was turned over to waiting police without incident.

Corral
1440 SE 17th St., Fort Lauderdale
Circa: 1980-1990

A neighborhood bar that occasionally had drag shows..

THE CORRAL

CONSTRUCTION PARTY

Can't Stop the Music
Can't Stop the Construction

VILLAGE PEOPLE

Can't Stop the Music

SUNDAY, JULY 27th
WEDNESDAY, JULY 30th

BEER BUST
25¢ Draft
BOTH NIGHTS

SPECIAL SHOW WEDNESDAY NIGHT
starring **LOWELL WILLIAMS**

Special men ... all the time makin it happen ... BE THERE
1440 S.E. 17th St. Causeway Ft. Laud.   463-9467

Corral
1700 N. Andrews Ave., Fort Lauderdale
Circa: 1998-2003

A men's bar with country & western dancing.

Costello's Gin Mill
2345 Wilton Dr., Wilton Manors
Circa: 2005-2009

The bar was attached to a popular restaurant owned by John Costello and John Lombardo. It was once Victor/Victoria and now is home to The Manor/Venue (see listings).

Cozmo's Lounge
2674 E. Oakland Park Blvd., Oakland Park
Circa: 2010-2011

From 5-9 p.m., it was a piano bar attracting an older clientele, and then a younger crowd would come in to see the male dancers until closing. It later became the Castle Lounge for a brief time (see listing).

Crescendo
3845 N. Federal Hwy., Fort Lauderdale
Circa: 1995

A cabaret.

Crossfire
2100 N. Dixie Hwy., Hollywood
Circa: 1983-1987

Also known as The Lone Star Saloon, *The Damron Guide* said, "looks promising." Robert Fronner recalls, "They had square dancing lessons."

Also at this location were Roadhouse and TeeJay's (see listings).

Cubby Hole
823 N. Federal Hwy., Fort Lauderdale
Circa: 1997-2019

Billed itself as "The best little butch bar in Fort Lauderdale." Dark and smoky, even after smoking in bars was officially banned. It opened early in the morning and featured a hard-drinking crowd of bears. It closed at the beginning of the COVID pandemic and is now home to Roxane's, a straight hipster hangout.

Billy H. said, "It was a man's bar no frills, a friendly group. I was younger than most, but the men did not make me feel out of place. I had great conversations with many men."

Bill Buff said, "It smelled like cigarettes and ass. You could get a blow job in there faster than you could get a drink from the bartender."

Cupcakes
1951 N. Powerline Rd., Fort Lauderdale
Circa: early 1990s

This was a women's pub. Club 1951 (also a women's bar), Eagle, Steel, and Uncle Charlie's (see listings) all occupied this space at various times. The building has since been demolished.

Curve Club
1025 N. Federal Hwy., Fort Lauderdale
Circa: 2000-2001

Located where Federal Highway and Sunrise Blvd. merge (hence the "curve"), it was known as a hustler bar. Lori Tanner says, "It was an after-hours hard-core place." The buildings in that area have since been demolished.

David's
502 E. Sunrise Blvd., Fort Lauderdale
Circa: 1988–1994

A neighborhood hangout. This space has also been home to Traxx, Phoenix, and, since 1997, Mona's (see listings).

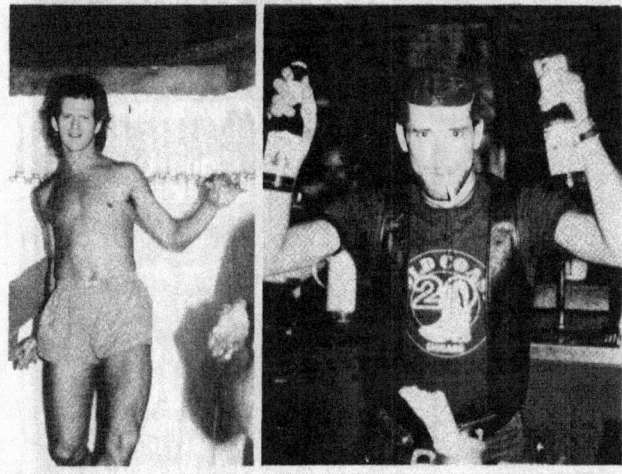

David's Bar is fast becoming "Party Headquarters" for the Ft. Lauderdale set. Bartenders John and Carl were honored at a recent party celebrating their anniversary with the bar, and last week *Torso Magazine* sponsored a talent hunt which brought out some of South Florida's finest specimins.

Deck
401 N. Atlantic Ave., Fort Lauderdale
Circa: 1995–1996

This was a piano bar in the Bahama Hotel on the beach, also popular for its Tea by the Sea Sunday tea dance.

Depot
1243 NE 11th Ave., Fort Lauderdale
Circa: 2009–2012

Took over the space formerly occupied by Bill's Filling Station (see listing). Other bars at this location include Two on a Match, Hector's, and Le Boy (see listings).

Depot Cabana Bar
2935 N. Federal Hwy., Fort Lauderdale
Circa: 2011–2013

Located in a motel, it was voted "Friendliest Bar in Fort Lauderdale" in 2012. DJ Karen Ward would spin at the monthly "She Tea." This was also home to Splash (see listing).

Dinopete's
4221 N. State Rd. 7, Hollywood
Circa: 2004–2006

Mixed, more straight than gay. A '50s vibe predominated with doo-wop music and a cabaret show at this supper club which hosted some LGBTQ events.

District
211 SW 2nd Ave., Fort Lauderdale
Circa: 1993–1996

Sometimes listed as 220 SW 3rd St., the building had entrances on both streets. John Manzi was one of the owners—he was also involved with Cathode Ray (see listing). It featured male dancers and was one of the spaces carved out of the old Backstreet (see listing). It was a late-night club that brought in many big-name dance club recording artists. This would later be home to The Lodge (see listing).

In 1994 the club hosted a debate between ACT-UP, represented by Michelangelo Signorile, and community groups who felt that gay people should dress more conservatively. It also hosted benefits for ACT-UP. This would later be home to The Lodge (see listing.)

Electra recalls, "I hosted a lot of shows there. One night we had a Carol Channing look-alike contest because Carol Channing was appearing at the Broward Center. Well, she came in and entered the contest as a joke. And she lost!"

Dock 501
501 SE New River Dr., Fort Lauderdale
Circa: 1988–1989

It opened as a floating restaurant and bar on a 165-foot former Coast Guard cutter.

The owners were Denis Turmer and Kevin Sharp. The site had been plagued with numerous businesses opening and closing quickly. Dock 501 was no exception. Despite a glittering grand opening in October 1988, covered by *hot shots Magazine*, it did not last six months.

Dog House
2505 W. Broward Blvd., Fort Lauderdale
Circa: 1977–1978

An after-hours club.

Doll House Lounge
1236 Federal Hwy., Fort Lauderdale
Circa: 1964-1980

This is now home to a popular BBQ restaurant.

Drynk
2255 Wilton Dr., Wilton Manors
Circa: 2018-present

A tiny spot with beautifully landscaped side and back patios, it features hand-crafted cocktails, handsome mixologists, and very chi-chi decor. It's a spot to see and be seen. Many interviewed about this bar echoed Larry D's feelings, citing the friendliness of the bartenders and "one of the best bartenders in Fort Lauderdale, Jay McCracken!"

Owned by the same people who run Patio Pizza and Bar (see listing).

Dudes
3270 NE 33rd St., Fort Lauderdale
Circa: 2004-2013

Sometimes advertised as "Dudes on the Beach," it was in a strip mall near the ocean and a group of condominiums known as Coral Ridge Towers with a strong gay demographic. It highlighted male strippers on one side and drag and cabaret on the other. It attracted an older crowd. Khris Francis would perform. Eric Rosenblatt and Wade Bolton bought the bar in 2012, it closed in 2013. *USA Today*'s 10 Best said, "Dudes takes the idea of a gay club up a notch with its charming, upscale atmosphere and piano bar and nightly specials."

Eagle
510 NE 13th St., Fort Lauderdale
Circa: 1990-1991

Sometimes listed as Florida Eagle or Fort Lauderdale Eagle, it opened on September 9, 1990. An ad on June 27, 1991, announced it was "moving to a new nest." It was ahead of its time—this area is now a hip neighborhood, and the space formerly occupied by the bar is now home to True Colonics Spa.

Eagle
Pompano
Circa: 2007-2008

A leather bar, unaffiliated with other Eagles, sometimes listed as Eagle in Exile using the address of another entrance. The address listed in the *Damron Guides* was incorrect as it was a private home. It could have been across the street 524/526 Sample Rd., a commercial building.

Eagle
2209 Wilton Dr., Wilton Manors
Circa: 2020 -present

A leather bar owned by Salvo Mule. It opened in the spot formerly occupied by Backstage, Bill's Filling Station/Bill's/B's, The Blue Parrot Lounge, Club Silver, Chardee's, The Palms, Southern Nights, and Wolf (see listings). The 8,000-square-foot bar has a large dance floor, a small bar called the Bear's Den, a small patio, and large open cruising areas. It seems to have found its niche and draws good crowds. It has hosted Florida Leather Week and Tropical Bear events.

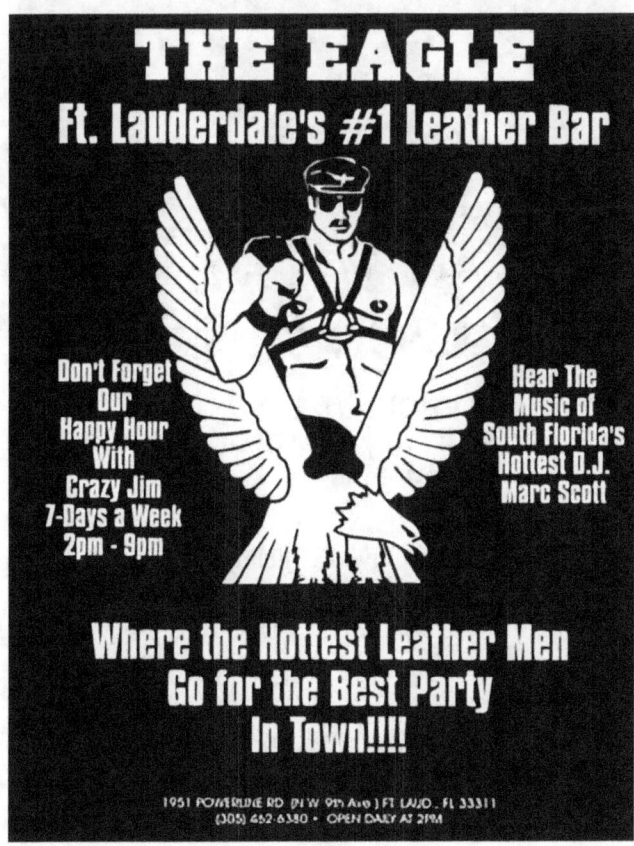

Eagle (Fort Lauderdale)
1951 N. Powerline Rd., Fort Lauderdale
Circa: 1991-2004

A leather bar, sometimes listed as the Florida Eagle or Fort Lauderdale Eagle. It hosted porn stars doing "private shows." It moved from 13th St. (see below) in July 1991. Other bars in the space include Club 1951 and Cupcakes (women's bars), Steel, and Uncle Charlie's (see listings). The building has since been demolished.

Elbo Room
241 S. Fort Lauderdale Beach Blvd., Fort Lauderdale
Circa: 1965-present

Mostly straight but listed as gay-friendly as far back as the 1960s. Walter Silverman recalls, "It was always busy, there were always people in there. You could pick up horny straight guys. It was very effective." It was featured in the movie *Where the Boys Are*.

Elements
3073 NE 6th Ave., Wilton Manors
Circa: 2004-2009

Mixed men's and women's dance club. Before Elements, it was Junkyard and is now home to Scandals (see listings).

Eleven
2229 W. Broward Blvd., Fort Lauderdale
Circa: 1981

The building has since been torn down.

Encounters
6060 Miramar Pkwy., Miramar
Circa: 1981

Only listed in *The Damron Guide* once, it now houses a vegetarian restaurant. This was also the location of Club Sappho (see listing).

End Up
3521 W. Broward Blvd., Fort Lauderdale
Circa: 1994-2000

A late-night dance club owned by Toni Barone (Electra called her a great gal, like a butch John Travolta kind of dyke) in the Romark Building, a five-story office complex. The bar was named because, at the end of the night, everyone would "end up" there. Previously home to GW's Place and Sleaze Alley (see listings).

Everglades (in Chainz)
1931 S. Federal Hwy., Fort Lauderdale
Circa: 1961-1999

The bar held its 25th-anniversary party in August 1986. In 1990 it went from beer only to a full liquor license. At one time it was listed as the oldest gay bar in Broward County. Its free Sunday buffets were very popular. Due to its proximity to the naval base, it was very popular with naval personnel and eventually, it was declared off-limits to them. Listed as Everglades in Chainz, then just Chainz (see listing) shortly before closing.

In June 1976, a young man attempted to rob the bar, but the bartenders, Maurice Lopez and Brian Alves knocked the gun out of his hand and beat him with a nightstick they kept behind the bar. They held him until the police arrived.

Clark recalls, "It was tired when I first moved to Fort Lauderdale in 1975. I think I was there once. There were only two people in there."

Electra says, "They had hurricane parties. They would turn on a fan and spray a hose through it."

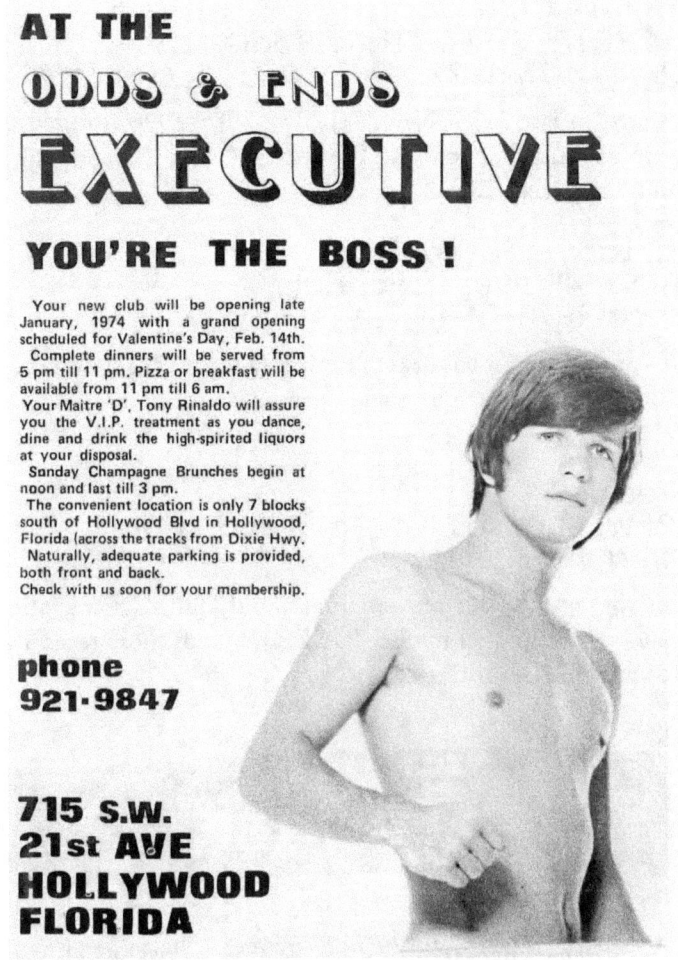

Executive Room (Odds & Ends)
715 SW 21st Ave., Hollywood
Circa: 1974–1979

It was owned by the same folks who owned Odds & Ends. A restaurant/cabaret, it held its grand opening on Valentine's Day, 1974. In October, it advertised its new manager, Jerry Fitzpatrick. It featured drag shows, "Ted Larson's Foxy Follies" with Tiny Tina, Angie Walker, Jeanine Harlow, Joey Knight, and Marc Sinclaire. Later, it was home to Hollywood Nights and Club Shadows (see listings).

Exit 21 (See Club 21)

Exit 66/Rock Bar
219 S. Fort Lauderdale Beach Blvd., Fort Lauderdale
Circa: 2009–2018

Cal Fortis and Ken Smith, the folks behind CroBar, opened the bar on March 15, 2009. It had five different bar areas and a pool, all decorated in Americana kitsch. It was listed in the *Fun Maps* gay guide, but it was mostly a "bro" bar.

Fantasy Club
714 SE 17th St., Fort Lauderdale
Circa: 1975-1977

Opened in late 1975. New Year's Eve 1975/1976 featured a complimentary buffet and a "Gayla Show" with Evan St. John, Sandy, and Trixie Taylor.

Fat Lady's/Fat Ladies
811 SE 14th Ave., Hallandale
Circa: 1976-1978

This was a women's bar next to Keith's. Different ads show both spellings of the name. Its grand opening was held on March 2, 1976.

Fireside
321 W. Sunrise Blvd., Fort Lauderdale
Circa: 1987

This space was a cabaret, restaurant, and lounge. It was also home to Georgie's, Impulse, Badd Boys, and, most recently, Slammer 321 (see listings).

Fireside
RESTAURANT & LOUNGE

"SPECIALS" In Our Restaurant	"SPECIALS" In Our Lounge
Tuesday • Wednesday • Thursday DAILY SPECIALS	Everyday — "HAPPY HOUR" 4-8 P.M.
Chicken Marango $7.95	$1.00—Well • Wine • Draft Beer
Pasta Du Jour 7.95	
Catch of the Day 7.95	Tuesday — Join "Eddie"
Prime Rib 9.95	.75¢ Our Singing Bartender
Includes House salad, veg. du jour homemade rolls	Punch for a night of country
Plus Our Regular Menu	Shooters
	Wednesday — Hump Day Special! Draft Beef — 75¢ 7-8 P.M.
Friday and Saturday **Carol Neal's Cabaret Show** *An Evening of Dining, Dancing or just drinking*	Thursday — "Ladies Day" 2 for 1 — Well, Wine, Draft 7-9 P.M.
Featuring Kelly Neal and more.	Friday — $1.00 Well • Wine • Draft 5-8 P.M. With Free Hor D'Oeuvres 5-7 "Listen For the Bartender's Bell" 5 Minutes Specials Throughout The Night Manager's Choice— 1.00
Sunday—"Talent Nite" Win dinner for 2 w/Bottle of Wine or 2 Free 1 Day Cruises on Sea Holiday *"Sign Up Now"*	Saturday — Last Chance Happy Hour 11-12 A.M. — $1.00 Well • Wine • Draft
WITH DINNER 20% OFF ANY BOTTLE OF WINE	Sunday — Late Afternoon Lite Bites $2.00 - 4-6 PM *Choice of:* Chicken Wings • Fried Zucchini Potato Skins • Fried Mushrooms Nachos • House Salad • Pizza Bread
"Check out our picture board and look for your face. Memories from the past year." "Take your shot with you."	**321 WEST SUNRISE BLVD.** (BETWEEN ANDREWS AND I-95) CALL: 462-FIRE FOR RESERVATIONS

Flamingo Bay
3148 NE 12th Ave., Oakland Park
Circa: 1987-1989

A cruisy video bar, it briefly rebranded as Bay City Station in March 1988. It may have been affiliated with Flamingo's. Roxanne's and Odds & Ends were also at this location (see listings).

Flamingo's
3148 NE 12th Ave., Oakland Park
Circa: 2004-2010

A neighborhood bar with food, also sometimes listed as Flomingos (sic). The grand opening was held on August 2, 2004. Roxanne's and Odds & Ends were also at this location (see listing).

Flip Flops
3051 NE 32nd Ave., Fort Lauderdale
Circa: 2010-2022

An LGBTQ-friendly restaurant and bar on the Intracoastal. It hosted a Sunday drag brunch and tea dance. "We miss that place," said Randy Clark.

A true dive, it closed in 2022 when its dock collapsed sending patrons into the water.

Flomingo's (see Flamingo's)

Flying Machine
Federal Hwy. and SE 28th St., Fort Lauderdale
Circa: 1975

It was a dining and dance hall with a large disco, owned by the same folks who ran the Marlin Beach Hotel. It was open from 9 a.m. to 4 a.m. daily and booked rock bands. According to Lori Tanner, The Copa (see listing) later opened in this space.

Follies
2960 N. Federal Hwy., Fort Lauderdale
Circa: 1977

This location was advertised in the June 1977 issue of *David Magazine* for auditions for "An Entertaining Restaurant and Tavern." Tangerine Disco and Montana were also at this location (see listings). It later became home to the Mason Jar restaurant, which was popular with the LGBTQ community before the building was torn down and the business relocated.

Curtain up! Light the lights!

WE'RE OPEN & READY!

WE'VE GOT SMILES, WE'VE GOT FOOD, DRINK & ENTERTAINMENT. WE'VE GOT TRUFFLES AND LOBSTER MOUSSE. WE'VE GOT SINGERS AND DANCERS, MUSICIANS AND MAGICIANS. WE'VE GOT SATIN AND SILK, TOP HATS, DIAMONDS AND LOTS OF FEATHERS. WE'VE GOT THE FOLLIES!

SO JOIN US FOR DINNER OR COCKTAILS AFTER...

because CAROL BREVAL, CHUCK LYONS and DELUXE want to entertain you.

EVENINGS, TUESDAY THROUGH SUNDAY
DARK MONDAYS
DINNER RESERVATIONS PLEASE

follies
An Entertaining Restaurant and Tavern
2960 N. Federal Hwy.   Ft. Lauderdale   563 4004

Full Moon Lounge
708-710 N. Federal Hwy., Fort Lauderdale
Circa: 1975

The lounge hosted an Aquarian buffet party in February 1975. An ad in *Travel With Pride* listed "Your hostess Estelle, formerly of the 1492." It is also the location of Lefty's and Haymarket (see listings).

COOK - OUT

THIS SUNDAY MAY 11
7—9 p.m
ALL BAR DRINKS .85 cents
CANNED BEER .60 cents
(TONY WILL BE HANDLING AND PREPARING ALL THE MEAT)

TAURUS PARTY

THURSDAY MAY 22nd
EVERYONE WELCOME
COME HELP ALL THE BULLS CELEBRATE.

ANNIVERSARY WEEK

SUN. MAY 18th THRU SAT. 24th
ALL BAR DRINKS .85 cents
CANNED BEER .60 cents
ALL WEEK

The Full Moon
The FRIENDLIEST and MOST TALKED ABOUT bar in Fort Lauderdale!
708 - 710 N. FEDERAL, parking in rear
763 - 8881

ESTELLE AND THE CREW WOULD LIKE TO TAKE THIS OPPORTUNITY TO THANK ALL THEIR CUSTOMERS AND FRIENDS FOR MAKING THIS PAST YEAR PLEASANT AND SUCCESSFUL.

Galleria G'Vanni
625 E. Las Olas Blvd., Fort Lauderdale
Circa: 1989-1992

The chi-chi restaurant and supper club featured cabaret performances, such as Monti Rock III. In 1991, a $350,000 portrait by the 16th-century Italian artist Raphael was stolen from G'Vanni's, which was known for its fine art collection. Years later, it turned up outside next to a delivery of bread. Police surmised that the thief had a change of heart or realized the painting could not be fenced.

Gallery (Big Bill's)
2889 W. Broward Blvd., Fort Lauderdale
Circa: 1971-1974

THE GALLERY
Ft. Lauderdale's Newest Show Bar
NOW OPEN 7 NIGHTS 5 P.M. TIL 4 A.M.
SHOWTIME 12 AND 2 A.M. EVERYNIGHT FEATURING LANA KUNTZ AND JAMIE

GRAND OPENING
JUNE 12, 13

the twins LANA and DONNA

DONNA DRAG

GUEST STARS: The River Queens from St Louis DONNA DRAG and CANDY

GO GO BOYS, DANCING

JAMIE
2889 W. BROWARD BLVD.

LANA KUNTZ
PHONE 583-9942

A drag show bar, with amateur go-go boy contests. The grand opening was June 12, 1971. An ad in in the January 1972 edition of *David Magazine* boasted a show featuring, "The unpredictable Mr. Michael, Totie, Aretha, Teddie, and Bobbie. The twins Lana and Donna, Jamie, Lana Kuntz, and Donna Drag." In 1974, it changed its name to Big Bill's (see listing) but kept the same format and owners. It closed soon after. The space later was home to Good Times (see listing).

Garth's
Hollywood
Circa: 1960s

Gary TB's Lounge
3799 N. Dixie Hwy., Fort Lauderdale
Circa: 1977–1978

The disco featured drag shows.

Gaylord's
1753 N. Andrews Ext., Fort Lauderdale
Circa: 1974

It was advertised as being a "Different and unique atmosphere." This was also home to Andrews Extension, Anywayz, and Side Street.

Gelati Martini Lounge
2037 Wilton Dr., Wilton Manors
Circa: 2010–2011

Guy Lehoux and Barry Dotson owned this bar with light food service. It later became home to 13/Even (see listing).

Georgie's
321 W. Sunrise Blvd., Fort Lauderdale
Circa: 1989–1992

George Kessinger opened his piano bar and restaurant on May 2, 1988, years before opening the infamous Georgie's Alibi in Wilton Manors. Advertised as the "Largest gay bar in Fort Lauderdale," it featured many cabaret acts and hosted numerous benefits. In late 1992, in response to the country music craze, it changed its format to a country-western bar and changed its name to Badd Boys (see listing). This location was home to many queer clubs, including The Fireside, Impulse, and most recently, Slammer 321 (see listings).

Georgie's Alibi/Alibi Monkey Bar (see Alibi)

Glitz
2100 Hollywood Blvd., Hollywood
Circa: 1991-1994

A piano bar and disco with drag shows—Nikki Adams directed the shows. Other bars at this location include Ladies' Loft, Cookie's Intimate Lounge, and Zelda's (see listings).

Glory Holes
1954 NW Powerline Rd., Fort Lauderdale
Circa: 1981-1982

A BYOB spot with male strippers and an active backroom scene.

GLOW Lounge
1116 W. Broward Blvd., Fort Lauderdale
Circa: 1988-1993

A neighborhood bar next to a police station with a drag show called Glamorous Ladies of West Broward. It was also home to Bottom's Up, Johnny's, and 11 Nightclub (see listings).

Godmother's
2077 Pembroke Rd., Hollywood
Circa: 1986

A women's bar.

Gold Coast
2471 E. Commercial Blvd., Fort Lauderdale
Circa: 1995-1998

A piano bar.

Good Timers Pub
200 W. Broward Blvd., Fort Lauderdale
Circa: 1986

This was also home to the bar Backstreet, which was open at the same time and rented space to Good Timers Pub, and later to Storm and Club Q (see listings).

Good Times
2889 W. Broward Blvd., Fort Lauderdale
Circa: 1975-1983

The bar held a limbo contest on June 28, 1975, and offered a free buffet the next day. A late-night bar, it advertised as Fort Lauderdale's only 4 a.m. bar, offering male strippers, just as its predecessor in this space, Gallery/Big Bill's did (see listings).

Gregarious
2033 Wilton Dr., Wilton Manors
Circa: 2013-2014

A short-lived dining and drinking establishment, that, judging by Yelp reviews, didn't get either right.

Grotto
1914 E. Oakland Park Blvd., Fort Lauderdale
Circa: 1975-1997

The bar's grand opening was advertised as February 1 in a 1975 issue of *David Magazine*. An ad in *Travel With Pride* from 1975 invited everyone to "Come cruise and dance." The bar changed ownership in 1993 and added New to its name. In 1980 *TWN* wrote, "A very butch place...It's amazing what a coat of black paint over everything and some license plates and hubcaps will do for a place."

Robert Fronner recalls, "This was my home bar for a while. It had a pool table, jukebox, and a couple of video arcade games. It was a very small neighborhood bar with a good mix of people and very friendly. The owner was Canadian (lived in Canada).

The main bartender was partial to deaf guys. Pitcher Billy was a fixture here. Night Train was our choice for "shots" as this was a beer/wine bar."

Later home to Le Bar (see listing). *The Damron Guide* has the years of operation of these bars overlapping, but it's more likely Grotto closed in 1995 and was not deleted from the magazine.

Grotto-Riverside
602 SW 12th Ave., Fort Lauderdale
Circa: 1987–1988

Formerly the Riverside Pub (see listing).

G Spot
2031 Wilton Dr., Wilton Manors
Circa: 2017–2018

Lisette Gomez co-owned this lesbian bar. Jennifer S. attended the opening, "G Spot Bar is a brand-new all-girl bar in Wilton. There hasn't been one for several years now, so the excitement of this bar opening was huge! The place was packed wall to wall with ladies partying. It even spilled out into the streets. It was awesome!"

Other bars at this location include Ballz, Pint, Circuit, and Club 2031 (see listings). At the same time, Sidelines (see listing) operated out of this address and exceeded G Spot by one year. It is a large bar, and it appears they shared a space and a liquor license.

GW's Place
3521 W. Broward Blvd., Fort Lauderdale
Circa: 1991

A BYOB club in the Romark Building, which was also home to Sleaze Alley and The End Up (see listings).

Gym
901 SW 27th Ave., Fort Lauderdale
Circa: 1975–1977

An ad in a January 1976 *David Magazine* read, "In memoriam George P Long, known and loved by all as Mona." Later this space would become home to Helen's Hole and Boots (see listings).

Gym Sportsbar
2287 Wilton Dr., Wilton Manors
Circa: 2015–present

The Florida outpost of the bars in NYC and WeHo. It has a loyal following among sports fans, shows games on its screens, and sponsors many sports teams.

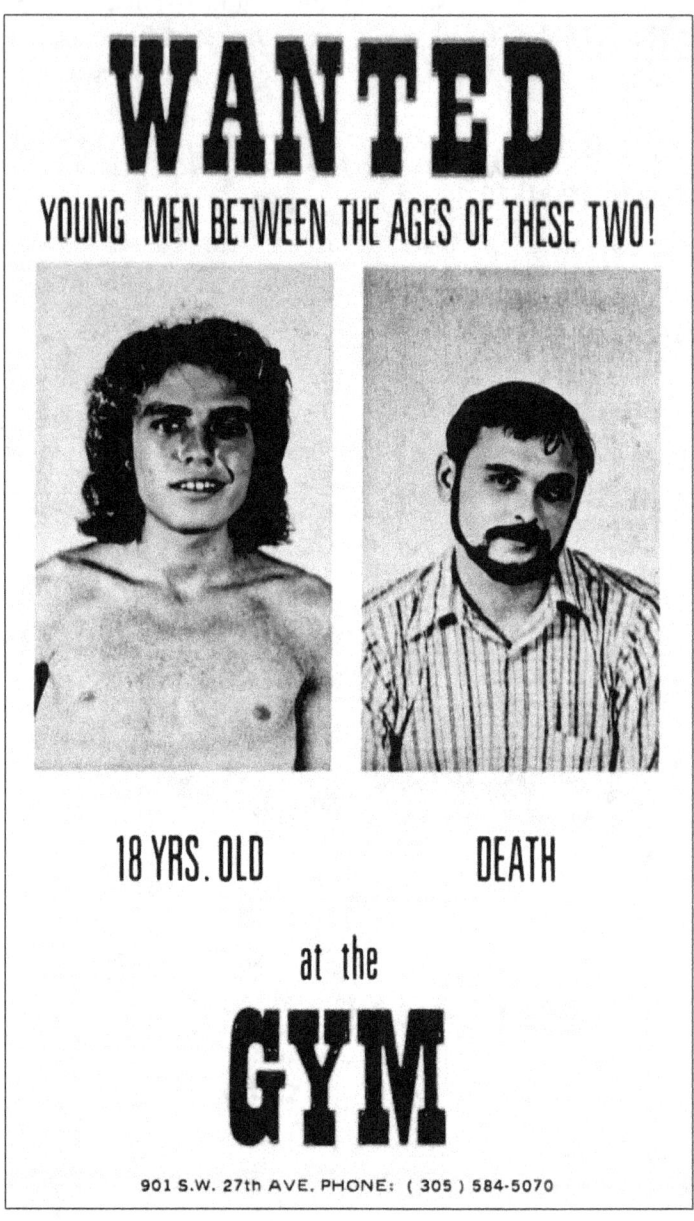

Gypsy's Cabaret
2750 E. Oakland Park Blvd., Fort Lauderdale
Circa: 2000

The cabaret, owned by Paul Pavone and partner Tony DeLuise, put on shows for seniors during the week but also featured special events such as Bi-Curious Saturdays, Love Jones poetry slam, and a Friday night event called Women for Womyn. Formerly home to Club Xanadu and Whale & Porpoise (see listings).

Male 'Girls' Still Entertain In Lewd Show At Club Ha Ha

The controversial Club Ha Ha in Hallandale again is receiving attention because of the lewdness of its entertainment despite an amended circuit court order that the establishment must conform to the same moral standards observed in other night clubs.

Club Ha Ha was ordered closed late last winter after Circuit Judge Tedder ruled the place a public nuisance. Probation Officer Tuppen had entered suit against the club, charging that female impersonators were putting on a show that was "lewd, indecent and nasty." The amended reopening order was issued later.

Turbulent history of the club continued recently when a petition for a writ of mandamus against the City of Hallandale to enforce the issuance of a liquor license to the night spot was granted by Circuit Judge Chillingworth to Charles [Babe] Baker, owner of the club.

Baker reopened his club this week, and Broward countians were anxious to know what manner of show he would substitute for the chorus line of female impersonators which provided entertainment last season.

They found their answer in women dressed in short order. Men dressed in women's gowns, wearing long wigs, high heels and heavily coated with make up, are the featured performers in a 70-minute show which is first presented starting at about 11 p. m.

Local nightclubbers noted that some of the lewdness of last season's show is lacking, but that basically the entertainment follows the familiar pattern.

1945

CLUB *the Original* HA! HA!
of NEW YORK

Where GAYETY KNOWS NO RESTRAINT

GALA OPENING
Wednesday Night Jan 16

BABE BAKER PRESENTS
Francis Dunn   Pat Clayton
Brooks Twins   Leon LaVerde
Bennett Green   Jackie Lee
George Oliver   Al Berl
Johnny Mangum
KEN MAYER
And His Band

NO COUVERT

Smartest and most Sophisticated Entertainment in Florida

DIRECTLY IN FRONT OF HOLLYWOOD KENNEL CLUB

'Babe' Baker Sentenced By Court Order

Club Ha-Ha Operator Guilty Of Contempt

Charles [Babe] Baker, operator of Club Ha-Ha, Hallandale night spot, was ordered to pay a $250 fine or to serve 30 days in jail after Baker was found guilty by Circuit Judge Tedder late Tuesday of contempt of court.

Baker was charged in a petition for contempt citation signed by Attorney H. J. Lather with ignoring a court order permanently restraining the Club Ha-Ha from presenting any kind of entertainment that was lewd, indecent or below moral standards observed by similar places of amusement.

After a parade of witnesses had been heard during the four-hour hearing in Judge Tedder's chambers, Lathero asked that Baker be held in contempt, and declared that presentation of female impersonators at Baker's club is "intolerable" in this county.

Robert C. Lane, attorney for Baker, asserted that the show recently presented at the club since its opening this year was not lewd or indecent and moved for discharge of the defendant on grounds that no evidence of contempt had been submitted.

Lane further pointed out that the supreme court, in upholding Judge Tedder's previous injunction against the club, had ruled that while any show tending to corrupt public morals could be enjoined, the use of men impersonating women was not in itself illegal.

In giving his decision, Tedder said he had expected that the case again would come up in his court, because the supreme court's findings might be construed as giving Baker a right to continue presenting the same type of entertainment as had been found objectionable in the past.

The court affirmed Baker's legal right to present a show featuring female impersonators. But the ruling was that the entertainment still was of a lewd, indecent and nasty character.

Tedder said he believed Baker had become so accustomed to the atmosphere of the club that he actually saw nothing wrong with the show and "actually believed he was running a clean show."

But he ruled that there had been a violation of the court's restraining order and that the defendant's own witnesses' testimony had showed the show presented this year was substantially the same as that of last year.

Baker's attorney indicated there might be an appeal of the court's findings to the state supreme court.

1945

It's Our Opinion--

Female-Impersonator Shows Not for Broward.

A GROUP of citizens visited this department Monday and inquired of us as to what could be done to prohibit County night clubs from featuring all female-impersonator floor shows.

We immediately suspected the group had reference to the Club Ha Ha, as we, too, had seen the announcement of opening this week in a Miami newspaper.

Taking the Club Ha Ha on its past performances we offered three procedures which they could follow:

1. Appear in a body before the Hallandale City Commission with proof that the type of show presented at the Club Ha Ha is not in the best interests of the people of Broward County and suggest that the club's liquor license not be renewed.

2. If turned down by the City of Hallandale, repeat the performance before the County Commission with the same request.

3. If the County refused to listen to their plea, then have a group of five to ten persons attend one of the performances, equip themselves with eye-witness testimony and go into court for an injunction to close the place.

NIGHT CLUBS TOO INTIMATE. Personally, we can't see the need of that type show in this County. We've seen some very high type female-impersonator acts back in the days of vaudeville, but the actors were always on the stage and never mingled with the audience. Night clubs are too intimate for such entertainment, especially, when the entire show consists of nothing but female impersonators.

We don't mind reporting that we received numerous complaints last season from citizens and visitors about the Club Ha Ha shows. And it's a known fact that the military placed the club out-of-bounds for service men. That's reason enough for scrutiny of planned entertainment of the club for the coming season by our officials before they issue liquor permits.

This department never intended to set itself up as a governor of what "type" night club entertainment was best for habitants of the pleasure palaces. We've always felt that if an adult [any person three-times-seven] had to have music, girls and comedians with his meal that was his business, but when people continually complain about certain types of entertainment then it's time to call a halt.

If, and when, the Club Ha Ha decides to present shows such as other clubs do in the County we'd be the first to sidetrack our complaint, but until they do we think we are duty-bound to speak out and warn mothers and fathers that an all female-impersonator show is not the right kind of entertainment for our youngsters.

1946

Club Operator Faces Hearing

Charles [Babe] Baker, operator or the Ha-Ha club in Hallandale, will appear before Circuit Judge Tedder Dec. 17 to show cause why he should not be held in contempt of court in continuing operation of the club on what is alleged to be the same basis as when an injunction was issued by the court late last winter.

The injunction issued by circuit court was later modified when the case was carried to the state supreme court. The modification permitted shows of the same moral standard as in other clubs in the area.

The motion for the contempt hearing was made by Attorney J. H. Lathero, who represented Probation Officer Frank Tuppen in the original complaint against the club.

The injunction was granted on the basis that the show presented at the club was lewd and destructive to public morals. The present show, it was claimed, features female impersonators.

1945

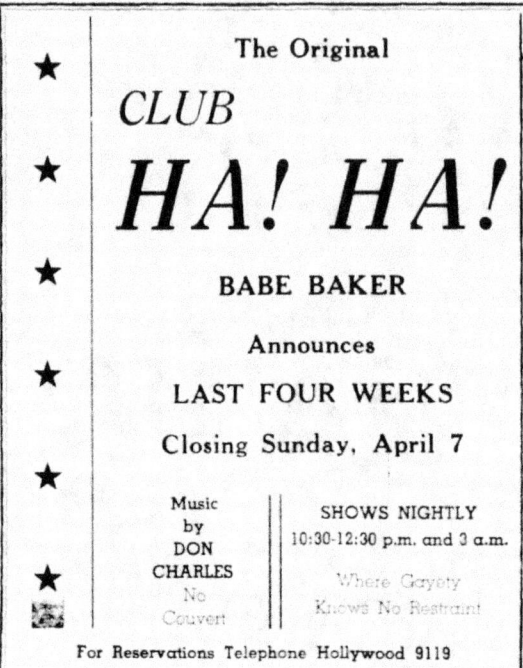

★ The Original

CLUB

★ HA! HA!

BABE BAKER

★ Announces

LAST FOUR WEEKS

Closing Sunday, April 7

★

Music by DON CHARLES No Couvert

SHOWS NIGHTLY
10:30-12:30 p.m. and 3 a.m.

Where Gayety Knows No Restraint

For Reservations Telephone Hollywood 9119

Service Boys Barred From Club Ha Ha

Army and Navy Boards Issue Joint Order That Club is Out Of Bounds to Them

Army and Navy personnel are deprived of the privilege of visiting the Club Ha Ha located south of Hollywood on Federal highway, according to a joint order of Army and Navy Disciplinary Control Boards declaring the club out of bounds to the service men.

The restrictions are signed by Maj. William B. Martin, provost marshal of the Fourth Service Command, and they order Military Police and Shore Patrol to see that the order is enforced. The order declares the club is not suitable for personnel to visit.

"For the best interests of the military service," said Maj. Martin, "men are not permitted to visit the establishment."

Complaints voiced by persons living in Broward county have described the club as "Raw," "Too Sophisticated," and "Too Different."

When Club Ha Ha representatives applied for a liquor license in Hallandale, they were at first refused a permit. Then the Broward County Commission, meeting at Ft. Lauderdale, approved the application for a permit. The council of Hallandale followed up by granting a license.

Danny Daniels, master of ceremonies at the club, describes it as "Florida's most sophisticated nightspot for diversion seekers."

Jackie Maye has been a headliner there for several seasons and is again this season. In some of the shows presented he dresses in a white satin gown and impersonates a woman. He wears a long-bobbed, black wig, artificial eyelashes, makeup, red fingernails, sparkling earrings and high-heeled shoes to add to the entertainment of the "glamour boys."

Then Jackie, wearing a red satin, short length dress, with black net stockings, and high-heeled bow-tie shoes, plays the part of Sadie Thompson in a Club Ha Ha version of "Rain."

1945

Male 'Girls' Still Entertain In Lewd Show At Club Ha Ha

The controversial Club Ha Ha in Hallandale again is receiving attention because of the lewdness of its entertainment despite an amended circuit court order that the establishment must conform to the same moral standards observed in other night clubs.

Club Ha Ha was ordered closed late last winter after Circuit Judge Tedder ruled the place a public nuisance. Probation Officer Tuppen had entered suit against the club, charging that female impersonators were putting on a show that was "lewd, indecent and nasty." The amended reopening order was issued later.

Turbulent history of the club continued recently when a petition for a writ of mandamus against the City of Hallandale to enforce the issuance of a liquor license to the night spot was granted by Circuit Judge Chillingworth to Charles [Babe] Baker, owner of the club.

Baker reopened his club this week, and Broward countians were anxious to know what manner of show he would substitute for the chorus line of female impersonators which provided entertainment last season.

They found their answer in short order. Men dressed in women's gowns, wearing long wigs, high heels and heavily coated with make up, are the featured performers in a 70-minute show which is first presented starting at about 11 p.m.

Local nightclubbers noted that some of the lewdness of last season's show is lacking, but that basically the entertainment follows the familiar pattern.

1945

Ha Ha Club
Federal Hwy., Hallandale
Circa: 1933-1947

Charles "Babe" Baker opened the female impersonator show lounge in Hallandale after his Ha Ha Club in New York City was forced to shut down after harassment by local politicians. The club faced similar harassment soon after opening in Florida. Frank Tuppen, a juvenile probation officer with political ambitions, filed a complaint against the venue. He argued that the club's performers were "sexual perverts" who had embedded "in the minds of the youngsters" who lived in the area. In March 1947, a Florida court ordered it to close, declaring it a public nuisance.

Baker appealed to the Florida Supreme Court, but in October 1947, the state supreme court upheld the injunction in its 1947 decision State v. Federal Amusement Co. It affirmed the lower court's decision that the club was a public nuisance stating, "Men impersonating women" in performances that are "nasty, suggestive and indecent" injure the "manners and morals of the people." The Club burned to the ground shortly thereafter, and Barker moved to Leon & Eddie's in Miami Beach (see listing). Governor Ron DeSantis used the ruling in 2023 to ban drag shows in the state of Florida.

The ban was overturned by Florida's Supreme Court in 2024.

Hamburger Mary's
2449 Wilton Dr., Wilton Manors
Circa: 2002-2006

The popular chain opened, but within a few years, the local owners quit the franchise and re-opened it as Rosie's Bar & Grill (see listing). In October 2004, actors Robert Gant and Peter Paige, then starring in *Queer as Folk* made an appearance at the restaurant to encourage people to register to vote. The bar/restaurant focused on live music and drag queens, as it still does.

Hamburger Mary's
2426 Wilton Dr., Wilton Manors
Circa: 2021-2024

The franchise operation opened a location in Wilton Manors directly across the street from Rosie's, which used to be a Hamburger Mary's. It was fraught with problems from the beginning. They bought the business just a few weeks before Stonewall Pride and struggled to open in time. They opened but were not fully staffed or prepared and never caught up (or caught on).

In 2023, Hamburger Mary's filed a lawsuit challenging a new law by Governor Ron DeSantis banning drag performances where children may be present, citing a "chilling effect" on First Amendment rights to free speech as guaranteed by the US Constitution. US District Judge Gregory Presnell rejected the

state's request to dismiss the case and granted an injunction temporarily blocking the law.

Under-staffed and under-trained, service was abysmal, and the food was awful. The business was only able to remain in operation by importing big-name drag names for shows. The owners eventually sold to the Canadian chain, The Well (see listing). Previously this location was home to Sidelines, Matty's, and Rumors (see listings).

Hannibal's
201 SW 2nd. St., Fort Lauderdale
Circa: 1985-1986

A hustler bar. This colorful space (orange and purple striped wall, a royal blue ceiling, gold trim) was formerly home to Bobby Winn's and later Regatta (see listings).

Haymarket
710 N. Federal Hwy., Fort Lauderdale
Circa: 1999-2002

It was known as a hustler bar before it was closed by the sheriff citing the sale of drugs and lewd acts. Formerly the location of Lefty's and Full Moon Lounge (see listings).

Heaven
3937 N. Federal Hwy., Fort Lauderdale
Circa: 1982-1983

Tim Miller remembers, "It was a beautiful bar with a sunken dance floor and bubbles would rise out of it. Rumor had it that it was taking away the Copa's business and they sabotaged it by putting garlic in the air conditioning vents."

Hector's
1243 NE 11th Ave., Fort Lauderdale
Circa: 1984

Other bars at this converted gas station include Two on a Match, Depot, Bill's Filling Station, and Le Boy (see listings).

Helen's Hole Bar
901 SW 27th Ave., Fort Lauderdale
Circa: 1980

It advertised go-go boys. According to one patron, "It was exactly as the location of The Gym and would later be home to Boots (see listings).

Hemingway's of Hollywood
219 N. 21st Ave., Hollywood
Circa: 1992

The building was once Hollywood City Hall and later a police station. It was later rumored to be owned by Al Capone and, at times, a brothel. It was also home to the Manhattan Lounge and Mankind, and X IT which used the Dixie Ave. address (see listings).

Hideaway
2022 NE 18th St., Fort Lauderdale
Circa: 1988–2007

Ads featured a leather guy and boasted drag shows. Lori Tanner recalls that it was a local, neighborhood, bar. Electra remembers, "It was owned by Ray, he was so sweet. Miss Puddin was the show director there. It was a tiny bar, dark and seedy. There were never more than a dozen people in there. Toni Barone used to host an underwear auction there. It was just a sweet neighborhood bar."

Hollywood Nights
715 SW 21st Ave., Hollywood
Circa: 1984

A dance bar. It lost its license because it was required to serve food. When inspected, it was found only to have a case of canned soup and one bowl. It was previously the location of The Executive Room and would later house Club Shadows (see listings).

Hombre
2500 W. Oakland Park Blvd., Oakland Park
Circa: 2011

A country-western-themed bar.

Hunters
2232 Wilton Dr., Wilton Manors
Circa: 2013–present

This popular dance club has expanded to fill four storefronts of the building and in 2024, added an adjacent coffee shop. It is one of the most popular bars in Wilton Manors. Its Sunday "Studio 54" tea dance features classic disco hits and attracts crowds of all ages. It features two bars and an impromptu outdoor lounge that spills into the parking lot. Kitty Meow (Shaun Palacious), in an interview with GayBarchives' Art Smith, said, "Mark Hunter and his establishments have always been top tier. In South Florida and in Wilton Manors in particular. I was on the board of the Pride Center for many years. Every time we would do a special event, he would come aboard and be the presenting sponsor. He has the vision to be such a part of the community. Ultimately, it brings visibility to our community. He gets it. He totally gets it."

Mark Hunter, in an interview with GayBarchives' Art Smith, explained why he opened one of his bars and ended up moving to Wilton Manors. "One of the reasons why I wanted to open here is that it had a vibe that was very laid back. I felt like I was at home. It's a gay Mecca. It had a growing gay population; the city government was very supportive of the gay community."

This space was formerly home to (Atomic) Boom (see listing).

Hysteria
2234 Wilton Dr., Wilton Manors
Circa: 1993–1994

Opened by Mark McKinley and Jaclyn Simon, it barely lasted a year. This space, now occupied by Hunter's expansion (see listing), was also home to Otherglades and Saigon (see listings).

I-Beam (Club)
3045 N. Federal Hwy., Fort Lauderdale
Circa: 1996

A dance club with videos. Electra, said, "It looked like a ski lodge. it was across the street from Target. I hosted a talk show on Monday nights. I'd bring in all sorts of folks to talk about their lives, drag hookers, hustlers, a guy that did piercing."

It was also home to JR's and The Mineshaft (see listings).

Impulse
321 W. Sunrise Blvd., Fort Lauderdale
Circa: 1994

This space has been home to many queer clubs since the 1970s including Georgie's, Badd Boys, The Fireside, and most recently, Slammer 321 (see listings).

Ice Palace
4200 N. Federal Hwy., Fort Lauderdale
Circa: 2004

Tiffany Arieagas had a show every Thursday. Also was home to Lord's, Russell's, and Moby Dick.

Infinity Lounge
2184 Wilton Dr., Wilton Manors
Circa: 2014–present

A martini lounge with a very devoted following. It is owned by Ken Hill and known for its craft martinis, named by *The Sun-Sentinel* as having some of the best martinis in the Fort Lauderdale area. It's quite small but has a large patio facing Wilton Dr., making it a popular spot for people-watching.

J's Bar
2780 Davie Blvd., Fort Lauderdale
Circa: 1999–2022

Easygoing women's bar, drawing a Black and Latino, blue-collar crowd, with happy-hour specials and various events, including poker, karaoke, and DJs. One of Fort Lauderdale's longest-running queer clubs.

Jackhammer
1725 N. Andrews Ext., Fort Lauderdale
Circa: 2007–2014

When it closed, it was supposed to move into the old Boom space, but the partnership did not work out.

Jackhammer
1901 N. Powerline Rd., Fort Lauderdale
Circa: 2001–2007

This location was sold, and it moved to a new location (see above).

Janbar's
5460 N. State Rd. 7, Fort Lauderdale
Circa: 1990

The grand opening was in August 1990, according to *The Sun-Sentinel*, which billed it as a supper club. Ads touted, "Your hosts Jan and Barb." Later home to Pink Tails and Rumors (see listings).

January's (see Jimmy January's)

Jet Set
109 SW 2nd St., Fort Lauderdale
Circa: 2009

It was mostly straight, but it was only gay on Wednesdays. This space was also home to Q (see listing).

Jillybeans
3732 N. Andrews Ave., Oakland Park
Circa: 1993-1994

A women's bar, this is now home to a popular Mexican taco joint.

where consistency is our priority......

Days may be cloudy or sunny, but we're always right on the money.

With new dinner specials every week
Great entertainment (Terry Hammond
7 nights, Karen Ann Wed.-Sun.)
Fun Nites Mon. & Tue. Talent Nite
Comfortable atmosphere, never stuffy!
Friendly service

We're with you always.

We're with you rain or shine.

Always support your gay owned businesses.

January's
restaurant and lounge

1 Block west of I-95 on Davie Blvd. Fort Lauderdale, FL 33312 Reservations 587-0938

Jimmie's Cabaret
1103 E. Las Olas Blvd., Fort Lauderdale
Circa: 2005-2007

A men's bar with drag shows. It was next to Cathode Ray (see listing). Nikki Adams was the show director.

Jimmy January's
2335 Davie Blvd., Fort Lauderdale
Circa: 1983-1992

A large restaurant, it had a piano bar where Skip Arnold and Terry Hammond, two popular local entertainers, performed. It added a second-floor bar called Rafters (see listing) and rechristened itself January's. A new I-95 overpass made it impossible to get to and it closed soon afterward. Randy Clark recalls, "That was Prince Leo De Lignac's favorite place. (editor's note Prince Leon de Lignac, originally born Abraham van Leeuwen in Holland). He and his mother were Jewish, and during WWII he saved a lot of people from the Nazis and was given the title because of that. He was a colorful character. He made a fortune in publishing, lived in St. Tropez, and traveled a lot. He had a 200-foot yacht moored in Fort Lauderdale and he and his lover would go to Jimmy January's all the time."

JJ's (Den)
2283 Wilton Dr., Wilton Manors
Circa: 1984-1988

The first gay bar in Wilton Manors. It was a women's dance club and bar. It expanded and changed its name to The Otherside (see listing). Two popular bartenders were Julie McGowan and Sandy Lockwood. It later became home to Pub on the Drive (see listing).

Johnny's
1116 W. Broward Blvd., Fort Lauderdale
Circa: 1995-2008

Before moving to this location, the bar was located on Himmarshee and 2nd St. and was known as Johnny's Village Inn (see listing). It was famous for its go-go boys. John Moses sold the bar to Sean David in 2008. David also owned Le Boy (see listing). This space was also home to GLOW Lounge, Bottom's Up, and 11 Nightclub (see listings).

Johnny's Village Inn
219 SW 2nd Ave., Fort Lauderdale
Circa: 1980-1994

Opened on August 1, 1980, by John Moses as a stripper bar. It was located on the ground floor with an opening on the corner of the block. Robert Fronner said, "It was a go-go hustler bar at both locations."

Various other clubs occupied the upstairs space, which had a separate entrance on another street.

Johnson's
2340 Wilton Dr., Wilton Manors
Circa: 2017–present

A high-end strip club owned by Matt Coluga, former manager of Swinging Richards in Atlanta. Known for well-built dancers. PJ's Cocks & Tails was previously at this location (see listing).

JR's Bar
3045 N. Federal Hwy., Fort Lauderdale
Circa: 1998

This was home to the short-lived I-Beam and Mineshaft (see listings).

JR's Place
Federal Hwy., near Sheridan, Hollywood
Circa: 1989

No specific address was listed in their ads.

Jungle
545 S. Federal Hwy., Fort Lauderdale
Circa: 1993–98

It was co-owned by lawyer, publisher, and activist Norm Kent, along with Stephen Whitney and Zak Enterline (who later opened Ramrod). Kent would go on to start two LGBTQ publications (*The Express* and *South Florida Gay News*). It was a stripper bar. This was formerly the site of Tunnel Bar.

Junkyard
3073 NE 6th Ave., Wilton Manors
Circa: 2002–2004

The grand opening was held on August 9, 2002. A sleazy space featuring strippers and dancing. After Junkyard closed it was Elements and is now the home to Scandals (see listings).

Juno's
2312 NE 26th St., Fort Lauderdale
Circa: 1993–1995

A women's bar, it was owned by the same people who previously operated Buddy's (see listing). Lori Tanner remembers, "Buddy's was an old man bar, and they weren't doing any business, so they thought, 'Why not make it a lesbian bar?' So, they hired me to run it." Different publications have this open at times overlapping with Phoenix (see listing). This was previously the site of Lefty's II (see listing).

Karnival Beach Club
900 Sunrise Ln., Fort Lauderdale
Circa: 2009

Owned by siblings Karry, Holly, and Joe Lucas, it was a women's bar right off the beach. Wide open, it had a long bar on the main floor and a dance floor upstairs. Fridays were Latin nights, and Saturdays were for the boys.

Keith's Cruise Room
813 SE 1st St., Hallandale
Circa: 1969–1978

A popular late-night spot (it was open until 6 a.m.), with drag shows. It attracted a young crowd and was cruisy and very

MR. BILLY BRIDGES

It's that time of the year again ! Guys in South Florida are warming their buns for the second annual MR BUNS contest at KEITH'S CRUISE ROOM in Hallandale. Billy Bridges MR BUNS '71 will be on hand to present the award to the lucky winner. The true winners will be the customers at the bar that night as they are treated to that daring, dazzling display of derrierres.

MISS CRUISE ROOM DANIELLE HALLANDALE, FLORIDA

popular. In 1975, it held a Mardi Gras party which culminated in the crowning of Miss Mardi Gras. Another popular event was the all-gay Dating Game hosted by Tiny Tina. It celebrated its 6th anniversary on October 13, 1975, with an all-star show featuring. "Rachel Wells (Miss David '74), Emore (Miss Universe '74), Roxanne Russell (Miss Florida '74) and Jerry Day as emcee."

Gloria Gaynor made her first South Florida appearance at the bar on February 20, 1975.

Keith's of Hollywood
219 NE 21st Ave., Hollywood
Circa: 2005
A gay-friendly, dance club.

Kicks
2008 Wilton Dr., Wilton Manors
Circa: 1999–2016

A lesbian sports bar owned by Carol Moran. It was named "Best Lesbian Bar by *The New Times* in 2002, stating, "You'll find ladies of every stripe in the rainbow flag here, from lipstick lesbians to girl-next-door types, coexisting (or competing, as the case may be) in harmony." This location is now the garden room at Tropics (see listing).

KY Club
4446 NE 20th Ave., Fort Lauderdale
Circa: 1988–1989

Two men from Kentucky opened this neighborhood bar, hence the name. It had pool tables. The grand opening was held on February 3, 1989.

Ladies' Choice Lounge
800 N. Federal Hwy., Hallandale
Circa: 1978

According to an ad in *She Magazine* from 1978, Wednesday was showcase night, but *The Damron Guide* lists the Backroom (see listing) at this location from 1977 until 1981. Ladies' Choice could be the women's nights at the Backroom and not a separate bar.

Cathy Johnson says, "This was before my time, but a lot of my friends went there a lot."

Lou's also occupied this space (see listing).

Ladies' Loft
2100 Hollywood Blvd., Hollywood
Circa: 1980–1990

A women's dance bar on the second floor. It featured drag shows. It was described as a swinging disco that offered a buffet on opening night. Offering a steel dance floor, mirrored walls with lights and sounds to disco all night. Ads touted "Diane Bronson, the Craxy Mixologist." This was also home to Cookie's Intimate Lounge, Glitz, and Zelda's (see listings).

Laser Wolf
901 Progresso Dr., Fort Lauderdale
Circa: 2011-present

Craft beer, wine, and hard cider only, hipster, a mixed crowd that is mostly straight but very LGBTQ friendly. This is a multi-storefront plaza that also hosts Patio Pizza and Bar (see listing).

Lauderdale Beach Hotel & Bar
101 S. Atlantic Ave. Fort Lauderdale
Circa: 1977-1978

Opened to compete with Marlin Beach, a pool bar, one of seven (Pool Bar, Wonder Bar, Gogo, 10¢ A Dance, PS Disco, and Koko, a show bar). It was a popular gathering spot, owned by the publishers of *Blueboy Magazine*. In April 1977, two hundred guests staying at the hotel had to be relocated after a fire caused extensive damage. It was the third fire in less than a month—all three were considered arson.

LOS INVITAMOS A BAILAR!

El Gato Tuerto y por supuesto TROPICANA.

Te acuerdas de La Habana en los '50 o te han contado?

The Lauderdale Beach, frente al mar te trasladara a un magico y único ambiente tropical: El Nacional, Capri, El Floridita,

Servicio y comida incomparable en The Roxy Restaurant. Con fantastico entretenimiento hasta el cierre.

El mas extraordinario sistema de sonido y luces en nuestra increible discoteca "10c a Dance"

Nos encantaria invitarlos a bailar en este romantico mundo de ayer con ritmo de mañana.

THE LAUDERDALE BEACH HOTEL
frente al mar
101 S. Atlantic Boulevard, Ft. Lauderdale

LC Dacrons
556 SW 27th Ave., Fort Lauderdale
Circa: 1985

Le Bar
1914 E. Oakland Park Blvd., Fort Lauderdale
Circa: 1995-1997

A neighborhood bar, it was once home to the (New) Grotto (see listing). *The Damron Guide* has the timelines for the bars overlapping, but it is more likely that The Grotto closed in 1995 and wasn't deleted from *Damron*'s database.

Le Boy
1243 NE 11th Ave., Fort Lauderdale
Circa: 2015-present

A tiny bar along the railroad tracks, its main draw is strippers, mostly Latin. Opened by Sean David in the space formerly occupied by Bill's Filling Station, it has a large patio. David sold the bar to Charles Horton, who also owns Lit (see listing). Other bars at this location include Two on a Match, Depot, and Hector's (see listings).

Lefty's
710 N. Federal Hwy., Fort Lauderdale
Circa: 1977-2001

Opened on September 8, 1977, and owned by Lefty Meyer, it attracted a young crowd. In April 1988, Lefty's advertised as the longest happy hour in town: 1 p.m. to 1 a.m. On Tuesday, Thursday, and Sunday, well and wine drinks are $1. The police closed the place in 2001 for drugs and lewd act violations. It is also the location of Full Moon Lounge and Haymarket (see listings).

Lefty's
JUST ONE MORE

A Cruisy Bar
Reasonable Prices

Taffy's Happy Hour 1 p.m. to 7 p.m.
All Bar Drinks $1.00
Seven days a week

710 N. Federal Highway, Ft. Lauderdale
761-0660

Parking in rear   Open 1 p.m. to 2 a.m.

Lefty's II
2312 NE 26th St., Fort Lauderdale
Circa: 1984–1993

The grand opening was February 2, 1983. *The Damron Guide* read, "looks promising."

The was also the site of Buddy's, Juno's, and Phoenix (see listings).

Legends
1950 Wilton Dr., Wilton Manors
Circa: 1998

Nikki Adams remembers, "It was owned by Larry and his husband, I can't remember his name. They had delicious food, and they would put on shows."

After the bar's closing, it was a laundromat, then a thrift store, and is now home to a deli.

Libations Nightclub
3460 N. Andrews Ave., Fort Lauderdale
Circa: 1989–1999

The grand opening was September 21, 1989.

Limelight
10001 N. Federal Hwy., Hallandale
Circa: 1997–1999

Peter Gatien's first Limelight opened in Broward County almost 10 years before the famed New York City club. It burned down after a mysterious fire in 1999. Rather than reopening, Gatien chose to relocate the bar to Atlanta in 1980. He then opened the New York location in 1983 and the Chicago and London locations in 1985. This was also the location of Rumsbottom's (see listing).

Lips
1421 E. Oakland Park Blvd., Oakland Park
Circa: 2007–Present

Before RuPaul's Drag Race there was Lips. Part of a five-outlet franchised mini-chain; Lips is a supper club with a Vegas-style drag show with the performers as servers. The clientele ranges from busloads of seniors to gay boys, it hosts numerous benefits for the LGBTQ community. The later shows tend to be bawdier. Former occupants of this space include Omni and Xenon (see listings).

Listen
2440 Wilton Dr., Wilton Manors
Circa: 2018–2019

Two women opened the bar after Chardee's Lounge (see listing) closed. They lasted just a few months shy of a year, and shortly thereafter Lit opened (see listing). 2440/New Moon and Progress (see listings) previously occupied this space.

Lit Bar
2440 Wilton Dr., Wilton Manors
Circa: 2019–present

Lit attracts a hip crowd and has a large outdoor back patio and parking lot. The bar offers trivia contests, karaoke nights, and cornhole (a beanbag game) tournaments. The original owners opened right before the COVID pandemic. After making it through the pandemic, they sold Lit to Charles Horton, who also owns Le Boy (see listing). There is a free shuttle that runs between the two bars. This spot was formerly occupied by 2440/New Moon, Progress, Listen, and Chardee's Lounge (see listings).

Little Jim's
3038 N. Federal Hwy, Fort Lauderdale
Circa: 1983–1992

Located in a strip mall, this location has been the home to many gay bars since the 1960s. Little Jim's was the Florida outpost of the Chicago bar of the same name, owned by Jim Gates, who moved to Fort Lauderdale. It was a neighborhood spot with a group of devoted regulars. Other bars that occupied this space were Bushes, Simba's, and now Smarty Pants (see listings). All have sometimes used the address 2400 E. Oakland Park Blvd., which is another entrance to the mall.

It opened in September 1991. Sean Tenant remembers that it was "...on the second floor above Johnny's original location (see listing), you would have to go up these narrow steps to get to the bar. It was owned by Jimmy Fanning, the man who owned Jimmy's (see listing). This space also housed the District (see listing).

Loft
420 N. St. Rd. 7, Plantation
Circa: 1999–2000

A leather bar.

Loose Caboose
99 SW 11th St., Fort Lauderdale
Circa: 1984

Located in a very desolate part of town, it was certainly off the beaten track.

Lord's (Knight Club)
4200 N. Federal Hwy., Fort Lauderdale
Circa: 2000-2003

The bar featured male dancers, drag, karaoke, and bingo. According to listings in *The Damron Guide* and *Gay Yellow Pages* Lord's and Russell's (see listings) both occupied this space from 2000-2003. Earlier, this was also the location of Moby Dick and later, Ice Palace (see listings).

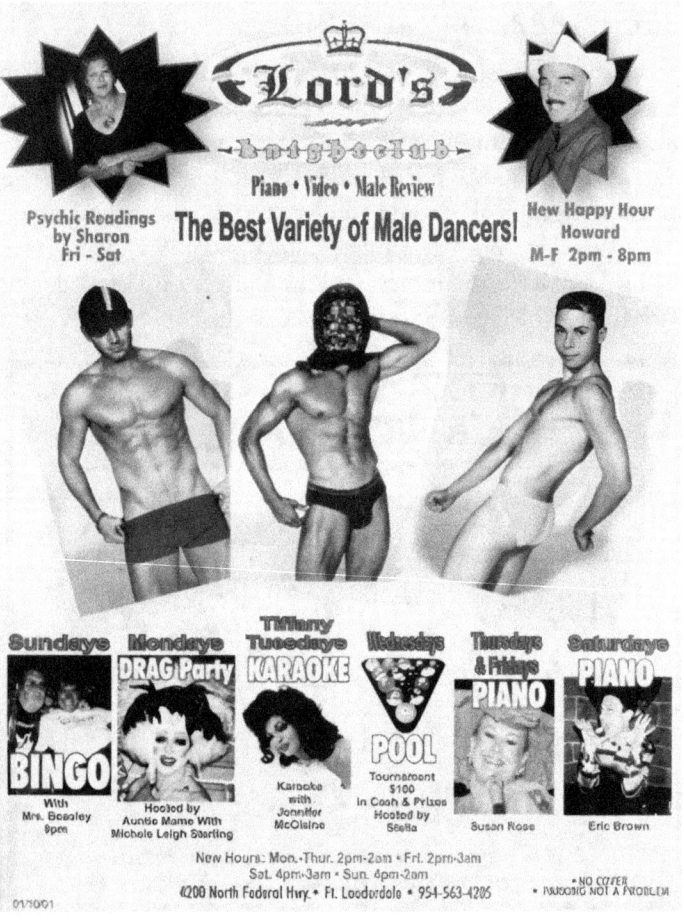

Lou's
800 N. Federal Hwy., Hallandale
Circa: unknown

This location was also home to Backroom and Ladies' Choice (see listings).

Louise's Venus
2520 S. Miami Rd., Fort Lauderdale
Circa: 1991-2008

A women's club attached to the Coliseum.

Lower Deck Disco
17 S. Atlantic Ave., Fort Lauderdale
Circa: 1990

Located in the Marlin Beach Hotel complex (see listing). It was known locally as the "Poop Deck."

Lucifer's Inferno
3485 N. Federal Hwy., Fort Lauderdale
Circa: 1984-1986

A disco, piano bar, and restaurant, across from Coral Ridge Mall. Tim Miller saw Sylvester perform there. A City Furniture store sits on the site now.

Malebox
825 W. Sunrise Blvd., Fort Lauderdale
Circa: 1993-1996

Known as a bar with strippers and hustlers, it was opened by Joe McCallion, a Boston entrepreneur who ran into tax problems with the IRS. Paul Hugo took over the bar, turning it into a successful neighborhood locale and selling it to Ed Cosman. It closed soon afterward.

Man's Western Country
1915 N. Powerline Rd., Wilton Manors
Circa: 1981

A "butch" men's bar with go-go dancers.

Manhattan Lounge
219 N. 21st Ave., Hollywood
Circa: 2004-2010

A mixed gay/straight dance club. The building was once Hollywood City Hall and later, a police station. It was later rumored to be owned by Al Capone and it was, at times, a brothel. This was also home to Mankind, Hemingway's, and X IT which used the Dixie Ave. address (see listings).

Manhattan's
20 SW 3rd Ave., Fort Lauderdale
Circa: 1998

Manhattan South
6890 Powerline Rd., Fort Lauderdale
Circa: 2004-2008

A country western dance club. This was later the location of the Black Banana (see listing).

Mankind
219 N. 21st Ave., Hollywood
Circa: 2000-2004

The building was once Hollywood City Hall and later a police station. It was later rumored to be owned by Al Capone and, at times, a brothel. It was also home to the Manhattan Lounge, Hemingway's and X IT which used the Dixie Ave. address (see listings).

Manor
2345 Wilton Dr., Wilton Manors
Circa: 2010-present

A multi-level, multi-room banquet facility as well as a late-night dance club. In its early days, it provided a home to Rising Action, Wilton Manors' LGBT Theater Company. It has also served as the location of many community fundraisers and benefits over the years. The Venue is the main bar. A "performance lounge" named Only Friends was added in 2023. Previously home to Costello's Restaurant and its Gin Mill bar and Victor/Victoria (see listings).

Maracas
3001 N. Federal Hwy., Fort Lauderdale
Circa: 2009-2011

Once a thriving bar with a deteriorating motel behind it, it hosted many conventions for larger men and those attracted to them. It was well-known for its $2 Margarita Monday specials. It was from the same team that operated Lips. The space is now abandoned.

Marandola's
1201 S. Federal Hwy., Fort Lauderdale
Circa: 1974

Restaurant, dancing, and cabaret billed as "An intimate gay spot for dining, dancing, and entertainment. With Neil Martin at the piano."

Marlin Beach Hotel
17 S. Atlantic (A1A, also known as Fort Lauderdale Beach Blvd.), Fort Lauderdale
Circa: 1977–1992

The hotel complex, located across the street from the beach, had numerous bars; a poolside bar, a lower-level disco with windows into the pool, and a roof-top piano bar. There was a tunnel leading from the hotel to the beach so that one didn't have to cross busy A1A. The restaurant also sometimes featured supper club-like shows. An ad in an undated publication from 1977 called *Michael's of Florida* touting the restaurant read, "Join us for dinner...Charles Nelson Reilly, Joan Blondell, Florence Henderson, Barbara Britton, Selma Diamond, and Ann Miller have!"

Among the bar names that were used throughout the years were the Deck, affectionately nicknamed Poop Deck by locals, Club 17 South, and Paragon. An ad in a 1975 issue of *Travel With Pride* stated, "By popular demand! Tea is now served twice a week! Every Saturday and Sunday 3-6 p.m."

Tom Bradshaw called the Marlin "The center of entertainment and cultural life." Richard Sedlak, who came out in 1973, agrees, "The community was pretty well centered around the Marlin Beach Hotel."

Tim Miller remembers, "Sundays were the big day. You'd start with a tea dance at the pool bar at Marlin Beach. Then at 6:00, that would close, and you would go down to Poop Deck, the lower-level bar, with a view into the pool. That would go until 7:30 or so. Then you'd head west of I-95 to Tacky's, and party there until 10 or so, then to Backstreet until two in the morning, and end up at Copa, which was in an unincorporated part of Broward County and stayed open until about five in the morning."

Vivian Oliva recalls, "I saw Grace Jones there. It may have been the same week she was at the Copa. But she drove into the lower bar, under the pool, on a motorcycle to start her show."

Martini's Cabaret
2500 Wilton Dr., Wilton Manors
Circa: 2004-2010

A lesbian bar. This space, at the north end of Wilton Drive, has been vacant for years.

Matty's at Wilton Park
2100 Wilton Dr., Wilton Manors
Circa: 2019-2022

This iteration of the club opened after the other Matty's closed (see below), with different owners. It was popular with the over-60 crowd early in the evening and had a few young regulars late at night. It closed following the COVID pandemic. The New York City bar, West End Lounge (see listing) opened an outpost at this location in April 2024.

Matty's on the Drive
2426 Wilton Dr., Wilton Manors
Circa: 2009-2012

It was forced to close after George Kessinger, one of the owners, was found in violation of a non-compete clause with Georgie's Alibi, which he had sold to other investors. It later changed its name to Rumor's, which then closed. It was followed by Sidelines, Hamburger Mary's, and The Well (see listings).

Melody Lounge
1819 Wiley St., Hollywood
Circa: 1991-1993

A neighborhood bar owned by Georgine Murdock, frequented by men and women.

Michael's
715 S. 21st Ave., Hollywood
Circa: 1977-1978

The lounge was open twenty-three hours a day. In January 1978 it hosted "America's foremost impressionist" Arthur Blake, and in May 1978, "Lynne Carroll as Liza Minnelli."

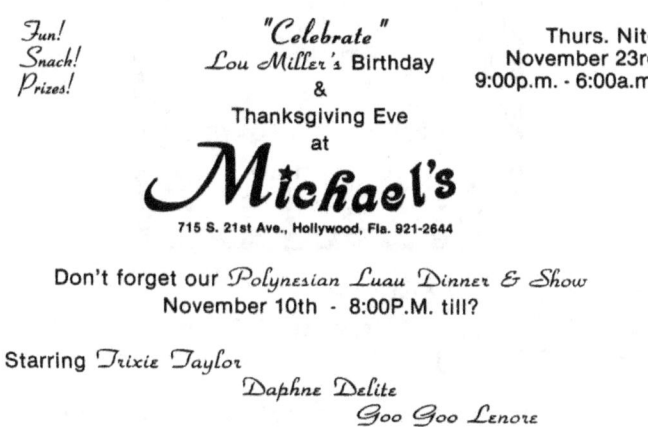

Mineshaft
3045 N. Federal Hwy., Fort Lauderdale
Circa: 1997-1998

A short-lived leather bar. Formerly the I Beam and JR's (see listings).

Moby Dick
4200 N. Federal Hwy., Fort Lauderdale
Circa: 1997-1998

This was a men's neighborhood bar owned by Wayne Gibson, who was one of the original owners of Cathode Ray (see listing). It was also the site of Russell's, Lord's, and Ice Palace (see listings).

Mona's Cocktail Lounge
502 E. Sunrise Blvd., Fort Lauderdale
Circa: 1997-present

A neighborhood bar owned by Jerry Schultz, Mona's Cocktail Lounge and Lisa's Backyard has been a popular gathering spot and local watering hole since 1997. It was previously the location of David's, Traxx, and Phoenix (see listings).

Monkey Business
2740 N. Andrews Ave., Wilton Manors
Circa: 2007-2022

A neighborhood bar in a strip mall that opened at 7 a.m. and sometimes hosted drag shows. It closed shortly after the COVID pandemic began.

Montana
2960 N. Federal Hwy., Fort Lauderdale
Circa: 2000

The Tangerine Disco and Follies (see listings) were previously located here. Later, the building became home to the Mason Jar restaurant, which was popular with the LGBTQ community before it was torn down and the restaurant relocated.

Naked Grape
2163 Wilton Dr., Wilton Manors
Circa: 2008-2018

An upscale wine bar with food that closed down due to the COVID pandemic. Now home to Apt 9f (see listing).

New Connection
3050 NE 26th Terr., Fort Lauderdale
Circa: 1987

It advertised "Male dancers 7 nights a week, Wednesday is *Dynasty* night." Clubhouse Connection (see listing) was previously open at this location and connected to a bathhouse.

New Moon
2440 Wilton Dr., Wilton Manors
Circa: 2005–2014

A lesbian bar run by Carol Moran, who previously owned Kicks and would go on to open 13/Even and Apt. 9f (see listings). When she first opened it, she called it 2440 (see listing). Judy Ireland remembers, "Beverly McClellan was a regular onstage there for years, (probably singing mostly for tips) and everyone loved her. She went on 'The Voice.' Tragically, she died of cancer in 2018."

This space would later house Progress, Chardee's Lounge, Listen, and Lit (see listings).

New River Lounge
501 S. New River Dr. E., Fort Lauderdale
Circa: 1988

It opened as Dock 501 and changed its name two months later. Even though it featured four bars—a cabaret, patio, disco, and video room—it couldn't make a go of it and closed shortly after the name change.

No Manors
2246 Wilton Dr., Wilton Manors
Circa: 2023–present

Steve Bialos opened the bar in September of 2023. Located in the corner of The Shoppes of Wilton Manor's strip mall, which also houses Alibi/Monkey Bar, Hunters, and Tap that Ash (see listings). It has three rooms—the first room has low-slung couches with a platform behind, and the main bar has five bartender stations along with high-top tables. A smaller room in the back with a wall-to-wall yellow sofa has table service and may be booked for private events. Thursday nights are women's nights.

Odds & Ends (Annie's)
3148 NE 12th Ave., Oakland Park
Circa: 1971–1982

A women's bar, sometimes called the O&E Club. It hosted drag shows. An ad in *David Magazine* from 1974 read, "Presenting Mr. Crystal and his Footlight Fakes."

Robert Fronner worked as the bar's manager for a short while. "Odds & Ends (Annie's) was a lesbian bar, and then for a fleeting time, it was a drag show bar. It had a pool table and jukebox. It was your typical small neighborhood bar. The owners squeezed out every drop they could from the place and resold it back as a lesbian bar."

This was also home to Flamingos, Flamingo Bay, and Roxanne's (see listings).

Odds & Ends II
1416 S. Federal Hwy., Fort Lauderdale
Circa: 1971-1975

Advertised in *David Magazine* 1971 as Jay & Carol's Odds &

Ends II boasting "a mixed bar." After Pat bought it in 1972, it was listed as "for boys."

Odyssey South
451 N. State Rd. 7, Plantation
Circa: 1988

An "Opening Soon" ad appeared in the February 18, 1988, edition of *Hot Shots* for this outpost of a New York club. It opened in April. Shangri-La formerly occupied this space (see listing).

Office
7126 Stirling Rd., Hollywood
Circa: 2002

A short-lived bar. Office appears in bar listings for August and September 2002, but it disappears after that. Cloud 9 (see listing) would later open at this address.

Office II Lounge
2590 S. State Rd. 7, Miramar
Circa: 1965-1977

Listed in the April 1972 issue of *David Magazine* as "Under new management. Vince & Brad."

Off the Hookah
111 SW 2nd Ave., Fort Lauderdale
Circa: 2015

The hookah bar opened in this space when the Voo Doo Lounge (see listing) closed after 12 years.

Omni
1421 E. Oakland Park Blvd., Fort Lauderdale
Circa: 1988-1999

An ad in *David Magazine*'s March 1988 issue read, "Ed (Cossman), Scott, and Staff invite you to Omni." Scott was Scott Holland of *Hot Shots Magazine*. It was a disco and piano bar, with male dancers. It closed in August 1999. The space formerly housed Xenon and now is home to Lips (see listings).

Oops! (see Tops)

O'Reilly's Cyber Café
1609 E. Commercial Blvd., Fort Lauderdale
Circa: 1998

Mixed men and women.

Otherglades
2234 Wilton Dr., Wilton Manors
Circa: 1998-1999

This space, now occupied by Hunter's (see listing), was also home to Hysteria and Saigon (see listings).

Otherside
2283 Wilton Dr., Wilton Manors
Circa: 1988-1997

The first LGBTQ bar on Wilton Drive. Bev McMahon was the owner and Dana Ford was the manager. Originally opened as JJ's Den (see listing) and afterward was sometimes listed as JJ's Otherside. The bar had multiple storefronts, and McMahon kept adding more storefronts, expanding the bar. It was a women's bar, but male-friendly. Later home to Pub on the Drive (see listing).

Our Place (aka Our House)
1608 E. Commercial Blvd., Fort Lauderdale
Circa: 1997

A neighborhood women's bar, it featured occasional entertainment.

Oxygen
2660 E. Commercial Blvd., Fort Lauderdale
Circa: 1998

Oz
1010 S. Federal Hwy., Dania Beach
Circa: 1982-1983

The bar advertised go-go boys.

Palms Restaurant & Cabaret
2209 Wilton Dr. Wilton Manors
Circa: 1987-1989

A cabaret/restaurant also opened a women's bar, The Blue Parrot, which didn't take off and was converted into the Palms' cabaret room. Other clubs at this location include Backstage Lounge, Bill's Filling Station/Bill's/B's, The Blue Parrot Lounge, Club Silver, Chardee's, Eagle, Southern Nights, and Wolf (see listings).

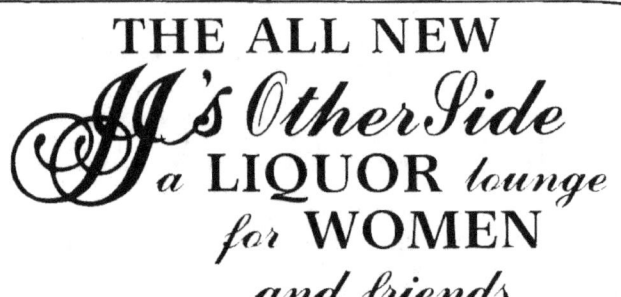

Panache
17 S. Atlantic Ave., Fort Lauderdale
Circa: 1987

One of the many names for the bars in the Marlin Beach Hotel (see listing). Debbie Jacobs and other dance divas performed there.

Paradise
2975 N. Federal Hwy., Fort Lauderdale
Circa: 1997-2000

Partners
625 E. Dania Beach Blvd., Dania
Circa: 1985-2000

This was a women's bar but male-friendly. It held its second anniversary party on June 20, 1987. Beach Betty's, Second Time Around, and Champagne Taste were also at this location (see listings).

Pat's Odds & Ends-see Odds & Ends II

Patio Pizza and Bar
901 Progresso Dr., Fort Lauderdale
Circa: 2022-present

Operated by the people who own Drynk on Wilton Drive (see listing). Popular for its large patio. Mixed gay and straight. Brian D describes it as, "A beautiful place with a big open interior bar area and a huge shared outdoor seating area. They have plenty of seating and a fire pit to gather around."

This is a multi-storefront plaza that is also home to Laser Wolf (see listing).

Pecs
1550 N. Federal Hwy., Fort Lauderdale
Circa: 1988

A dance club with male dancers, and dining. The grand opening was held on May 28, 1988. Paul Parker performed on July 3, 1988. Tim Miller remembers, "The bartenders were all gorgeous and they put a lot of money in the bar."

Another patron recalls, "It had a large number of investors, and each thought he was the owner. They all gave contradicting directions to people. It was only open for about a year."

Phases
2829 W. Broward Blvd., Fort Lauderdale
Circa: 1975–1979

An ad in the November 22, 1975, issue of *David Magazine* advertised a Thanksgiving dinner menu and promised the bar would be "open soon" with "Your host and manager Doug, formerly of Venture Inn." The grand opening was held on December 28th, 1975. Other clubs at this location include Bam and Torpedo Bar (see listings).

Phoenix
502 E. Sunrise Blvd., Fort Lauderdale
Circa: 1994–1996

This was also the location of David's, Traxx, and Mona's.

Phoenix
2312 NE 26th St., Fort Lauderdale
Circa: 1994–1996

Different publications have this open at times overlapping with Juno (see listing). This was previously the site of Lefty's II and Buddy's (see listings).

Pier
3333 NE 32nd St., Fort Lauderdale
Circa: 1999–2000

A dance club and cabaret. It was located on the Intracoastal. The bar was the site of three arson attacks. On the third attack, the police apprehended the arsonist and prints tied him to the previous attacks. They were not able to charge it as a hate crime, but he was imprisoned. The building has since been torn down and is the site of a Marriot Residence Inn.

Pink Tails
5460 N. State Rd. 7, Fort Lauderdale
Circa: 1993

A neighborhood bar on the second floor, where everyone knew everybody else. They did shows despite how small it was. This was also home to Janbar's and Rumors (see listings).

Pint
2031 Wilton Dr., Wilton Manors
Circa: late 2018–early 2019

Opened by Sean David, who pivoted to the name Pint when the city would not let him open his stripper bar Ballz (see listing). This space has also been home to Circuit, Club 2031, G Spot, and Sidelines (see listings).

Pitts
Federal Hwy. & SE 28th St., Fort Lauderdale
Circa: 1977–1978

In the rear of the Copa (see listing), a leather/Levi club with a separate entrance.

PJ's
3635 N. Andrews Ave., Oakland Park
Circa: 2018–2021

A neighborhood bar with a diverse crowd. PJ is a popular bartender with a loyal following (see multiple bar listings).

PJ's Cocks & Tails
2340 Wilton Dr., Wilton Manors
Circa: 2014–2016

Now home to Johnson's (see listing).

PJ's Corner Pocket
924 N. Flagler St., Fort Lauderdale
Circa: 2006–2013

A neighborhood bar. Often listed in directories as PJ's Interracial Club.

PJ's Corner Pocket
2705 N. Andrews Ave., Wilton Manors
Circa: 2023–present

A diverse group of regulars enjoys this neighborhood bar.

Progress Bar
2440 Wilton Dr., Wilton Manors
Circa: 2014–2017

This was formerly the site of the 2440/New Moon, followed by Chardee's Lounge, Listen, and Lit (see listings). It was an outpost of a popular Chicago bar that never caught on.

Promenade Deck
4240 N. Galt Ocean Dr., Fort Lauderdale
Circa: 1988

A piano bar, with a poolside happy hour.

PS Disco
2023 Pembroke Rd., Hollywood
Circa: 1977–1979

A women's dance club. This club was located next door to Tops (see listing).

Pub on the Drive
2283 Wilton Dr., Wilton Manors
Circa: 2012–present

Originally known as The Village Pub, Michael Connell bought in and became partners with Alex Sadeghi, and they changed and name to The Pub in 2021. It is now billed as Pub on the Drive, featuring live entertainment, drag shows, and game nights. It also serves breakfast, lunch, and dinner. Michael Connell passed away in late 2023. After Mike Connell's death, George Kessinger (of Georgie's Alibi-see listing) stepped in to help manage the bar. The building was previously the site of JJ's Den and The Otherside (see listings).

Puddle's Corner
South Federal Hwy. & 28th St., Fort Lauderdale
Circa: 1983

Purple Shamrock Pub
1816 University Dr., Plantation
Circa: 2000

Q
109 SW 2nd St., Fort Lauderdale
Circa: 1994

A dance club. This space also was home to Jet Set (see listing).

Rafters (see Jimmy January's)

Ramrod
1508 NE 4th, Ave., Fort Lauderdale
Circa: 1995–present

A leather bar famous for its monthly "Pig Dance," it is one of the longest-running LGBTQ bars in Fort Lauderdale. Andy V. says, "It's a kind of 'anything goes' attitude that sets it apart from any other bar in the region. Even with the city sort of forcing the bar to clean up its image (or activities that go on inside the bar), it still has its edge to it."

Marqus is a fan, "Without a doubt, the best, if not the only real gay leather bar in all of South Florida. I've been to them all, and none begin to compare with the Ramrod. It offers some updated disco music, happy hours, a pool table, and a nice quiet outdoor patio type of bar. Every night is a special night from 'Battle of the Bulge,' 'bare butt,' 'pig dance,' and 'caged hunks,' just to name a few. It draws a good cross-section from the leather and gay community. There are some dark corners and areas, but any activity is discouraged and generally does not happen. As for age groups, basically thirty-something on up. This is definitely not your twinky, raver, go-go, A-List type of establishment. And yes, during the tourist season the place gets packed to the proverbial rafters with 'fresh meat.'"

Rascals
310 NE 13th St., Fort Lauderdale
Circa: 1989

Entered from a side parking lot.

R Bar
2217 N. Federal Hwy., Hollywood
Circa: 2005

A women's bar. Zachary's (see listing), another women's bar, was open in this space earlier.

Rebel Wine Bar
3520 NE 12th Ave., Oakland Park
Circa: 2022-present

It is not a gay bar, but it has many LGBTQ staff and a mixed crowd. It is an intimate bar serving wine and beer in an upscale setting. It offers art shows in conjunction with Arts United. Chad D says, "It is just large enough for a decent-sized crowd, but not so large that you feel lost in a sea of faces."

Red Barn
3491 W. Sunrise Blvd., Fort Lauderdale
Circa: 1970-1971

Entertainment and dancing. An ad in *The Fort Lauderdale News* in 1970 boasted, "Chunga and Keni Carson, formerly of the Jewel Box Revue are now appearing at The Red Barn Friday and Saturday Nights!" Although vacant, the red barn is still standing, adjacent to a flea market and drive-in theater.

Regatta
201 SW 2nd St., Fort Lauderdale
Circa: 1984

Other bars in this space include Bobby Winn's and Hannibal's (see listings).

Rendezvous
120 E. McNab Rd., Pompano Beach
Circa: 1978-1993

A BYOB dance club. It offered monthly lectures on everything from human sexuality to the use of hypnosis to stop smoking.

Riverside Pub
602 SW 12th Ave., Fort Lauderdale
Circa: 1986

Later home to The Grotto-Riverside (see listing).

Roadhouse
2100 N. Dixie Hwy., Hollywood
Circa: 1977-1983

It held its grand opening in January of 1977 and featured dancing and go-go boys. In *David Magazine* of April 1972, the This Week With David column advertised the bar as, "The largest, cruisiest oval bar in South Florida!" It was formerly the site of TeeJay's and would later become Crossfire (see listings).

Chateau Madrid. From 1964 to the early 1970s it was Fort Lauderdale's top entertainment spot, featuring such entertainers as Rosemary Clooney, Buddy Greco, Tony Martin, and Louis Armstrong. In 1976 the Chateau Madrid manager was under investigation and died in a mysterious plane crash. The club closed and fell into disrepair. In 1991 a new investor opened it as a gay club, with a restaurant and a rotating bar. The Rooftop was popular on Friday nights and had a bartender named Crazy Richard, recalls Tim Miller. The space now sits empty above Citibank.

Rooftop Disco
3101 N. Federal Hwy., Oakland Park
Circa: 1991

Located in the architecturally significant Kenann Building, the eighth-floor nightclub and dining venue originally opened as

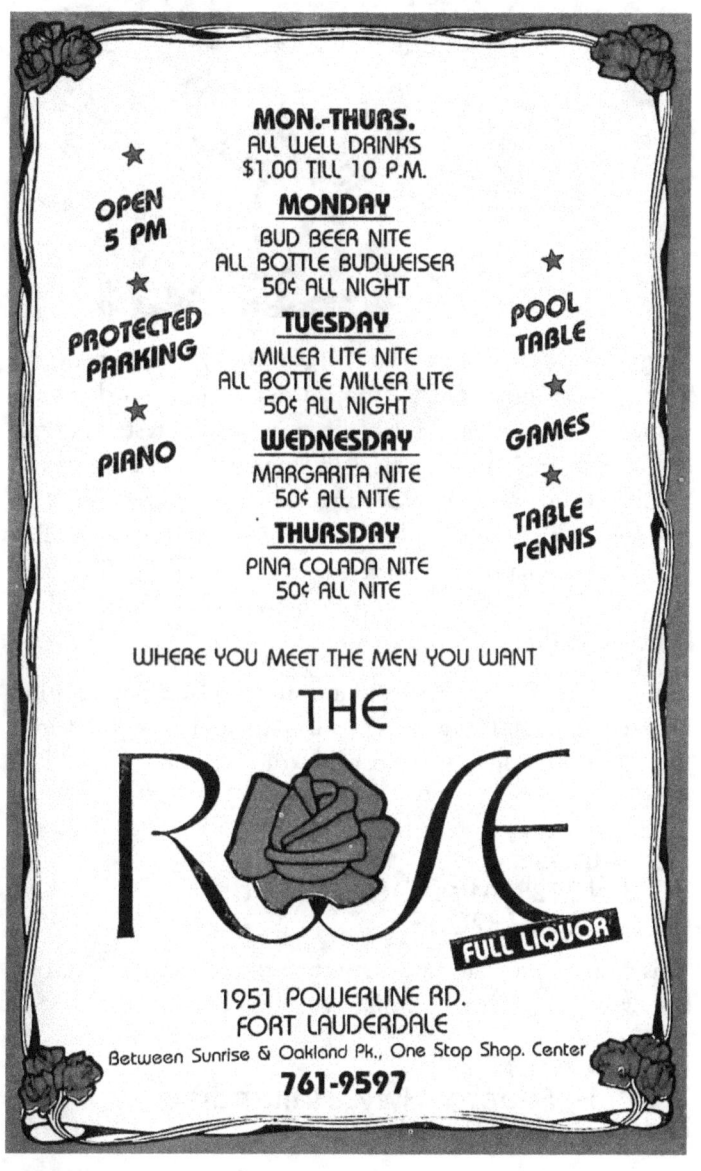

Rose
1951 N. Powerline Rd., Fort Lauderdale
Circa: 1987–1989

A neighborhood bar with go-go boys, pool tables, and dining.

Rosie's Bar & Grill
2449 Wilton Dr., Wilton Manors
Circa: 2006-present

Originally opened as a Hamburger Mary's (see listing). In 2004, owner John Zieba dropped out of the franchise and reopened as Rosie's. It is easily the most popular restaurant and bar in Wilton Manors, especially known for its burgers and Sunday brunch. It was featured on an episode of *Real Housewives of Miami*. In bar listings, it is often named "Best Gay Bar." Its hamburgers are also award-winning. The large patio has been described as "A tropical oasis in the middle of Wilton Manors.

Johnny Q says, "I always recommend this place. Been coming here for years, and it's always good. Standard fare, good drinks, friendly staff, super-gay. Rosie's is the place to see...and be seen!"

Roxanne's
3148 NE 12th Ave., Oakland Park
Circa: 2007-2009

This was a men's bar with drag shows. The various Flamingo bars were also at this location (see listings).

Rumbottoms
10001 N. Federal Hwy., Hallandale
Circa: 1975-1977

A mixed straight and gay disco with drag shows. An ad in the January 11, 1975, issue of *David Magazine* touted, "Dance to Calhoun, New York's #1 group, Friday, Saturday and Monday."

In July 1975, club operator Dean Sarafianos proposed to the city of Hallandale that he be allowed to erect a large tent on city property near the club to produce shows. The proposal was denied.

On September 28, 1975, it hosted the Mr. Groovy Guy contest. The bar later closed and became the first location of Peter Gatien's legendary Limelight nightclubs (see listing).

Rumors
5460 N. State Rd. 7, Fort Lauderdale
Circa: 1993-1994

This space was home to a dance club with a mix of men and women. Janbar's and Pink Tails (see listings) were also at this location.

Rumors
2426 Wilton Dr., Wilton Manors
Circa: 2013-2019

Located in a strip mall on Wilton Drive. It had a small but loyal following. It took over the space once occupied by Matty's on the Drive (see listing). This space later became home to Sidelines, Wilton Manor's second incarnation of Hamburger Mary's, and then The Well (see listings).

Russell's
4200 N. Federal Hwy., Fort Lauderdale
Circa: 2000-2002

According to listings in *The Damron Guide* and *Gay Yellow Pages*, Russell's and Lord's (see listing) both occupied this space from 2000 to 2003 as a neighborhood bar offering karaoke, bingo, and Male Dancers. Earlier, this was the location of Moby Dick and, later, Ice Palace (see listings).

Rustlers
3419 N. Andrews Ave., Fort Lauderdale
Circa: 1991-1993

A country and western bar, it opened on June 27, 1991. It was also the location of Club Pierre (see listing).

Ruthie's Fun Palace
702 SW McNab Rd., Pompano
Circa: 1969-1978

It was a BYOB bar. An ad in a 1975 issue of *David Magazine* touts the club's 6th anniversary, while an ad from that same year in *Travel With Pride* announces the grand opening of Ruthie's Golden Garter at this address. The manager was Gary Keele. Some guides and directories give this address for both Ruthie's Fun Palace and Ruthie's Golden Garter (see listing below). It was advertised as the only 4 a.m. bar in Pompano.

Ruthie's Golden Garter
Oakland Park at Federal Hwy., Fort Lauderdale
Circa: 1966-1978

At some point, it may have consolidated with Ruthie's Fun Palace (see listing above). Some guides and directories give the McNab address for both places. In the October 18, 1976, issue of *David Magazine*, the McNab address is listed in an ad for Halloween with the Miss Golden Garter contest on November 1, and the Mr. Buns contest on November 12, 1977. The strip mall at Oakland Park and Federal

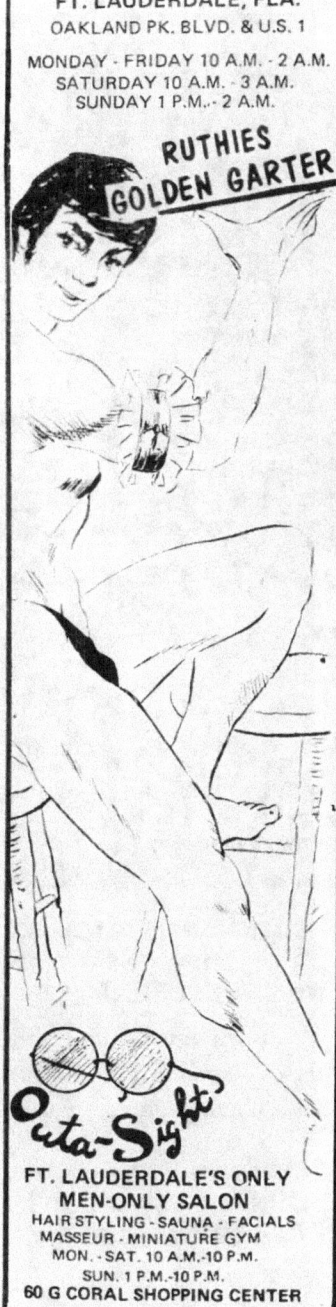

FT. LAUDERDALE, FLA.
OAKLAND PK. BLVD. & U.S. 1

MONDAY - FRIDAY 10 A.M. - 2 A.M.
SATURDAY 10 A.M. - 3 A.M.
SUNDAY 1 P.M. - 2 A.M.

RUTHIES
GOLDEN GARTER

Outa-Sight
FT. LAUDERDALE'S ONLY
MEN-ONLY SALON
HAIR STYLING - SAUNA - FACIALS
MASSEUR - MINIATURE GYM
MON. - SAT. 10 A.M.-10 P.M.
SUN. 1 P.M.-10 P.M.
60 G CORAL SHOPPING CENTER

Highway was home to Little Jim's, Simba's, and Bushes and is now the location of Smarty Pants.

Saigon
2234 Wilton Dr., Wilton Manors
Circa: 2009-2010

Tim Miller jokes, "We used to call it 'Soon Gone' because there was never anybody in there." This space, now occupied by Hunter's expansion (see listing), was also home to Otherglades, and Hysteria (see listings).

Saigon
4301 N. Federal Hwy., Fort Lauderdale
Circa: 2004-2010

SAIGON

MORE THEN JUST A NIGHTCLUB...
...finally, the destination you have been "impatiently" waiting for.

DANCE TO ARTISTICALLY MASTERED SIGHTS & SOUNDS
Authentic Sushi Bar
Private "Invitation Only" Opening
Get on our VIP list, register online at www.saigonFL.com

SAIGON
www.saigonFL.com
4301 North Federal Highway
954 876 0412

Saint
1000 State Rd. 84, Fort Lauderdale
Circa: 1997-2003

A dance club, Paul Hugo and Brett Tannenbaum closed the Coliseum (see listing) to open Saint. The DJ was Lazro Leon. It had an outdoor volleyball court and a large dance floor. The club hosted foam parties, teen nights, and an event called "Purgatory." In 2001, the club's manager Kai-Uwe Their was arrested for hiring a hitman to murder the club's bookkeeper because he thought she was telling the owner lies about him. The Stud and Uncle's (see listings) also occupied this location.

Saint
1509 NE 4th Ave., Fort Lauderdale
Circa: 2004-2005

Saloon
219 SW 1st Ave., Fort Lauderdale
Circa: 1971-1986

Located next to Zanzibar bookstore. An ad in a 1971 *David Magazine* reads, "Your hosts Jimmy, Fluffy, Chad, and Father." Its motto was "The best place to come."

In 1980 a patron of the bar was murdered in the parking lot by what *The Sun-Sentinel* described as "...a baby-faced drifter in bib overalls without a shirt." In the article, bartender David Lindroth said, "The bar has been open for 20 years [sic] and we've never had anything like that happen before. We're all family here."

THE SALOON

"The Best Place To Come"

219½ S.W. 1ST AVE.
FT. LAUDERDALE, FLA.

525-2524

Jimmy Fluffly, Chuck and Father

Saturn
20 N. Federal Hwy., Fort Lauderdale
Circa: 1991

Scandals Saloon
3073 NE 6th Ave., Wilton Manors
Circa: 2007-present

South Florida's largest gay country and western bar with a large outdoor patio, line dancing lessons, and poker games. Very popular on Sunday afternoons, when the outdoor patio of packed pec-to-pec. The bar offers poker tournaments, line dance lessons, drag shows, and cowboy strippers. Jessica Channing is the in-house diva. This space was previously home to a stripper bar called Junkyard then Elements (see listings).

Sea Monster
2 New South River Dr., Fort Lauderdale
Circa: 1998-2010

Under the Andrews Ave. drawbridge, it was owned by Toni Barone and David Rodgers and was known for Sunday tea dances and male dancers. Saturday was Women's Night, and the opening night party was held on November 5, 1998. Vivian Oliva remembers, "We used to go there a lot when we came up from Miami. We didn't go to the women's bars in Fort Lauderdale. We were all lipstick lesbians from Miami, and we didn't like the look of the lesbians in Fort Lauderdale."

Labor Day Sunday T Dance

The Hottest Most Fun T-Dance in Town
$2 Drinks All Day All Night*
Free BBQ on the Patio from 7pm-9pm
Doors Open at 6pm
Dance Floor Opens 7pm
*well & domestic

No Cover
Free Parking

The HOT Sounds of DJ Billy Hallquist

2 S. New River Dr. West
Ft. Lauderdale • 954.463.4641
(under the Andrews draw bridge, formerly "Squeeze")

Broward to 3rd Ave. - Go South to 6th St. Make a Right, Go Past the Courthouse, cross Andrews Ave., and make first right after Andrews Ave.

Sea MONSTER

Second Time Around
625 E. Dania Beach Blvd., Dania
Circa: 1982-1984

It was open until 1984, although it was still listed in *The Damron Guide* in 1985. This was also the location for Beach Betty's, Champagne Taste, and Partners (see listings).

Secrets
4509 Pine Island Rd., Sunrise
Circa: 1995

A small bar located in a strip mall.

Shangri-La
451 N. State Rd. 7, Plantation
Circa: 1984-1987

Its grand opening was in January 1985—Freda Payne and Sylvester performed there. Michael Bende and Lawrence Weiner were listed as the corporation's owners. It was originally a women's dance club, but when business lagged, it changed to a mixed bar. The Plantation police raided it in 1984 and it lost its license. DJ Steve Knoll remembers that the owner, John DeSanto, still opened the bar the next day, but since he couldn't sell drinks, he gave them away.

Robert Fronner said, "It was a disco, probably the nicest club in West Broward. For the brief period it was open."

The Odyssey South opened there in 1987 (see listing).

WEDNESDAY
FRI., FEB. 13TH

NICE 'N WILD

Singing their hit "DIAMOND GIRL" and more...

Coming
Wed., Feb. 18th &
Fri., Feb. 20th

"THE DICE GIRLS"
Leah Landis - Lauren Grey

Singing their hits:
"Starlight", "Putting the Night On Hold",
"Saturday Night", and their new hit, "Boys"

451 N. STATE RD. 7 (441)
FT. LAUDERDALE
587-5340
FORT LAUDERDALE'S ONLY COMPLETE ENTERTAINMENT COMPLEX!

Shero's Cabana Bar and Nightclub
1441 Powerline Rd., Pompano Beach
Circa: 2004-2005

It was a women's space owned by Anne Becall, with a bar in the front room and a pool table in the back. Cathy Johnson remembers that they had free drinks from 8-9 p.m., and everyone would try to get there early for the free drinks.

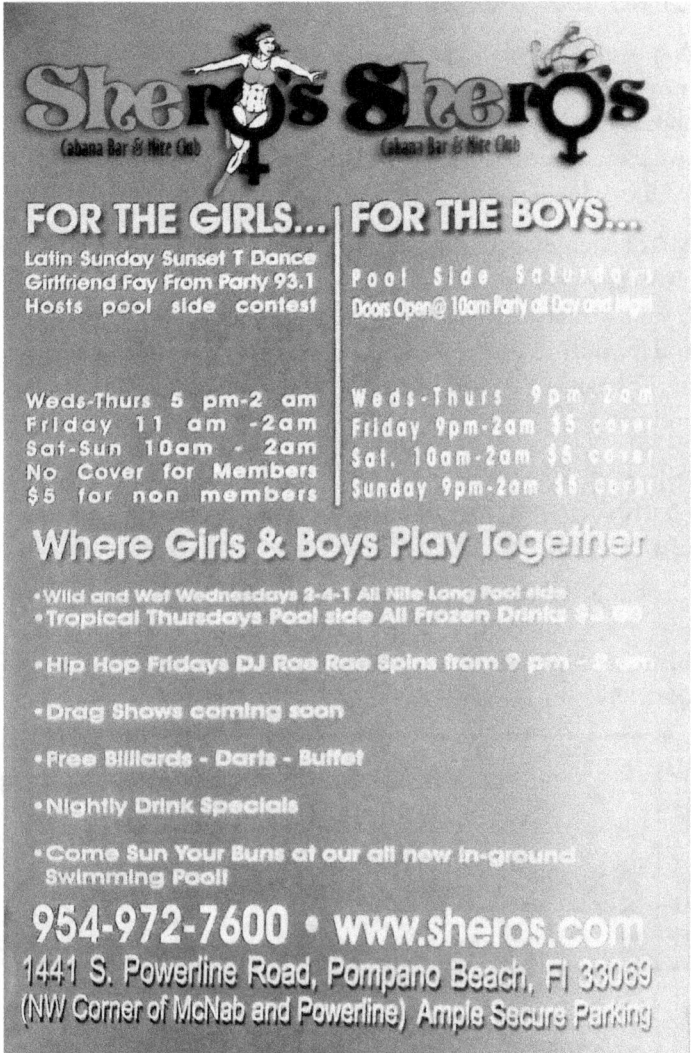

Side Street
1753 N. Andrews Ext., Fort Lauderdale
Circa: 1994-2000

This was a video bar with karaoke. Andrews Extension, Anywayz, and Gaylord's (see listings) were also at this location.

Sidelines Sports Bar
2031 Wilton Dr., Wilton Manors
Circa: 2013-2019

A sports bar owned by Laurie Whittaker. After months of renovations, she discovered the changes were made without permits, and not up to code standards. She also had parking issues and decided to close the bar and move to a location farther up the Drive (see listing below). Other bars at this location included Ballz, Pint, Circuit, Club 2031, and G Spot (see listings).

Sidelines Sports Bar II
2426 Wilton Dr., Wilton Manors
Circa: 2019-2021

A sports bar, it briefly re-opened (less than three months) after moving from a spot elsewhere on Wilton Drive (see listing above) into the space vacated by Rumors and Matty's. The space was later occupied by Hamburger Mary's and now, The Well (see listings).

Marqus remembers that during its brief tenure, "The general local reputation of Sidelines is that it was a lesbian bar. Though from my visits, I would agree, but only to a point. It was open and friendly to everyone, lesbian, gay or straight, though being in the heart of Wilton Manors, [it was] predominantly lesbian and gay."

Silver Fox
Hollywood Blvd., Hollywood
Circa: 1970s

The bar had dancing and entertainment from such acts as Reba and the Western Airz, The Versatiles, Guy Brooks & Irv, and Blanche Wallace, the Last of the Red Hot Mamas. Highballs were 85¢. The hosts were Jay and Larry Walsh.

Simba's
2400 E. Oakland Park Blvd., Fort Lauderdale
Circa: 1992-1996

Briefly open (a few months) in the same space as Little Jim's, Smarty Pants and Bushes (see listings). This space has been reported to have been home to queer bars since the late 1950s, although we have only been able to document as far back as 1983.

Slammer
321 W. Sunrise Blvd., Fort Lauderdale
Circa: 2009-present

A BYOB sex club in the space formerly occupied by many gay clubs including Georgie's, Badd Boys, Fireside, and Impulse (see listings). It was also home to Plato's Retreat, a straight swingers sex club.

Sleaze Alley
3521 W. Broward Blvd., Fort Lauderdale
Circa: 1991

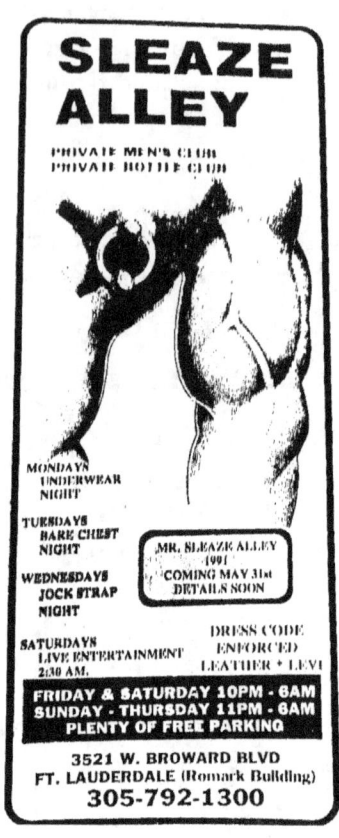

This was a private bottle club that later became home to GW's Place and The End Up (see listings).

Smarty Pants
2400 E. Oakland Park Blvd., Fort Lauderdale
Circa: 2004-present

A neighborhood bar with a devoted following, it opens early in the day and offers a Saturday brunch, trivia, and karaoke nights, as well as the occasional underwear party. Other bars at this location include Simba's, Bushes, and Little Jim's (see listings).

Southern Nights
2209 Wilton Dr., Wilton Manors
Circa: 2017-2018

It was part of the Southern Nights chain of men's dance clubs with bars in Tampa and Orlando. It held an amateur drag night called, "So You Think You Can Drag?" where first-timers were done up in drag with the help of professionals and then competed for a $100 cash prize. After mixed reviews, it closed. Other clubs operating in this space include Backstage Lounge, Bill's Filling Station/Bill's/B's, The Blue Parrot Lounge, Club Silver, Chardee's, The Palms, Wolf, and The Eagle. (see listings)

Spanky's
320 N. Federal Hwy., Fort Lauderdale
Circa: 1995–1998

A neighborhood hangout.

Spencer's Corner Bar
2390 Wilton Dr., Wilton Manors
Circa: 2020–present

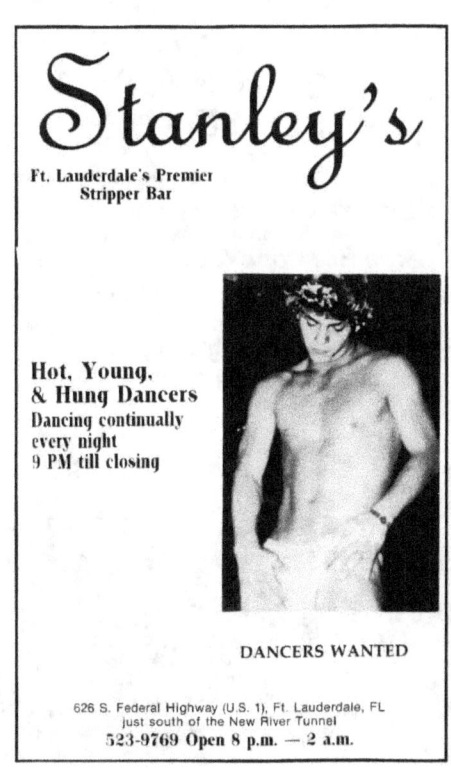

It is equal parts restaurant and bar. *Hot Shots Magazine* describes it as "The interior is open, clean, and modern, and features about a dozen tables and a huge bar with stools. The seating capacity is more than doubled by the addition of the beautiful, covered patio, which also boasts another full bar."

Splash
2935 N. Federal Hwy., Fort Lauderdale
Circa: late 1990s

Marqus said, "I wasn't exactly sure of its target market as it really didn't seem to have any particular focus except maybe as a bar/pool arrangement for locals and hotel guests which with hotel support may make it, but not as a standalone, as it didn't offer anything that anyone would go out of their way for, especially with so many other similar choices available." Formerly the location of Depot Cabana (see listing).

Stable
205 E. Oakland Park Blvd., Oakland Park
Circa: 2009–2015

A country and western-themed bar. Steve H remembers it as, "Nothing fancy, friendly staff, and cheap prices as gay bars go. Free pool on Sunday." It was bought by Scandals and the two merged into Scandals' location a few blocks away.

Stanley's
626 S. Federal Hwy., Fort Lauderdale
Circa: 1990–1997

It featured strippers and hustlers and, as one former patron described, was "Sleazy in the best way." The bar advertised "Hot and Hung dancers Every Night." Visions (see listing) would open in this spot soon afterward.

Stars
3299 N. Federal Hwy., Pompano Beach
Circa: 1989

A dance bar and cabaret, it hosted a Thanksgiving "orphans buffet."

Steel
1951 N. Powerline Rd., Fort Lauderdale
Circa: 2001–2012

It was affiliated with Jackhammer. On Oct. 12, 2007, The Broward Dept. of Health distributed free condoms at the bar. An Eagle also opened in this space, as did Club 1951 and Cupcakes (both women's bars), and Uncle Charlie's (see listings). The building has since been demolished.

Storm
200 W. Broward Blvd., Fort Lauderdale
Circa: 2000

Formerly Backstreet and Good Timers (see listings,) it hosted 2000 Pride South Florida. This was also home to Club Q (see listing).

Stud
3460 N. Andrews Ave., Fort auderdale
Circa: 1993–1997

It was a huge dance facility that included an outdoor volleyball court and a host of showcase performers. It also housed Club Matrix, a cabaret/drag room. Nikki Adams hosted whipped cream wrestling. It later became The Saint and Uncle's (see listings).

Student Prince
229 S. Atlantic Ave., Fort Lauderdale
Circa: 1964–1975

A small ocean-front bar near the gay beach.

Studio West
3543 Pine Island Rd., Hollywood
Circa: 1995

A dance club.

Swinging Richards
1350 SW 2nd St., Pompano Beach
Circa: 2013-2018

Managed by Matt Colunga, the bar featured nude male strippers. It moved to this location, an industrial area when it was forced to close in Miami (see listing).

Tacky's
2509 W. Broward Blvd., Fort Lauderdale
Circa: 1975-1993

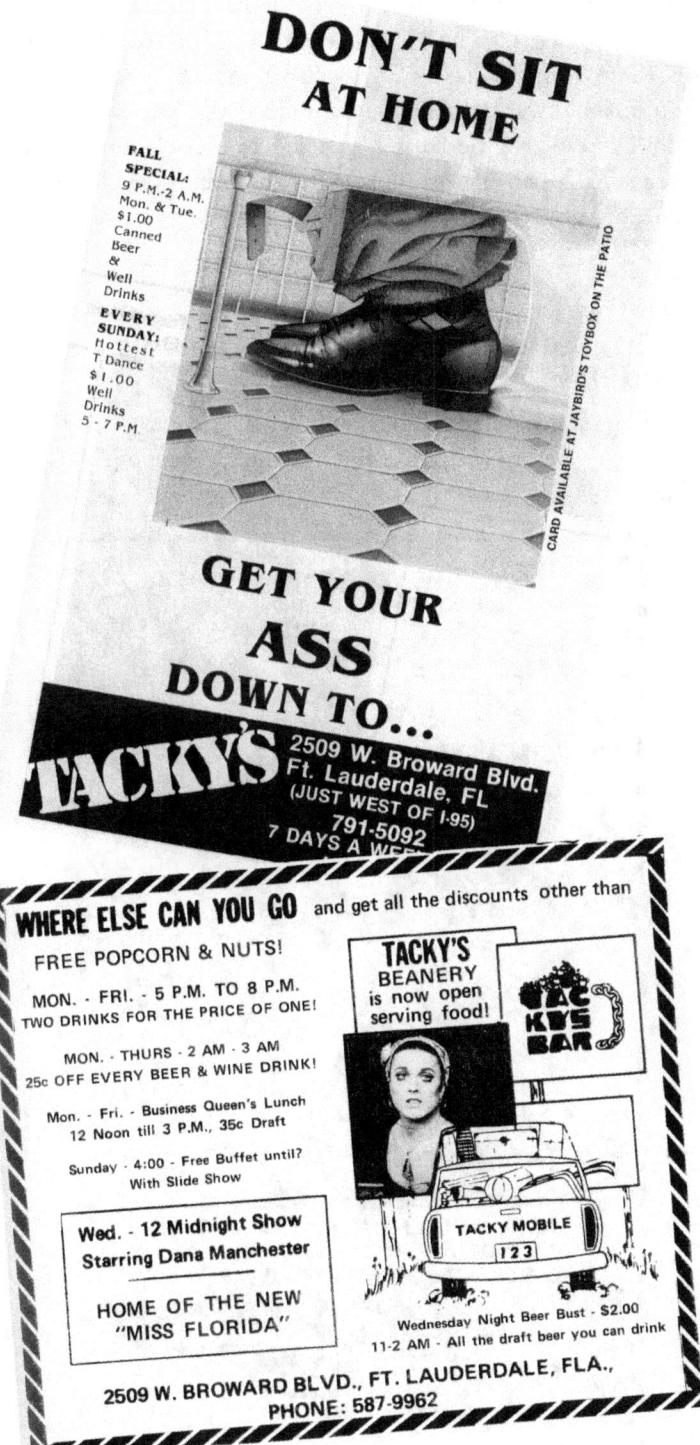

Owned by Jim Rakvica, the showroom was called The Doghouse. Christine Jorgensen performed there once, but Dana Manchester was the house diva. It featured dollar shots of Night Train. In 1985 it hosted the regional Mr. Drummer contest. Some report it was the site of a gay bar as far back as the 1950s. The "last call" song was always the theme song from "The Jetsons."

Robert Fronner remembers it for, "The sawdust and peanut shell-covered floor. It was a slightly sleazy bar with pool tables."

Later this space was home to 2509 West (see listing).

Tangerine Disco
2960 N. Federal Hwy., Fort Lauderdale
Circa: 1975-1977

An elegant restaurant and disco with extravagant shows with production numbers. It also had a bar called Upstairs. Dana Manchester, Angie DiMarco, and Nikki Adams performed there. John Castelli says, "I wanted to have a restaurant, disco, and a piano bar. I sunk a lot of money into it. It was ahead of its time, but it was too small to accommodate all the people who wanted to get in, so we opened the Copa (see listing). I opened dance bars just as the disco craze was exploding. The Copa became so successful, we decided to expand that brand, so we closed Tangerine."

An ad in the December 20, 1976, edition of *David Magazine* touted "Direct from the Continental Baths, Reno Sweeny's, and the Rainbow Grill...Laura Kenyon." Holly Woodlawn

appeared in concert in July 1976. Follies and Montana (see listings) were also at this location. This later became home to the Mason Jar restaurant, popular with the LGBTQ community before the building was torn down and the restaurant relocated.

Cathy Johnson recalls, "The lesbians all loved Dana Manchester."

Tap That Ash
2240 Wilton Dr., Wilton Manors
Circa: 2023-present

A cigar lounge and wine bar.

TeeJay's
2100 N. Dixie Hwy., Hollywood
Circa: 1971-1975

An ad for a grand opening ran in *David Magazine* in January 1973. It was open as early as 1971, so perhaps it had a new owner. It was known as a cruisy bar. In March 1975, the bar hosted the Bartender Awards for Broward and Dade County

COME SEE ME
2100 N. DIXIE HWY.
HOLLYWOOD, FLA.

with a special show by Marcia Rose and guests. The bar held a grand re-opening on May 21, 1976, and boasted a new dance floor, new lights and sound, and new ownership. Jess Monteguerdo recalls, "TeeJay Johnson was the owner, he used to do drag as Joan Crawford."

The Roadhouse and Crossfire were also at this location (see listings).

Thinkers
2929 NE 6th Ave., Wilton Manors
Circa: 1999

Tim Miller spills the tea on Thinkers, "It was a private club and you paid something like $5. When you first entered there was this room with bookcases filled with books, a couch, and a couple of chairs. It all looked very intellectual. There was a door behind one of the bookcases that led to a back room with booths and a bar. It was a cover for the backroom. It lasted almost a year before they got busted. I used to go there all the time."

Together
1800 E. Sunrise Blvd., Fort Lauderdale
Circa: 1980-1983

A restaurant and dance club. It appears to have dropped the s from the name in 1982. Later this was the location of Embassy Club/1800 East (see listing).

Tommy on the Beach
5th St. & Ocean Dr., Fort Lauderdale
Circa: 1989

Tops (Annex)
2027 Pembroke Rd., Hollywood
Circa: 1974-1984

It started as a mixed gay and lesbian club. An ad at that time touted, "Watch for our grand reopening on January 29." In 1978, it became a women's bar. Its women's baseball team was the team to beat. It was located next door to PS Disco (see listing).

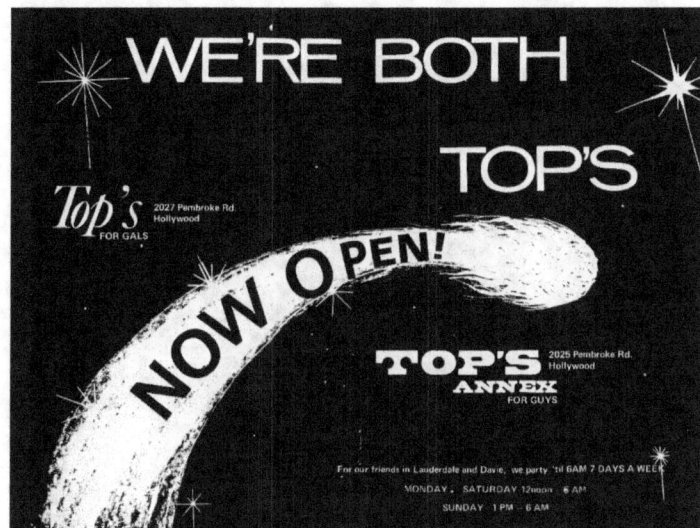

Torpedo Bar
2829 W. Broward Blvd., Fort Lauderdale
Circa: 2005-2015

In 2013, *The New Times* said of the bar: "Get hot and sweaty dancing all night with the boys at Torpedo. This gay dance club caters to a mostly younger male crowd, looking to party all night. It's open until 4 a.m."

Other clubs at this location include Phases and Bam (see listings).

Town Line
200 E. McNab Rd., Pompano
Circa: 1981

Traxx
502 E. Sunrise Blvd., Fort Lauderdale
Circa: 1980-1990

A small bar near the railroad tracks. In July 1980, the owner presided over a same-sex wedding. This space has also been home to David's, Phoenix, and, since 1997, Mona's (see listings).

Tree House
813 SE 1st Ave., Hallandale
Circa: 1984

Open late, it was located across from the train tracks in an underdeveloped area. It attracted a mostly straight, young crowd who liked heavy metal.

Tree Tavern
656 N. Andrews Ave., Fort Lauderdale
Circa: 1971-1975

Although the area is now a hot area for young singles, at that time it was mostly light industrial and almost deserted after dark. Ads at the time boasted "dancing til closing" and listed such entertainment as Fable, Hellstrum, Legs Diamond, and Hopney & Phineas, the Pride of Coconut Grove.

TRICK AT

THE TREE

BY THE TRACK

OPEN 7 DAYS A WEEK
7 P.M. to 2 A.M.

656 North Andrews Ave.
CORNER OF FLAGLER DR.
Ft. Lauderdale, Florida

Treetop Disco (see Club Caribbean)

Trixie's
600 S. Dixie Hwy., Hollywood
Circa: 2003-2010

Stanley (of Stanley's) and Carlos opened the drag show bar, which many interviewed identified as a place known for being able to pick up trans girl prostitutes.

Tropics Grille
2004 Wilton Dr., Wilton Manors
Circa: 1994-present

This cabaret bar and restaurant has gone through many owners over the years. In 1994, Chris Wilson was a partner, and Nate Horner was the chef and became a partner in 2007. Most recently it is operated by Bashir Khan, who also owns Scandals (see listing) and has partial ownership of Lips in Wilton Manors (see listing) and The Townhouse in New York City. It is very popular with the 60+ crowd for Friday cocktail hour, drawing as many as 300 men for a few hours, emptying at about 8 p.m. In 2022 Khan added Grille to the name. It was formerly home to Cape and Club Classics (see listings). It seems to have settled into a groove as a well-established cabaret and supper club with a devoted following of older gentlemen and their admirers.

Tunnel (Les')
545 S. Federal Hwy., Fort Lauderdale
Circa: 1975-1992

Originally opened as Les' Tunnel, it was listed in guides as a women's bar, but according to Lori Tanner, it appears to have had primarily male customers and was kind of a sleazy bar. This location was later the site of Jungle (see listing), partly owned by Norm Kent, later publisher of two LGBT publications.

TUNNEL BAR

ALL REGULAR DRINKS 75¢
(Except Premium Beer)
DRAFT 50¢ —All Day & All Night!
Bar Opens 9 A.M. Mon.-Sat., Noon Sun.

545 S. Federal Hwy., Ft. Laud., Fla. 761-9668

Two on a Match
1243 NE 11th Ave., Fort Lauderdale
Circa: 1980-1983

A women's club with a piano bar. An ad in the July issue of *David Magazine* touted new ownership in 1980, "Vinnie, Freddie, Phil & Clara." This space was also home to Bill's Filling Station, Depot, Hector's, and Le Boy (see listings).

"When Sunny gets Blue," she goes to...

Two on a Match

Fort Lauderdale's Intimate Friendly Piano Bar
'Where Connoiseurs of Fine Wine and Excellent Entertainment Meet
The talented Ron at the Piano!

1243 N.E. 11th Ave.
(N.E. 13th St. & 11th Ave.)
525-2897
OPEN 7 DAYS 6P.M. TILL 2A.M., 3A.M. ON SAT

Uncle Charlie's
1951 N. Powerline Rd., Fort Lauderdale
Circa: 2004-2005

It was a men's dance bar. Club 1951 and Cupcakes (women's bars), The Eagle, and Steel all occupied this space at various times. The building has since been demolished.

Uncle's (aka Uncles)
1000 State Rd. 84, Fort Lauderdale
Circa: 2007-2008

An ad in a 2007 issue of *Buzz Magazine* announced the grand opening. It was sometimes listed as Uncles without the apostrophe. The Saint and Stud were previously at this location (see listings).

Underpass
100 Ansin Blvd., Hallandale
Circa: 1995

A dance bar with shows. Scott Schildgen remembered, "The Underpass lasted five minutes. I saw singer Vicki Shephard perform there."

Electra remembers, "I was hired by the guys that owned it. It was a huge warehouse space. It had been a rock club and they got tired of the rough crowd. So, they redecorated it and had a gay night once a week. And then it closed a few weeks later."

Val's Catering Service
4003 N. Andrews Ave., Oakland Park
Circa: 1965

While listed as a catering company, it was operating as a gay bar. Acting on the complaints, police raided the club on April 18, 1966. Before the raid, the police alerted the news media, who were in the parking lot. In the club, they found 150 patrons mostly men and mostly white. Two straight Black couples told the police they came to "enjoy the show." A patron tried to escape the raid by smashing through a back door, then assaulted a cameraman for taking his picture. Four people were arrested for disorderly conduct and other minor charges. Since 1984 this has been the home to a popular South Florida landmark restaurant called Catfish Dewey's.

Venture Inn
1791 W. Broward Blvd., Fort Lauderdale
Circa: 1971-1975

Although open as early as 1966, the Venture Inn was a mainstream nightclub. An ad in April 1968 listed the bar for sale and although no information could be found on the sale, by 1969, the advertising took a decidedly "gayer" turn. Classified ads touted "Venture Inn any night for entertainment that is lively, different and crowded" and "Gay atmosphere and good food" and perhaps most tellingly, "Men - Know who? What? Where? Dig Venture Inn." By 1971, they were done being subtle. An article in *The Fort Lauderdale News* on

September 26 with the headline "Gays 'Need a Place' Find Many in Area" named the Venture Inn by name and described one of the drag acts. A restaurant, with dancing and a drag show. It was best known for nude male go-go boys on the bar. According to a former bar manager, "They didn't do it for the money, they just liked to expose themselves." In December 1975, Wayland Flowers and Madame performed there. The building has since been demolished and is home to a Salvation Army store.

Victor Victoria
2345 Wilton Dr., Wilton Manors
Circa: 1996–1998

Once home to Costello's and its Gin Mill bar, now the location of The Manor/Venue (see listings).

Victoria Park
908 NE 20th Ave., Fort Lauderdale
Circa: 1995

Named after its neighborhood, then a home to many in the LGBTQ community.

Village Pub (see The Pub on the Drive)

Villa Nova
532 Dixie Hwy., Hollywood
Circa: 1977–1983

A private club in a strip mall with a country and western/Levi theme, the bar's owner sued Hollywood Police for harassment in 1985.

Vinyl
721 N. Federal Hwy., Fort Lauderdale
Circa: 2004–2010

An after-hours club.

Visions
626 S. Federal Hwy., Fort Lauderdale
Circa: 1997–1998

A video bar with dancers opened where Stanley's (see listing) once operated. It continued with the theme of sleaze and go-go boys.

Voo Doo Lounge
111 SW 2nd Ave., Fort Lauderdale
Circa: 2004–2013

Sunday night drag show, but otherwise straight. Electra recalls, "It was a very 'bridge and tunnel' crowd. And then when they sold it to Dennis Rodman, all hell broke loose and that was the end."

Later Off the Hookah would take over this space (see listing).

Well
2426 Wilton Dr., Wilton Manors
Circa: 2024

The Wilton Manors outpost of a chain of bars in Ontario, Canada, owned by John Ribson and managed by Jason Basilico, formerly of Scandals. Ribson took over the location from the failing Hamburger Mary's (see listing), honoring the contracts for events the previous management team had in place. As this book went to press, he was renovating the space while keeping the bar open and changing the menu to feature such Canadian favorites as poutine. The focus will still be on drag performances. Previously this space also housed Sidelines, Matty's, and Rumors (see listings).

West End Lounge
2100 Wilton Dr., Wilton Manor
Circa: 2024-present

The New York City bar's outpost opened in March 2024 in the space that formerly housed Matty's on the Drive (see listing). The upscale lounge with a vintage Vegas vibe features live entertainment and craft cocktails.

Wet
401 S. Fort Lauderdale Beach Blvd., Fort Lauderdale
Circa: 2018

The reimagined Whiskey Blue in the W Hotel. It tried to attract a gay crowd but never succeeded.

Whale & Porpoise
2750 E. Oakland Park Blvd., Oakland Park
Circa: 1996-2000

Owned by a drag queen known as Miss Liz and her husband. It was advertised as female-owned and operated. It attracted a mixed crowd, many bi. This location was home to a lesbian club, Club Xanadu, for a few months, then back to Whale & Porpoise. This space also housed Gypsy's Cabaret (see listings).

Where the Boys Are
1224 S. Dixie Hwy., Hollywood
Circa: 1984-1996

Located in a strip mall.

Whiskey Blue
401 S. Fort Lauderdale Beach Blvd., Fort Lauderdale
Circa: 2012-2013

The bar at the W Hotel was mostly straight but gay-managed. It would later reopen as Wet (see listing). Many attempts were made to woo a gay clientele, none of which were successful.

Wilton Biergarten
2245 Wilton Dr., Wilton Manors
Circa: 2012

Ads and posters outside the club said it would open in the summer of 2010. It did not open until two years later and then closed after a couple of weeks. The space is now home to Club Xtra (see listing).

Wine & Stein
3919 S. State Rd. 7, Fort Lauderdale
Circa: 1965

On June 3, 1963, Broward Sheriff's Deputies raided the bar during the "Miss Wine & Stein" contest and arrested 17 men, many dressed in women's clothing. Their names, ages, and addresses were listed in the newspaper the next day. When the case came before a judge six weeks later, only two defendants showed up and they were declared innocent. In 1962 police were called to the bar when a motorcycle gang beat a doorman who refused them entrance. He suffered a broken jaw, several deep bruises, and a severe knife laceration that required him to be hospitalized. The police tracked down and arrested three of the gang members.

He Wouldn't Dance
Odd Party Brings Court's Snickers

Occasionally the sober decorum of a courtroom has to give way to a chuckle or two.

Yesterday in Court of Record before Judge Louis Weissing, was a case in point.

Criminal Investigator John J. Ryan was telling the judge how he and several other police officers took part in the June 2 raid at the Wine 'N' Stein Club, on S. State Rd. 7.

Seventeen men were arrested for disorderly conduct there, but failed to show up for trial.

At the time of the raid, according to Ryan, four of the men arrested were in women's clothing and vieing for "Miss Wine 'N' Stein" of 1963.

"Well, your honor, as we entered the place, we saw all these men dancing with one another," Ryan explained.

QUEEN'S THRONE

"Of to one side was a small throne surrounded with satin pillows and the party was just getting ready to select a new queen."

"A what?" asked Judge Weissing. "A queen," replied Ryan.

Standing next to Ryan in court and who also participated in the raid was Deputy George Murdock, a burly, giant size man standing at least a head and a half taller than Ryan.

He told the judge what he knew of the raid as did investigator Ed Clode.

Said Clode, trying to keep a straight face, "I was shocked your honor."

"Does anybody have anything else they want to say?" Judge Weissing asked.

DANCE REFUSED

"Only that Murdock here refused to dance with me," quipped Ryan.

The judge found the only two defendants who appeared for the trial innocent.

Deputy Clode said the establishment was closed the night of the raid by orders of the sheriff.

Wolf
2209 Wilton Dr., Wilton Manors
Circa: 2016-2017

Short-lived tenant in the space formerly occupied by The Backstage Club, Bill's Filling Station/Bill's/B's, The Blue Parrot Lounge, Chardee's, Club Silver, The Palms, Southern Nights, and currently, The Eagle (see listings).

Xenon Club
1421 E. Oakland Park Blvd., Oakland Park
Circa: 1985

When it opened, it was owned by Peter Mora and Patrick Krusto, two New York City club owners. It was later owned by Pedro Paredes, who was arrested by the FBI on fraud charges unrelated to the Club. This was once the location of Omni and is now home to Lips (see listings).

X IT Nightclub
219 N. Dixie Hwy., Hollywood
Circa: late 1990s-early 2000s

Saturday was women's night.

Ye Olde Tavern
503 E. Sunrise Blvd., Fort Lauderdale
Circa: 1984

Mixed men and women. The building has since been torn down and a Home Depot sits on this site.

Zachary's (Pub)
2217 N. Federal Hwy., Fort Lauderdale
Circa: 1994-2000

Initially a women's bar, it later became R Bar (see listing), also a women's bar.

Zanzibar
214 SW 1st Ave., Fort Lauderdale
Circa: 1964-1978

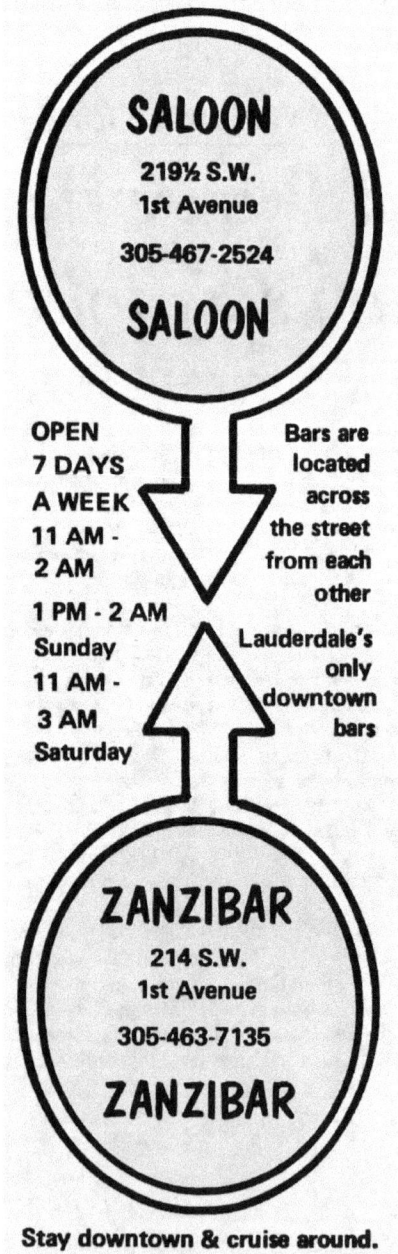

SALOON
219½ S.W.
1st Avenue
305-467-2524
SALOON

OPEN
7 DAYS
A WEEK
11 AM -
2 AM

1 PM - 2 AM
Sunday
11 AM -
3 AM
Saturday

Bars are located across the street from each other

Lauderdale's only downtown bars

ZANZIBAR
214 S.W.
1st Avenue
305-463-7135
ZANZIBAR

Stay downtown & cruise around.

WE'RE GETTING STRONGER EVERY DAY!
Happy Hour - 2 for 1 - 7 days, 5-10 P.M.
DISCO EVERY NITE TILL 4 A.M.

SUNDAY
LEVI-LEATHER NITE

MONDAY
CHICKEN OF THE WEEK
$50. CASH PRIZE

TUESDAY
GAY GONG SHOW
$50. CASH PRIZE

WEDNESDAY
DANCE-OFF
$50. CASH PRIZE

THURSDAY
SHOW NITE
DINA JACOBS

FRI., SAT. & SUN.
HOT INTIMATE DISCO

ZELDA'S
THE DISCO
DISCO NIGHTLY 5PM-4AM • 561-8988
4050 N.W. 9th Ave. (Powerline Rd.), Ft. Lauderdale
NO COVER
NO MINIMUM

Zelda's
4050 N. Powerline Rd., Oakland Park
Circa: 1978-1983

This was a dance club that originally opened as Bacchus (see listings), then changed its name to Zelda's Bacchus, then just Zelda's. Robert Fronner recalls, "It was Bacchus previously, then Bacchus became just the upstairs restaurant after they changed the name of the disco to Zelda's. It also had a piano bar where Miss Vicky (Keller) played and had "Name That Tune" contests."

The club was fighting the city of Oakland Park to retain its 4 a.m. license when owner Johnny DeLorenzo took on additional partners. A judge eventually ruled in the club's favor.

Zelda's Disco
2100 Hollywood Blvd., Hollywood
Circa: 1981

This space also housed Cookie's Intimate Lounge, Ladies' Loft, and Glitz (see listings).

Zu Bar
300 SW 1st Ave., Fort Lauderdale
Circa: 2002-2003

Sunday was its big night, with big-name DJs and dancing on its covered patio. A free buffet was included. This location was also home to Art Bar and The Living Room (see listings).

Restroom Peek Held Legal

Broward Circuit Judge L. Clayton Nance has upheld the right of police officers to secretly peep into public men's room during the investigation of alleged homosexual activity.

In an appeal from a Ft. Lauderdale municipal court conviction, Judge Nance ruled police have the right to use peepholes.

Nance's ruling came when Charles W. Brunty of Ft. Lauderdale appealed his conviction for indecent behavior. Brunty was arrested in a department store men's room last January by detectives who said they watched him commit an indecent act with another man in a closed restroom stall.

Police were looking into the stall from a second floor peephole.

Fort Lauderdale News, 1969

93

Miami-Dade County
The Birthplace of Florida's Queer Community

In many ways, Miami-Dade County was the birthplace of South Florida's queer community. Starting with James Deering's Vizcaya in 1912, to the "femmic" bars of the 1940s and 1950s, to the circuit parties of the 1990s, to cocktails at The Hotel Gaythering, a queer presence has very much been a part of the history of Miami.

An important part of the gay bar story is how the police reacted to their presence and operation. Post-prohibition bars offering female impersonators entertainment were just seen as part of the colorful nightlife of Miami. When, in 1939, the neighbors of one North Miami bar, La Paloma, complained to the police, particularly about the action taking place in the parking lot, the police ignored them. The neighbors then contacted the local Ku Klux Klan chapter, which raided and shut down the bar. Then the police started to pay attention. However, as there were no laws prohibiting cross-dressing or serving drinks to homosexuals, there was little they could do, unless they had complaints of "lewd and lascivious" behavior taking place. Since most of the "lewd and lascivious" behavior took place outside the bar (in the parking lot, the bushes, on the beach, or in private apartments), bar raids were infrequent.

After World War II, the number of "femmic" bars offering female impersonator entertainers grew. It was also becoming obvious that the customers of those bars, mostly men, weren't interested in the "girlie" show, but that they were interested in each other. Chief law officials called a meeting of the bars' owners and suggested that they offer the "warm beer treatment" to the "swishy" customers. Some of the entertainment reporters, however, argued that the bars were just a sign of Miami's "urban maturity." Even Miami's chief of police argued that the bars allowed his men to "keep an eye on that crowd."

The Miami Herald, seeing itself as an upholder of civic respectability, began a major press campaign against the "femmic entertainers." And in 1951 Miami passed a law banning female impersonators. Despite the law, the bars with their "swishy" clientele continued to operate and prosper. It was now evident that Miami had a large "pervert community." A murder, supposedly involving a "fight" over who was going to be the "queen" of the community, led to another "moral panic," enflamed by *The Miami Herald* in 1954. This time the city passed a law banning the serving of alcohol to homosexuals. The bars closed—but only for a few weeks.

By 1956, the bars were busy again, but without advertising. As for the "perverts," Miami's police chief said, "It's like brushing off mosquitoes, there's no great problem." The bars thrived into the 1950s and 1960s with infrequent raids.

The sexual revolution of the 1960s changed the social landscape. In 1972 both the Democratic and Republican Presidential Conventions were coming to Miami. This provided the opportunity for all the radical groups emerging in the 1960s, including the Gay Liberation Front and the Gay Activists Alliance, to come to

Miami to protest. Local bars provided food to the visiting gay activists, and local gay activists took this opportunity to challenge the laws banning cross-dressing and serving alcohol to homosexuals. As the social landscape changed, the activists had quick victories and both laws were thrown out.

The decades of the 1970s and early 1980s were challenging times for Miami nightlife and bars. Because of growing air travel attracting tourists to other warm-weather destinations (Hawaii, Las Vegas, the Caribbean) and the opening of Disney World in Orlando offering Florida tourists a more family-friendly Florida vacation, Miami's tourist-based economy went into serious decline. Some of the major hotels were declaring bankruptcy and many of the smaller ones, particularly in Miami Beach, were being converted into poorly maintained, cheap single-room residences for the growing number of retirees. Once glamorous Miami Beach was described by *Time Magazine* as a "geriatric ghetto" and a "seedy backwater of debt-ridden hotels, gaudy condominiums and decaying apartments," and Miami as "Paradise Lost." For LGBTQ people, the situation was even more dire as Anita Bryant, in 1977, conducted a major media campaign against them.

The newly cheap oceanfront real estate, however, held the seeds of the city's rebirth. In the dilapidated Art Deco buildings in South Beach, preservationists found a mission. And as they were doing across the country, gay men and some lesbians moved in and rehabilitated the decaying buildings. The cheap rentals in South Beach drew creative types and the empty ballrooms of the old hotels created spaces where mega-disco dance halls could be built, and trendy bars and restaurants opened. In the 1990s, South Beach became an international gay destination, with major circuit parties and massive beach parties.

Today the queer presence has melded into an ever-increasingly vibrant South Beach and Miami. The old favorites like Twist and the Palace have survived; others were reopened with new names and management. Despite the high rents, South Beach appears to be a gay mecca that will stand the test of time. A relative latecomer to Pride parades, Miami held its first city-sanctioned event in 2009. Since then, it has continued to grow and gain more support from city leadership and the increasing number of queer bars, restaurants, and businesses.

In 2008, the new Miami Beach Mayor Matti Bower created a Gay Business Development Ad Hoc Committee, with a mission to bring recommendations to the Mayor and City Commission on initiatives to be implemented and supported by the city regarding a variety of issues to ensure the welfare and future of the Miami Beach LGBTQ community. In January 2010, Miami Beach passed a revised Human Rights Ordinance that strengthened enforcement of already existing human rights laws and added protections for transgender people, making Miami Beach's human rights laws some of the most progressive in the state.

The 5 O'Clock Club, Miami, Circa 1936

2x2
201 NE 2ⁿᵈ Ave., Miami
Circa: 1974–1977

The bar consisted of three rooms: a country and western dance bar/game room, a piano bar, and a disco. Robert Fronner remembers, "It was also known as the '2 by 2.' All I can remember is they had a really cute bartender, who graced the cover of *David Magazine* once. It was around the corner from Hideaway and just down the street from the Double R" (see listings). This was the site of gay bars going as far back as the 1960s, including Roman Room, Rainbow, and later, Uncle Charlie's Downtown (see listings).

5th Street
429 Lenox Ave., Miami Beach
Circa: 1989–1993

A mixed bar, straight and gay, run by Michael Pellerin and Peter Thomas. It hosted concerts by dance divas and "boys nights," aka gay nights (Wednesdays) and women's nights (Thursdays). It was Miami Beach's most successful club with a primarily Black clientele. Among the performers who appeared at the club were Tania Maria, Nestor Torres, and Herbie Mann.

By 1991, there were complaints from neighbors about crimes occurring near the club and reports of numerous shootings, and the club was put on a six-month probation; it closed in mid-1993.

8½
1137 Washington Ave., Miami Beach
Circa: 1980–1983

A disco known for its Egyptian parties. In the 1970s this was the location of Miss Kay's Lounge, Calypso Lounge (see listings). It is now home to a Thai restaurant.

13 Buttons
2998 NW River Dr., Miami
Circa: 1977–1980

This Miami outlet of the Ft. Lauderdale bar was owned by Richard Trainor, who also owned Twist (see listing). Its grand opening was November 23, 1977. In 1980 it dropped the word Buttons and began being called 13 Disco. It closed soon afterward. Performer Nikki Adams remembers, "I worked at both locations, Miami was around longer than Fort Lauderdale. (The Fort Lauderdale location was open for a much longer period of time). They had a stage the size of a postage stamp and folks would really crowd in. You were right on top of them when you were performing. Denny O'Reilly was the manager, or maybe one of the owners, such a sweet man."

Electra remembers the owner's name differently, "It was owned by Eddie O'Reilly, who also owned Ozone. Daphne Delight was the drag queen who worked there. They had a movie screen and would show movies like Rocky Horror and Bette Midler concerts."

Jesse Monteagudo recalls, "You'd walk in, and you think, 'Where is everybody?' and they were all in the back room."

700 Club
700 S. Miami Ave., Miami
Circa: 1953

It was raided in 1953 by an undercover police officer who testified that the bar catered to, "young men who danced with each other, spoke with a lisp, and wore lipstick." The license was suspended and the club closed down.

821
821 Lincoln Rd., Miami Beach
Circa: 1997–2004

A local hang-out that was equal parts art gallery and bar run by Gerry Gubitosi (when it opened), featuring theme nights such as Crash on Fridays, Bent Saturdays, 8th Grade ('80s music) on Sunday, and cabaret on Thursdays. The bar's "After Beach Bingo" was popular. It hosted a fundraiser for SAVE, a gay political action group in 1997. Owner Larry Callendar closed the bar in May 1999 due to rent increases, according to an article in *The Miami Herald*.

This space was also home to Bulldog's and Peacock Alley (see listings).

1800 Lounge
1800 Bayshore Dr., Miami
Circa: 1965

Owner William Ader filed a complaint against the Miami Police Department saying the police were harassing his customers. According to *The Miami Herald*, Police Chief Glen Barron said, "The bar being in Coconut Grove, there's always the possibility of homosexuals." In 1965, TV and film star Brian Kelly was a regular at the bar as reported in *The Miami News* on June 13 and *The Miami Herald* on July 1. *The Miami News* on August 29 also reported Bobby Rydell hanging out at the bar.

6700 Lounge
6700 W. Flagler St., Miami
Circa: 1977–1979

The bar featured go-go boys. Tuesday was topless night, where the second drink was half-priced for shirtless men. This was also home to Flag Bar (see listing).

6700 lounge
Go-Go Boys
NITELY 9 P.M. to 2 A.M.
MONDAY—Topless Nite—2nd drink ½ price
NO COVER – NO MINIMUM WEEK NITES
6700 W. Flagler Street, Miami   Extra parking "in rear"

After Dark
163rd St. & Collins Ave., Sunny Isles Beach
Circa: 1978

Billed itself as "Provocative, Exotic. The only Oriental Disco-Lounge and Game Room."

Bar Owner Charges Police With Harassing His Place

By MILLER DAVIS
Herald Staff Writer

A Miami bar owner complained Sunday that one of his places is "harassed" nightly by platoons of police who poke flashlights in patrons' eyes, check the liquor license twice an hour and tune patrol car radios full pitch outside the club.

The accusation of harassing tactics was promptly denied by Miami Assistant Police Chief Glen Barron, who said the 1800 Lounge, 1800 N. Bayshore Dr., had been reported as a place where unsavory persons sometimes go.

At the same time, Barron conceded that police appearances six or seven times a night at a spot might be overdoing it, and said he will "have this corrected."

"I would cut those to two or three a night," said the chief of police operations. His boss, Chief Walter Headley, said he did not know of the frequent visits to the bar.

The complaint of harassment came from William Ader Jr., who also owns the just-opened 27 Birds Bar at SW 27th Ave. and Bird Rd.

"Saturday night," said Ader, a former Metro Zoning Appeals Board member and operator of six drinking spots in Dade, "the officers — in uniform mind you — came into the 1800 every 30 minutes while I was there with my attorney.

"A policeman was sitting outside in his patrol car, the red light flashing in circles and his radio blasting away. I asked him why.

"He said, 'I'm just assigned to sit outside!'"

Ader said the officer was "pleasant and courteous."

When the 27 Birds opened with a gala bustout Wednesday night, Ader went on, "the police — in uniform — were in there by 11 p.m. They came back twice the

next night, twice the next and Saturday night three times. I never did find out what they wanted." No violations were found, and no arrests were made, he said.

Barron was puzzled about this too, saying, "Well, the bar being in Coconut Grove, there's the possibility always of homosexuals."

Police checked the liquor and cigaret machine license here, too, with unrelenting regularity, Ader said.

During one week, Ader declared, "those police came into the 1800 between 60 and 80 times.

"They would prowl around and shine flashlights right into the eyes of my customers."

A spokesman for the Dade state attorney's office agreed that there were "indications of harassment," but added, "I do not with to comment on what may be police department policy." He said normal methods of investigating suspected vice in bars would revolve around the use of undercover agents — not uniformed police.

Ader and his lawyer, Tobias Simon, said an officer told them police checked bars that appeared "on a list they give us."

Chief Barron went along with this:

"Yes, we provided a list of places we felt needed surveillance." He reeled off the names of a dozen downtown and near-downtown saloons.

Ader said he has never brushed with the law, except for one violation the second year the 1800 Lounge was open.

"They found a drink on the bar five minutes after closing time," Ader said.

Simon said he would press the matter, taking Ader's complaints to State Attorney Richard Gerstein.

Ader said a Dade Circuit judge had already been advised of "this matter" and he

After Dark
238 Sunny Isles Blvd., North Miami Beach
Circa: 1989

It was a show lounge and a piano bar. Nikki Adams remembers, "They did a lot of shows and benefits. My boyfriend at the time, Jeff Sherman, was a bartender there."

This was also home to Tops (see listing).

Alibi
601 S. Miami Ave., Miami
Circa: 1954

It is unrelated to the Alibis in Palm Beach or Broward Counties. Police raided it in 1954 as part of a multi-bar crackdown by Miami-Dade County Sheriff Thomas J Kelly, who was quoted as saying, "We don't want perverts to set up housekeeping in this county. We want them to know that they're not welcome."

Nine Arrested In Bar Raid

Two persons today faced City Court charges of disorderly conduct and seven others charges of drunkenness after they were arrested in the Alibi Bar, 601 S. Miami Ave.

Detective Sgt. Tom Lipe and Detective Ben Palmer said the nine were suspected perverts. They also arrested the proprietress, Mrs. Merle Strader, 43, of 2464 NW 104th Ter., and charged her with allowing intoxicated persons to congregate.

Palmer said she was warned previously about allowing "undesirables" to congregate in the bar. He added the raid was in line with current city policy of breaking up congregations of suspected perverts.

Alley (Room) Lounge
1685 Alton Rd., Miami Beach
Circa: 1971–1972

This was a home for gay bars going back to the 1940s with Casbar. In 1971, it advertised "The Alley Kat Revue" every Friday, Saturday, and Tuesday at 11:30 and 2:15 and Sunday at 10:30 and 1:00. It was also the location of Delicate Frank's, Coral Room, Freddie's Piano Bar, and Onyx (see listings).

Ambassadors III
427 22nd St., Miami Beach
Circa: 1971–1974

Calling itself "Miami's most together disco," it featured go-go boys and a weekly Friday night dance contest. An ad encouraged patrons to "Exorcise Yourself from Boredom." In the October 1971 issue of *David Magazine*, it was reported that the club "... has done a beautiful job of remodeling the inside of the bar with a Gay Paree Nightclub effect." This space later became home to the Blind Fox Lounge (see listing).

Amnesia (International)
136 Collins Ave., Miami Beach
Circa: 1993–1998 & 2011–2013

It was a primarily straight but gay-friendly dance club, initially famous for its foam parties. Brothers, Andre and Gregory Boud, were listed as the owners. Lesley Abravanel, who used to cover Miami Beach's nightlife scene, described Amnesia as, "...unbridled hedonism from the children of the night born a bit too late for Studio 54." The owners were constantly battling with neighbors who filed police complaints about noise and crimes including theft and assault.

After five years, the space was leased to various other clubs, including Opium Den and Prive. It re-opened in 2011 after extensive renovations and was sold in 2013. Most recently, it has operated as Story, owned by millionaire Jeffrey Soffer of the Fontainebleau Hotel.

Edison Farrow recalls, "This was a fantastic venue with an open roof. There were tea dances on Sundays with outrageous drag performances by Damien Deevine, Daisy Deadpetals, Wanda, Connie Casserole, Chyna Girl, Sexcelia, and Shelley Novak. The DJ was David Knapp.

Anam's
3019 Coral Way, Miami
Circa: 2006–2012

A women's bar. *New Times* named it the "Best Gay Bar" of 2007 and described it as, "... an exclusive women's club, located on the second floor of a building on Coral Way. Hidden from the street, the only hint of Anam's existence is its name etched into a glass door in swirling cursive. Inside, dimly lit, stained-glass chandeliers shroud the bar in ambiguity, and faces are hard to distinguish among the shadows. For the most part, men aren't allowed in, and the crowd is usually Latin women anywhere from their late twenties to early fifties. Owner Olga Sanchez serves the drinks while her partner, Ana Pou, plays the bongos to the DJ's mix of salsa, bachata, and other Latin beats."

Angel Ultra Lounge
247 NW 23rd St., Miami
Circa: 2005–2010

Resident DJs David Solero and Quixx mixed the beats. The bar hosted special guests such as NBA stars Nick Van Exel, Sam Cassell, and James Posey for themed parties. Other events included Icy Saturdays, Milk and Honey Mondays, and Spank Thursdays.

Annex
6519 SW Bird Rd., Miami
Circa: 1988

It held its grand opening in March 1988, sometimes identified as Club Annex.

THE CLUB ANNEX

**The Celebration Continues
Thru March**

Free Drinks 9 P.M. - 11 P.M.
And Complimentary
Happy Hour Buffet 3 P.M. - 8 P.M.

Entrance Thru The Rear
With Enough Well-Lit And
Secure Parking For Over 500 Cars

6519 SW 40th St. (Bird Rd.) Miami
(305) 661-2333

Aquarius
9th & Lejeune, Miami
Circa: 1973

Area 51 (see Discotekka at Mekka)

Atlantic House
1716 Alton Rd., Miami Beach
Circa: 1990-1992

Nikki Adams performed there often. This was also home to the Mayflower Lounge from the 1940s-1970s (see listing). Lori Tanner remembers, "It was owned by Ernie Michaels. It was named after the place in Provincetown. It was way before South Beach became popular. Everyone called it The A House. It was a small, late-night dance club."

At the Boulevard
7770 N. Biscayne Blvd., Miami
Circa: 2009-2010

For a hot second, this was the most popular club in town, then just as quickly, it fell out of favor.

Azucar (Club)
2301 SW 32nd Ave., Miami
Circa: 2005-present

Originally opened as Sugar, it was a popular dance club, especially with the Latin community. *USA News'* 10/Best claimed, "You've never been to a better Latin drag club than the oh-so-memorable Azucar Nightclub. This ultra-hot gay Latin nightclub is just the place to go to enjoy the best drag entertainment off South Beach. Thursday nights are Drag War nights and the best queens come to battle it out for the prize, not to mention the bragging rights. If you're looking to get a lot of dancing, though you'll want to drop by on a Saturday night for Sabados Locos con Azucar."

Hannah H. said, "I came here with a large group of people around midnight. The place was dead, but we hung out on the patio where it seemed to be a bit busier. Cut to 2:30 in the morning, and suddenly a deserted stage area is transformed into a fully realized drag show. Most of the songs were in Spanish but there were a few Ariana Grande songs thrown in there. Every queen was giving it their all. This was not rookie shit."

This was formerly home to the Concorde Lounge and The Trip (see listings).

Bachelor's
820 SW 2nd Ave., Miami
Circa: 1972-1974

Sometimes listed as Bachelor's West. According to Jesse Monteagudo, "It was on the second floor and downstairs was a straight bar. It was later home to Second Landing." (see listing). Note: this is not affiliated with Bachelor's II (see below), even though they were open at the same time.

101

Bachelor's II
2847 Coral Way, Miami
Circa: 1972–1978

A second-floor bar, it was raided on March 19, 1972. Bill DuProest, a Miami police officer who was off duty with his wife at the bar, described to the *Miami News* how, in minutes, police swarmed the bar and harassed patrons. Disagreeing with his department's actions in this effort, DuProest quit his job.

On October 5, 1975, the bar hosted "Friends" with Michael St. Laurent, Neil Martin, Ernie Michaels, and special guest, David Vance.

Local entertainment writers sometimes confused it with Bachelor's III in Fort Lauderdale, which brought in mid-level names such as George Maharis, James Brown, and Kaye Stevens. When folks showed up for the show they were often very confused. The bar started listing itself as Bachelor's West.

Jesse Monteagudo recalls, "Though Bachelor's II then boasted 'the delightful piano stylings of the famed Walter Lena and Neil Martin,' to me it was just a place to grab a drink on my way to the nearby Club Miami Baths."

Ironically, given the name, this space was usually the home to women's bars including Blackie's Hideaway, Chez Louise, Mimi's, and Womyn's Town (see listings).

Backdoor Bamby
727 Lincoln Rd., Miami Beach
Circa: 2008

This was an event in a small bar behind Cameo. Score, Kremlin, and Tunnel 1437 (see listings) all called the main bar home. Cathy Johnson recalls, "Shelley Novak (aka Tommy Strangie) worked the door there. He's still active in the Miami club scene."

Bambu
645 Washington Ave., Miami Beach
Circa: 2007

EVO (see listing) later operated at this location.

Bang
1516 Washington Ave., Miami Beach
Circa: 1995

Classy Caribbean restaurant in the early evening, which then, later at night, converted to a music club with the Magic City Funk Factory, Gwen Johnson, and Euro-disco on Sundays. Celebrities such as Paloma Picasso and Kelly Lynch were often spied there.

Bar 14
1417 N. Washington Ave., Miami Beach
Circa: early 2000s

The Gay Yellow Pages lists Cockpit and Rocket as bars operating out of this space simultaneously. More likely, they were simply the names of events at the bar.

Bar 721
721 Lincoln Rd., Miami Beach
Circa: 2011–2012

Owners Dan Sehres, Martin Krediet, and Alan Randolph commissioned Robert Zemnickis to create a campy interior that simulated a 1970s Soho loft turned rec room, with scattered vintage pieces and plush sectionals around a faux fireplace. Shag carpets cushioned the floor and brick walls welcomed guests to watch a concert, listen to groovy tunes, shoot pool, order great wine, or a tableside keg.

Edison Farrow remembers, "I was the promoter for Hype Fridays at Bar 721 with DJ Smeejay. We had free vodka drinks from 9 p.m. to 10 p.m. It was during a great time in Miami Beach when we had 721, Mova, and Score all nearby for bar hopping."

Laundry and Black Sheep Bar (see listings) were also at this location.

Bar Code
653 Washington Ave., Miami Beach
Circa: 1994

It was a drag show dinner theater. Among the performers were Adora, Damian, Rober, Marsha Mallow, Marvella, Bridgette, Sexy, and Mother Kibble.

Bar Gaythering
1409 Lincoln Rd., Miami Beach
Circa: 2014–present

Located in the Hotel Gaythering, owned by Stephan Ginez and Alexander Guerra. The bar is decorated in MiMo style and located in a 1958 building in the heart of a Miami Beach gayborhood. The bar has a devoted following and is a see-and-be-seen spot. *Forbes Magazine* says, "Gaythering Bar is always thumping. Local craft beers and a carefully curated cocktail list featuring vintage classics punched up with local flair are the fare here, but this bar may be better for your ego than most gay bars thanks to the inspirational message board that helps keep the vibe ever positive."

Don't miss drag karaoke on Mondays ($5 margaritas will provide plenty of liquid courage) or trivia on Wednesdays if you know your stuff, but daily happy hours have you covered all week long.

Bar Room
320 Lincoln Rd., Miami Beach
Circa: 1999–2001

A straight bar with a monthly gay night run by Ingrid Casares and Chris Paciello in the old art deco Flamingo Theater. It was also popular with the leather crowd. It was the hottest club of the summer of 1999. By the fall of 2000, it was all over.

Bash
655 Washington Ave., Miami Beach
Circa: 1995–2007

A mixed gay and straight dance club. The owners included Sean Penn and Simply Red singer Mick Hucknall, with co-owner/manager Eric Omores at the helm, and Kitty Meow holding court. Bash ushered in a short-lived era of relatively unself-conscious enjoyment when it opened in April 1993. The space expanded the VIP-room concept and initiated many theme nights. The club was sold in 2007. "I guess what made it great was the mix of people. Back then everybody just wanted to have fun," the Senegal-born, France-raised Omores recalls wistfully. "It was nothing pretentious."

Dek 23 (see listing) would follow at this location with a popular Sunday gay night event, "Click."

Basin Street
1610 Alton Rd., Miami Beach
Circa: 1972–1981

Basin Street featured a piano bar, cabaret, go-go boys, and drag shows. The bar opened as a primarily Black club. It became a gay club in 1972 under new management. In January 1975, it held its 3rd anniversary with a buffet and show featuring

Donnie Jay, Bobbie Ramone, Crystal Beed, Camille St. Lawrence, and special guest star Cecelia Valdez. This was also the location of Club Benni and Red Carpet Lounge (see listings).

Bay City Station (see Flamingo Bay)

BBC
323 23rd St., Miami Beach
Circa: 1977

Its grand opening was on August 3, 1977, with a special guest DJ Hub. It was owned by the same people who owned the Glory Hole bar in Chicago. It advertised itself as Miami Beach's first leather-Levi dress code bar and featured three bars. It lasted about six months. This space has been a gay bar since the early 1970s, serving as home to Billy's Back Lounge, Billy's Backroom, Dinghy, Duck's Pastime, Groove Jet, Joseph's, Little Al's, Miss Kay's, Rain, Teran's, and WOW (see listings).

Berlin
666 Washington Ave., Miami Beach
Circa: 1998

Electra says, "It was kind of like a gay Gilligan's Island back then, all those bars along Washington Ave. You'd just pop from one to another. I stopped going when all the Eurotrash came in. It wasn't gay anymore."

Billboard Live
1500 Ocean Dr., Miami Beach
Circa: 2001-2004

Party organizer Jeffrey Sanker was behind this men's dance club financed by the Billboard Organization. It opened to great acclaim, then suddenly shuttered, filing bankruptcy two months after opening.. Dolce and Sky Bar (see listings) would take over this space and use the Collins Ave. entrance as their address.

Beach Head
1510 Alton Rd., Miami Beach
Circa: unknown

Billy Lee's
1718 Alton Rd., Miami Beach
Circa: 1960s

A supper club featuring drag shows across the street from Onyx (see listing). Film star Martha Raye sometimes hung out there. In *The Miami News* from March 1, 1960, columnist Herb Rau reported, "Spotted at Billie Lee's Back Room in the Mayflower Hotel in Miami Beach; ex-governor Charlie Johns." This was notable because the Johns' Commission, officially The Florida Legislative Investigation Committee, was established by the Florida Legislature in 1956, during the era of the second red and lavender scare. Like the more famous anti-Communist investigative committees of the McCarthy period in the United States Congress, the Florida committee undertook a wideranging investigation of allegedly subversive activities by academics, Civil Rights Movement groups, especially the NAACP, and suspected communist organizations Having failed to find communist ties to Florida civil rights organizations, to gain continued funding it began to focus on a more vulnerable target: homosexuals, who at the time were widely believed to be a threat to national security, as well as a threat to youth. Students and faculty were fired or forced to resign from Florida universities, especially the University of Florida. Charlie Johns was the leader of a group of rural legislators who dominated the Florida Legislature.

The Sun-Sentinel reported in 2019 that the committee "...employed entrapment and blackmail...and unrelenting cruelty."

The bar lost its liquor license after a series of raids on gay bars in 1962.

Billy's Back Lounge
323 23rd St., Miami Beach
Circa: 1990

A neighborhood bar with pool tables. This space has been a gay bar since the early 1970s, serving as home to BBC, Billy's Backroom, Dinghy, Duck's Pastime, Groove Jet, Joseph's, Little Al's, Miss Kay's, Rain, Teran's, and WOW (see listings).

Billy's Backroom
323 23rd St., Miami Beach
Circa: 1971

This was a bar located behind Wild Bill's Steakhouse.This has been a gay bar since the early 1970s, serving as home to BBC, Billy's Back Lounge, Dinghy, Duck's Pastime, Groove Jet, Joseph's, Little Al's, Miss Kay's, Rain, Teran's, and WOW (see listings).

Bit & Bridle
8237-39 NE 2nd St., Miami
Circa: 1989-1990

A leather bar with strippers. Gracey's Tavern took over this space (see listing).

Blackbird Ordinary
729 SW 1st Ave., Miami
Circa: 2022-present

Mostly straight hipsters. The bar specializes in hand-crafted cocktails and a diverse beer selection. Tuesday night is for lesbian and non-binary folks. Named one of the 100 best bars in Miami by *New Times* and highly praised by *Conde-Nast Traveler*. It underwent a total renovation in early 2024 but has managed to keep its outsider vibe.

Blackie's Hideaway
2847 Coral Way, Miami
Circa: 1978-1981

A women's bar. This space was also home to several other women's bars, including Chez Louise, Mimi's, and Womyn's Town, but it also housed the men's bar, Bachelor's II (see listings).

Black Sheep Bar
721 Lincoln Rd., Miami Beach
Circa: 2009-2010

Although it only lasted from about January to July, for a while this was a hopping spot with DJ Rekha Malhotra whose claim to fame was mixing tracks for Wyclef Jean. Others running the turntable at this spot were DJ Wreck, Ash-Rock, Mad Mc and Juan Bashead. The ubiquitous Shelly Novak was at the closing night party.

Laundry and Bar 721 (see listings) were also at this location.

EVERYBODY'S GOING TO THE BLIND FOX FOR THE BIGGEST HALLOWEEN GALA!

SATURDAY OCT. 1st

Blind Fox   427-22nd STREET   MIAMI BEACH, FLORIDA 33139
Ph. 305/672-9659   GEORGE MOCKBEE Manager

Blind Fox Lounge
427 22nd St., Miami Beach
Circa: 1975-1978

Owned by Dekbert Livermore and Roy Speer. George Mockbee was the manager. Herb Rau, writing in his entertainment column in *The Miami News* on October 27, 1975, ran an item about the Blind Fox stating, "Blind Fox disco on 22nd Street in Miami Beach is every Wednesday night a scene of dance contests whose participants are transexuals. And a local transexual who underwent a sex-change operation in 1974, dropped the assumed name of Linda Mitchell and is now known as Lisa Hyden." Previously, this was the location of Ambassadors III (see listing).

Blue
222 Espanola Way, Miami Beach
Circa: 2000-2005

A mixed gay and straight club with drag shows. This would later be home to Kill Your Idol (see listing).

Blue Parrot Bar
145 NE 1st St., Miami
Circa: 1969

Thirty men were arrested in a raid in 1960. However, all charges were dropped, according to an article in *The Miami Herald*.

Blue Waters Hotel Lounge
4th off Collins on Ocean Tr., Miami Beach
Circa: 1976

An ad in *David Magazine* in October 1976 read "Miss Kay's Back in Action. P.S. Freddie is here too!"

Boardwalk
17008 N. Collins Ave., Miami Beach
Circa: 1985-2001

A male strip club open 23 hours a day, founded by Victor Zepka. It was in an unincorporated part of Miami-Dade County and was popular in the late '80s and all through the '90s. In the early 2000s the city, which moved its city hall to the same plaza the Boardwalk was in, didn't want bars in that area. After struggling with the city for more than a year, Zepka decided it was time to close the Boardwalk. Approximately six months later, in April 2002, he opened the Boardwalk in Fort Lauderdale in an old Flannigan's restaurant (see listing in Broward County).

Bond Street Lounge
150 20th St., Miami
Circa: 2008-2013

Located in the basement of the Townhouse Hotel, this was a sushi bar early in the evening, and a cocktail lounge later.

videos, pool table, back room for men only, and a landscaped outdoor patio." In June 2008, *The Miami Herald* described it as, "An easygoing drinking dive bar that caters to gay hipsters."

Theme nights included Hipsters (Fridays), Party Monster (with DJ Fernan D (Saturdays), pool tournaments (Mondays), and Queen Cabaret with guest artists (Thursdays).

Buccaneer Disco
16051 N. Collins Ave., Miami Beach
Circa: 1977-1979

Located in the Winward Resort, it featured drag shows regularly and advertised them in mainstream newspapers, such as *The Miami News*. In 1977, it advertised upcoming appearances by Wayland Flowers, Donna Summer, Michael Greer, Gotham, and Morgana King. In May of 1978 a production of "The Boys in the Band" was staged in the bar." In 1979 an arsonist set a fire in one of the dressing rooms and returned days later to set another one. The first fire spread, causing the evacuation of 24 guests; the second fire was put out quickly, causing little damage.

Bonfire
1060 NE 79th St., Miami
Circa: 1992

The bar offered dancing and entertainment to a mixed crowd of men and women. This location has housed several queer clubs over the years including Club Milord, Cupid's Cabaret, Sandal Club, and Zippers (see listings).

Bongo's Cuban Café
603 Biscayne, Miami
Circa: 2004-2010

The restaurant and bar that hosted LGBTQ events and parties including, Fuego! With DJ Lazarus Leon. Not to be confused with singer Gloria Estefan's now-defunct restaurant of the same name.

Boy Bar
1220 Normandy Dr., Miami Beach
Circa: 2004-2010

A small storefront neighborhood/dive bar. Club Fly identified it as, "A neighborhood cruise bar with full liquor service,

Buck's Lounge (aka Buck15 Lounge)
707 Lincoln Rd., Miami Beach
Circa: 2007-2012

Located above a Chinese restaurant, it was a gallery and bar. Thursdays "The Simple Life," were gay nights hosted by Edison Farrow for four years, along with Chyna as the "Door Goddess" and DJ Daisy Deadpetals spinning a mix of hip-hop, '80s, rock, and dance. Edison Farrow remembers, "There was a line to get in every Thursday for seven years. There was incredible energy. People would dance on the couches and literally swing from the rafters."

A news item from the time read, "This party attracts a fun, young, hip, fashionable crowd in this intimate New York City style Lounge."

Bulldog's
821 Lincoln Rd., Miami Beach
Circa: 1993-1994

This bar attracted a leather crowd. This space was also home to 821, Snap and Peacock Lounge (see listings).

Bunkhouse
6535 Bird Rd., Miami
Circa: 1994-1996

Cabaret
233 12th St., Miami Beach
Circa: 2014

The bartenders and servers performed at this cabaret co-owned by Edison Farrow and Ed DeCaso. Farrow said, "Every employee was an incredibly talented singer. Most are successful singers now, and many have been on *American Idol* and *The Voice*. We had singers, piano players, burlesque dancers, drummers, and saxophone players. There were also special performances with Leslie Jordan, Coco Peru, and Molly Ringwald."

Frommer's Travel Guide described it as, "an intimate, old-fashioned piano-bar style experience in the middle of sometimes overwhelming Clubland. And besides crooners and musicians, they throw in a little old-school burlesque, even circus acts."

Cabaret
1801 N. Collins Ave., Miami Beach
Circa: 2017-2023

Located in the Shelborne Hotel, *Miami Community News* reported that "Singers, dancers, and piano players rotate between bartending and singing while working the crowd." In August 2017, it held a birthday party for Madonna—she did not attend. Throughout its run, it periodically held nights in honor of singers/performers such as Elton John, Prince, George Michael, and Whitney Houston. . It closed in March 2023, a casualty of the COVID pandemic.

Cactus Lounge, aka Cactus Club
2041 Biscayne Blvd., Miami Beach
Circa: 1950-2004

Owned by Roger Claudius Farrell Sr., a straight man. It was the first Black-owned gay bar in Miami and, at one time, the oldest gay bar in Miami-Dade County. It held a 40th-anniversary party on September 23, 1990.

Electra recalls, "The guy who owned the bar also owned all the houses between the bar and the beach. He wanted to open it as a resort of some sort. I did shows there every Sunday. They filmed scenes for the movie *There's Something About Mary* in one of those houses."

Club D (see listing) operated in this space for a brief time in the late 1980s.

Café Con Leche (see KGB)

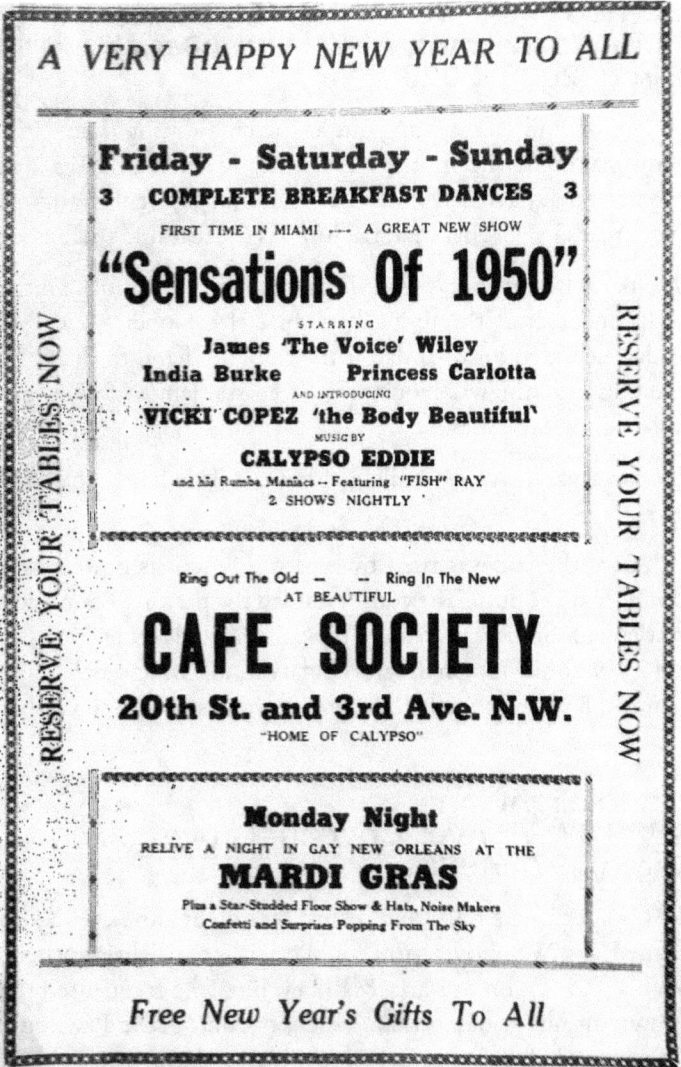

Café Society
20th St & 3rd Ave., Miami
Circa: 1930s – 1950s

The star performer in the drag show was Princess Carlotta. One patron recalled, "To go there and see him in his fabulous gowns was really something. The mainstream news press reported on Princess Carlotta, never realizing that she was a he. The bar is sometimes referred to as Calypso Club.

Cage
901 S. Miami Ave., Miami
Circa: 1999–2000

Calypso Club (see Café Society)

Calypso Lounge
1137 Washington Ave., Miami Beach
Circa: 1977

Featuring Walter Lena on the piano on Saturday, Sunday, and Monday and shows with Diana Dox, Tina Christie, and Rick Rivera. This was formerly Miss Kay's and would later become 8½ (see listings).

Cambridge
2547 Coral Way, Miami
Circa: 1978–1980

Popular local bar celebrity Vivian (of Chez Vivian, see listing) was the face of this restaurant with a disco upstairs. The grand opening was on Valentine's Day 1978, with special guest entertainers Chuck Lyons, Vicki Keller, and Rick. It billed itself as a "dining room/cruise bar."

Cameo
1445 Washington Ave., Miami Beach
Circa: 2006-2020

Rhiannon and Kesha hung out at the club during their 2010 tour, making it the spot for celebrities to chill. In 2013 Ace Hood and DJ Khaled hosted a Memorial Day party and on New Year's Eve of that year, L'il Jon was the featured performer.

The party had groovy '60s-style psychedelic projections on the walls and lots of thumping bass. In 2014, rapper/singer Flo Rida celebrated his birthday at the club. On hand to share the evening with him was Houston Rockets star James Harden and a slew of pretty ladies.

Electra says, "It wasn't really gay, but the little bar at the back was."

In 2015, the bar was sued by a patron who was beaten by a bouncer at the door. The court awarded the patron a $5 million settlement. Shortly thereafter, the bar was sold to new owners. IN 2019 Young Jewish Singles held its annual Matzo Ball at the Cameo. It closed shortly thereafter. It was also home to Crobar (see listing

Candlelight Inn
2869 SW 7th Ave., Coconut Grove
Circa: 1974-1980s

It was a members-only club owned by Bob Stickney, who also owned The Warehouse. You could often spot celebrities there, such as Roy Cohn or Barry Manilow. Jim, who frequented the restaurant and cabaret, said, "The Coconut Grove Playhouse was around the corner, so a lot of actors hung out there...I remember having dinner with Tennessee Williams."

Vivian Olivo agrees, "It was a really nice place to have dinner, really elegant. It had a nice ambiance. You would go out to dinner there, then go out to the bars afterward. A classy place, it was expensive, and people dressed up. This was the '80s.

In her memoir, *Traveling on the Path of Joni Mitchell*, Ann Powers notes that folk singers performed in "neighborhoods centered on nightlife typified by the Grove, where crash pads for musicians and actors were everywhere...and gay enclaves like the Candlelight Inn dotted the avenues...by the time the folk revival had started, the Grove was ready...and so were the singer-songwriters of Greenwich Village, eager to hop down the coast and shed their sweaters for the winter. One of those early Grove adopters was Joni."

In January 1976, gay rights activist Leonard Matlovich spoke at a brunch at the Candlelight Inn organized by the Society for Individual Rights (SIR), a gay rights organization.

Nikki Adams recalls, "It was the first really elegant gay restaurant in the area."Cap's

Cap's
1289 NW 119th St., Miami
Circa: 1977

A pre-opening celebration was held on June 15, 1977, with a special show featuring Glen Elliot. It was a restaurant, lounge, disco, and denim bar.

Carnival Bar
137 NE 3rd Ave., Miami
Circa: 1950s-1975

Originally known for a rough trade crowd, it was targeted in the bar raids of 1954. In later years, it became a popular Latin hangout. In 1975, the bar ran classified ads in *The Miami Herald* stating, "Lost Our Lease" and listing bar equipment for sale. Although *The Damron Guide* lists the bar in 1997, it probably closed in 1975, as there is no information listed for it after that date.

Cas-Bar
1685 Alton Rd., Miami Beach
Circa: 1940s-1961

Located in the Sea Shore Hotel, near the beach, it was operated by a woman named Shirley. Men and women would stop by after a day on the beach for the free buffet. A wall was painted black, and patrons would trace their handprints on the wall and put their names inside the prints.

A 1961 classified ad listed the bar's assets for sale.

Since then, this area has become the site of many gay bars, including The Alley (Room) Lounge, Coral Room, Delicate Frank's, Freddie's Piano Bar, and Onyx (see listings).

Cattle Co.
343 SW North River Dr., Miami
Circa: 1981-1982

A leather bar with a nice patio, the business was registered to Clifford Lincoln and Michael Latterner. Later home to Old Town (see listing), also a leather bar.

CB's Pub
3660 NW 79th St., Miami
Circa: 1978

A women's bar run by Jean Hudler. It offered entertainment on weekends.

*** WELCOME TO C.B.'s PUB

3660 N.W. 79 St. Miami

Entertainment on Fri. & Sat.

***

Celebrations
4225 NW 167th St., Miami Gardens
Circa: 1985

Attracted a diverse crowd.

Charles Hotel Bar
1475 Collins Ave., Miami Beach
Circa: 1954–1965

It was mostly a women's bar but was welcoming to men. One of the many bars raided in August 1954 by Miami-Dade County Sheriff Thomas J Kelly.

Charlie's (see Uncle Charlie's)

Cheeks
7005 Biscayne Blvd., Miami
Circa: 1987–1988

This was a neighborhood bar. Southpaw, Jamboree, and Stables (see listings) would later open at this location.

Cheers
2490 NW 17th St., Miami
Circa: 1988–2005

This was a neighborhood lesbian bar, sometimes listed as Cheers/Diversions. It had a decent-sized dance floor. Men were welcome. Cathy Johnson reminisces, "This was my bar. It started as a video bar, then they expanded and put in a dance floor. There was a lot of cocaine going around in those days. It was more of a mixed bar, for both men and women." This was also to Mixers, Sebastian's, and Sappho's (see listings).

Cheers (the World)
5922 S. Dixie Hwy., Miami
Circa: 1987–1995

Jan Harrold's bar attracted a young crowd. Friday was salsa, merengue, house music, disco, and classics. Sunday was 50¢ draft beer night and Wednesday was leather fetish fantasy. In 1992 a production of *Vampire Lesbians of Sodom* was staged at the bar.

Vivian Olivo remembers this bar well: "It was during the time of MTV, and Cheers was a big deal. There were TVs everywhere and music videos playing. It was an oval-shaped bar. It had a dance floor and a little outdoor patio and then another bar in another room off to the right."

This space has been home to many bars, including Club Climax, Club 5922, Splash, and Steel (see listings).

Chelsea
944 Washington Ave., Miami Beach
Circa: 1995

Before it became a chic boutique hotel, the bar was well-known as a hustler hangout.

Cherry Grove
2490 NW 17th Ave., Miami
Circa: 1987-1993

This women's bar hosted the official women's party after the 1989 White Party. Cathy Johnson has fond memories of Cherry Grove, "They had pool tournaments, and they had BBQs on Sundays. There was a big dance floor. The bar was down the left side of the room, and on the right was the pool table."

Vivian Olivo says, "Louise [Boivin] who owned Chez Louise (see listing), also owned Cherry Grove."

Nikki Adams remembers, "Louise owned that bar. I did a lot of drag shows there. They loved us."

According to Lori Tanner, Louise Boivin did not own Cherry Grove but managed the bar.

Chez Louise
2847 Coral Way, Miami
Circa: 1983-1987

It was a mixed crowd of women and some men. Lori Tanner remembers, "It was owned by a straight couple, but Louise Boivin was the manager and the face of the bar."

Cathy Johnson recalls, "I went there when I first started going out. It was dark and I was nervous."

This space was home to several women's bars, including Blackie's Hideaway, Mimi's, and Womyn's Town, but it also housed the men's bar Bachelor's II (see listings).

Chez Pepe
5950 S. Dixie Hwy., Miami
Circa: 1964

It was owned by Henry Leitson, who also owned the Candlelight Inn in Coconut Grove. He purchased the former Dante's (see listing) and switched the cuisine from Italian to French/Continental. During the early 1960s, some venues were not explicitly gay, but for those "in the know," one could go there to meet other gay men. Chez Pepe was one of those places. A restaurant that was popular with the ladies who lunch and who dine, and in the late evening, it was popular with gay men. The cocktail lounge had a reputation for being a place to meet other gay people. It opened on May 7, 1964.

China Club
1450 Collins Ave.
Circa: 1987-1988

The same management of China Club in New York took over the space formerly occupied by Warsaw and Ovo (see listings). A focal point was the giant fish tank in the center of the room

with live sharks. After extensive renovations, the club opened in time for Halloween in 1987 with an appearance by the Rock Group Nerve Damage. The Four Tops appeared for Christmas weekend, and the cast of *Cats* did an AIDS fundraising benefit on December 27. Its dedication to serious rock music didn't find a following and by August of 1988, owner Danny Fried was looking for a buyer, although he vowed to keep the club open on weekends until he did so. He declared bankruptcy and the club's assets were sold off in November of 1988.

Christopher Street
1763 Coral Way, Miami
Circa: 1980

It hosted the Miss Southern USA Contest on August 4, 1980.

Circus
401 Ocean Dr., Miami Beach
Circa: 1950s-1959

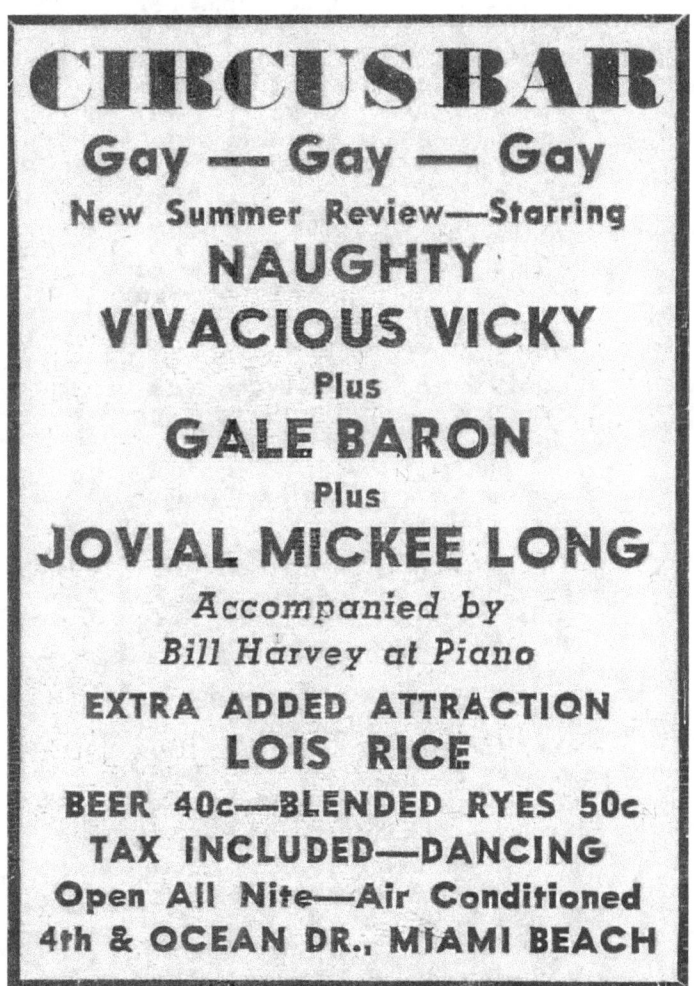

A drag show bar that attracted a mixed crowd. The ads promised "Gay Gay Gay." It was raided by the police numerous times. In 1950 three performers were charged with "wearing clothing unbecoming to their sex" and charged $50 apiece. In 1954, as part of a multi-bar crackdown by Miami-Dade County Sheriff Thomas J Kelly, who was quoted as saying, "We don't want perverts to set up housekeeping in this county. We want them to know that they're not welcome." A Miami judge overruled the police officers and gave the bar back its liquor license. In 1956 it was declared off-limits to military personnel. By 1958 there was a classified ad listing the bar for sale, and soon after that, there were no news items about the bar at all.

3 Convicted As Female Impersonators

Three female impersonators were convicted in Miami Beach city court today despite the expressed fears of their attorney that the ruling might open the way to prosecution of men wearing shorts on the beach.

The defendants were Frank Quinn, 32, of 335 Ocean dr.; Jay Colby, 30, of the Somerset hotel, and Gene Michaels, 26, of the Adams hotel. All were arrested at the Circus Bar, 401 Ocean dr.

* * *

Colby and Quinn were arrested both Saturday and Sunday nights, while Michaels was arrested only on Saturday.

All three were charged with wearing clothing unbecoming to their sex, while an additional charge was filed against Quinn for singing lewd songs in an indecent manner.

Colby and Quinn were fined $50 apiece by Judge Daniel P. Galen, and Michaels was fined $25 and costs.

* * *

Attorney Charles Courshon, defending the trio, declared that the question of whether clothes were becoming or not becoming to a man's sex was entirely a matter of opinion.

"If you can convict this man (Michaels) because he had his shirt tucked up, then you can convict any man who sits on the beach that way," he said.'

"If you can convict him because his trousers do not come to the ankles, then you can convince any man on the beach who wears shorts."

Assistant City Attorney Irving Cypen, however, argued that the entire effect of the costume was that of a woman's dress.

Clayton's
427 Jefferson Ave., Miami Beach
Circa: 1990

Only open for one month, then changed its name to Scratch (see listing).

Clover Club
118 Biscayne Blvd., Miami
Circa: 1940s–1953

The Clover Club featured big-name performers and lavish production numbers; it was in the heart of the downtown hotel district. In January 1953, one of the most popular local entertainers and burlesque dancers, Joanne Gilbert, identified and exploited a loophole in the 1952 legislation regarding crossdressing and nudity: it did not apply to women. She swapped out her scanty burlesque costume for a pair of masculine britches and a shirt. Such resistance led commissioners to change the law in 1956 to include both women and men from being "in a state of nudity or in a dress not customarily worn by his or her sex."

On March 9, 1947, the bar, as well as two others, Club Jewel Box and Zissen's (see listings) were raided for presenting drag shows.

Club 49
4901 SW 8ᵗʰ St., Miami
Circa: 1983–1984

Club 245
245 22ⁿᵈ St, Miami Beach
Circa: unknown

This was also home to Club Nu, Heaven, and Onyx Room (see listings)

Club 1235
1235 Washington Ave., Miami Beach
Circa: 1988.

Sometimes known just as 1235, it opened in 1986 as Z (see listing) as a teen dance club, but by 1987, Thursday was the only night for those under 21, and it had changed its name to Club 1235, re-opening amid a lot of fanfare. An ad in Hot *Shots Magazine* from August 7, 1987, read, "Coming Soon Grand Opening."

Garage rockers The Mooney Suzuki will play at Revolver's Friday party at Club 5922 in South Miami.

been home to many bars, including Cheers (the World), Climax, Splash, and Steel (see listings).

In 1988, a new management team was brought in to redecorate the place, rebrand it, and start bringing in big-name acts; Siouxie and the Banshees were the first name act to perform in August 1988. New management was brought in again, along with a new focus (not gay) and the bar was renamed Passion in August 1990.

Nikki Adams remembers the bar, "It was a huge space and beautifully decorated."

Electra concurred, "...the floor could retract, and there was a swimming pool underneath.

Prince had once also owned a club in this same space club called Icon (see listing).

It had a brief surge of popularity but eventually closed on Columbus Day weekend in 1988. This address was home to Icon, Mansion, Paragon, Glam Slam, Level, and Z (see listings).

Club 5922
5922 S. Dixie Hwy., Miami
Circa: 2001–2002

An underground music scene dance club, it was gay night on Thursday, and an all-ages show on Sunday also drew many LGBTQ kids. It was an indie-rock kind of crowd. The place has

Club Bagdad
NW 36th St. at 38th Ave., Miami
Circa: 1930–1938

The grand opening was held, on June 6, 1930. A pansy bar with female impersonators. An ad in *The Miami Herald* from 1934 advertised "All New Show Direct from Chicago $1 Admission Includes Ale, Ice and Sparkling Waters and Eight New Beauties."

Club Benni
1610 Alton Rd., Miami Beach
Circa: 1940s-1954

The bar's owner, last name Klein, no first name listed in the interview, claimed Club Benni was the first gay bar in Miami, "Our nightly drag show had visits from pianist Liberace, playwright Tennessee Williams, television host Robert Q. Lewis and socialite John Jacob Astor VI. In those days, it was a little frowned upon, but to me, it was strictly a business. I happen to be married with children. What do I care if somebody's gay or not? People came to the bar to relax. Some of them were famous. Some of them weren't.'

The bar closed in 1954 when its liquor license was revoked. This was the location of Basin Street and Red Carpet Lounge (see listing).

Club Benni Denied License Renewal

Liquor license renewals were granted to five Miami Beach bars late this afternoon and one, the Club Benni, mentioned in a Miami News series as a hangout for homosexuals, was denied. Renewals for liquor licenses were granted the Harem, Little Club, Paper Doll and Life Bar. A beer and wine license renewal was granted to the Night and Day Club.

Club Boi
Various Locations, Miami
Circa: 1998-present

This is an itinerant bar party that caters to Black men of South Florida. It has hopped around several locations, including Club 1216, and 1060 NE 79th St. in Miami (the site of several queer bars). For the past eight years, it has been ensconced at The Villa, 3632 NW 25th St., Miami.

Club Climax
5922 S. Dixie Hwy., Miami
Circa: 1993-1994

A bar drawing a diverse crowd, Monday was the erotic banana eating contest hosted by Tiny Tina, Wednesday was the hot legs contest, Friday was women's night and Saturday was Country Western night. The place has been home to many bars, including Cheers (the World), Club 5922, Splash, and Steel (see listings).

Club D
2041 Biscayne Blvd., Miami
Circa: 1989

This bar started as Cactus Club but the name was briefly changed to Club d' Caribbean. It was then renamed Club D for a few months but reverted back to Cactus Club (see listing). It offered live music, was located on the Intracoastal, and had a boat permanently moored dockside with a bar on it.

Club Deep
621 Washington Ave., Miami Beach
Circa: 1998-2007

"Mystica" was women's night at this primarily straight club, known for over-priced drinks. On weekends it attracted a primarily Latin crowd. The dance floor sat atop a 2,000-gallon aquarium where koi swam under your feet as you danced.

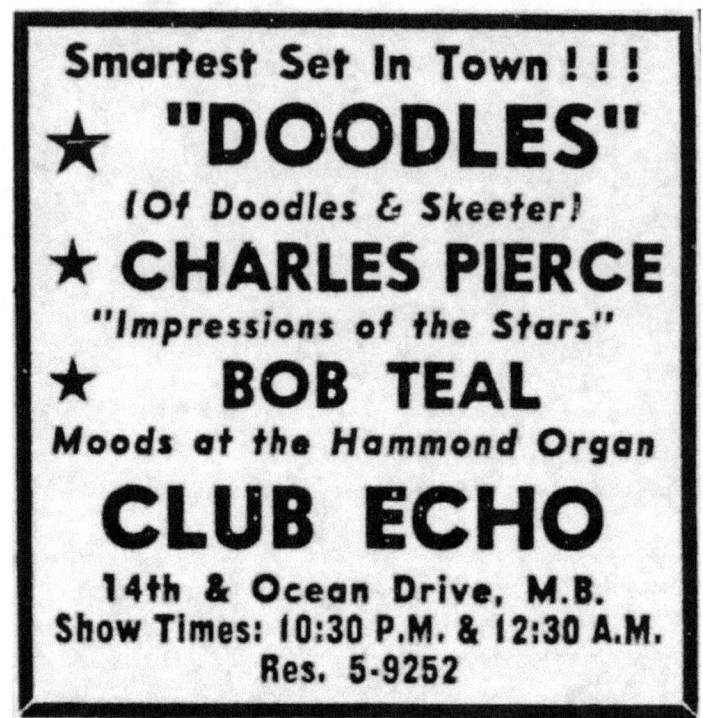

Club Echo
1446 Ocean Dr., Miami Beach
Circa: 1950-1970s

A 1956 description of "A Guide to Miami After Dark" read, "Club Echo—This small intimate club has quite a local following among the gay set. It's very restrained since Miami prohibits female impersonators. But the entertainers of both sexes do come off with some entertaining antics. Reservations are needed since the Echo is always crowded."

It was among the bars targeted in the 1954 purge of "powder puffs" by then Miami-Dade County police chief Kelly. Before that, it, along with the Jewel Box, had been a favorite among Miami's smart set.

It was one of the places famed "Male actress" Charles Pierce, first performed outside of San Francisco.

Club El Patio
1717 NW 17th Ave., Miami
Circa: 1989

Its grand opening was in January 1989. It featured three dance floors, bars, and a restaurant. It was also home to Womyn's Town, Pier 17, and Peter's (see listings).

Club FX
3025 NE 188th St., Aventura
Circa: 1996-2002

The grand opening on November 29, 1996, featured DJ Chaz spinning New York house music until 6 a.m.

Clubhouse Connection
229 SW 8th St., Miami
Circa: 1978-1990

A bathhouse that also served beer and wine. The Sunday tea dance was popular.

Club Jewel Box
512 NE 15th St., Miami
Circa: 1939-1947

Owned by Danny Brown and Doc Brenner, a gay couple who brought the concept to Miami from Tampa, where they operated a similar venue for a decade. Doc sometimes sang and performed in skits (as a man), Danny was the show's emcee, and they also played at The Fountainbleu for many years.

The show's headliner was Angie Walker, billed as the many faces of Angie Walker. While most of the staff was gay, it catered to a straight audience.

Raided by police in 1947 for drag shows, it closed a few years later. The Jewel Box performers formed a traveling revue touring the country. The revue was made up of a diverse group that included African Americans, Latinos, Native Americans, and whites, which was unusual for the times before the Civil Rights Movement. Brown and Brenner retired to Hallandale, where they died a few months apart in 1976.

In the late 1940s, the club was demolished to build the Jordan Marsh in Miami.

DANNY BROWN

Danny and Doc's Jewel Box was created by Danny Brown and Doc Benner in 1939 in Miami Beach, Florida. They have been partners for 16 years. Previous to their first Jewel Box, Doc Benner was a dancer and Danny Brown was a master of ceremonies. They had their own units out for quite some time, then in 1937 they took their first group of Female Impersonators on tour. Since then they have often been called the Ziegfields of Impersonators. They have started so many tal-ented youngsters on the road to success and have created more new talent than any one else in this field. Their Jewel Box has become world famous and is considered one of the country's most beautiful night clubs. Their shows have been known for their clean production and outstanding costumes, young, fresh and good performers. Besides the Jewel Box they have three units on tour now through the Middle West. Through that medium they are able to get the best of all talent for their Miami Club.

DOC BENNER

JEWEL BOX REVIEW PERFORMERS

MR. BILLIE HERRARO

The Brazilian Gypsy Rose Lee — and he well deserves that title.

MR. RALPH GILBERT

Has been featured for many years in some of our finest supper clubs and theatres in his act called "Twisted Rhythm."

MR. LESTRA LA MONT

Has been world famous for many years as the Paper Fashion Plate. He creates and makes all his costumes of crepe paper and is an outstanding performer.

MR. ART WEST

Who has celebrated his thirty-fifth year in show business and as a comedian.

CLUB JEWEL BOX
FEATURES
AMERICA'S FOREMOST
FEMALE IMPERSONATORS
512 N.E. 15th St.   Ph. 9-3100

MR. LEON LEVERDE

Started in show business at the age of six with his mother and dad and has played every important theatre in the world. Is considered the country's finest male toe dancer and has held the title of star for many years.

MISS TOMMY WILLIAMS

Tommy Williams has been in show business for about ten years, most of which has been in and around Hollywood where she is a great favorite and a strong attraction. She spent the better part of last year in one of Mexico City's finest night clubs, where she was a great sensation. Tommy's services are in great demand all over the country. Before entering show business Tommy studied at Iowa State Teachers College, holds a Bachelor of Arts Degree and has two years of pre-medical education to her credit. She was forced to give up the further study of medicine because of lack of funds. Medicine has lost a potential surgeon but the theatre has gained a great singer.

MR. KAYRL NORMAN

Known to the world as the Creole Fashion Plate. When Mr. Norman's name is mentioned that means show business. He was one of the greatest performers of our time. When Mr. Kayrl Norman passed away the world lost a great artist.

MR. JOHNY MANGUM

Went to a party in New York where Mae West was the guest of honor. That was the beginning of Johny's career as Mae offered him a job in one of her shows. He has worked in all of the smart clubs in the country.

TY TANIC

He is considered to look and act more like Mae West than she does herself.

MR. NICKI GALUCHI

Nicki was a feature of a big-time circus for ten years as the prima donna and tight wire dancer. He has been called the Male Lily Pons due to his beautiful natural soprano voice.

MR. GEAN EVOL

Formerly of the vaudeville team of Love and Hate and is now known as the male Fannie Brice. Evol, his last name, is Love spelled backward.

MR. HARVEY LEE

From a secretary in the United States Treasury Department to a headliner in night clubs is quite a jump, but Harvey Lee made it without a falter on the way. After four years as a secretary, Harvey opened at the Club Richman in New York City and created such a sensation that he was billed as the "world's most beautiful male in women's clothes today." Harvey received a great honor at the beginning of his career when he was asked to appear at the first of the President's Birthday Balls in Washington. Made a short subject for Warner Bros. Vitaphone Co. in New York titled, "City Slicker."

MR. BILLY RICHARDS

From New Orleans and truly a fine artist, not just as a singer, but as a costumer as well.

MR. BOBBIE BELL

A brilliant East Indian Notch Dancer and he has also become famous for his costume designing.

MR. FRANCIS DAVID

Often called the Body Beautiful.

MR. JACKIE MAYE

Who has stepped right in line of the late Julian Eltinge and the Creole Fashion Plate Kayrl Norman. Mr. Maye is considered by all critics to be one of America's greatest artists and our leading female impersonator of our time.

MR. DEL LeROY

Just about ten years ago, a beauty contest was held, but only for legs. The girls lined up on the stage and the curtain was lowered to knee length and the one with the most beautiful legs was awarded the prize. Were the judges amazed when the winner proved to be a boy. Del LeRoy! He had entered as a gag and it ended up with being the beginning of a career. Since then Del has been billed as "The Boy with the Million Dollar Legs."

MR. FRANCIS RUSSEL

Sophisticated singer of sophisticated songs.

MR. BOBBIE JOHNSON

Who has been famous as a dancer and was hurt. Shows his showmanship by being greater. He now sings sophisticated comedy tunes and is a must on anyone's list.

Club Magic
17290 Biscayne Blvd., Miami Beach
Circa: 1990

An ad in *Hot Shots* of October 10, 1990, touted "Coming Soon with Ozzie Wheaton performing."

An "Opening Soon" ad in *The Miami Herald* in August touted "Los Sucios, Joey C, with the hot new single on Power 96, "All I'm Asking".

Ladies' nights were Wednesdays and Sundays, and Thursdays were for rock. Salsa dance lessons were held on Sundays. The Chippendales were promised to be arriving soon. If they arrived, the club wasn't there. It closed by the end of the year.

Club Milord
1060 NE 79th St., Miami
Circa: 1985-1989

A disco with shows and male dancers, it was owned by the same people who owned Karleman's (see listing) and was sometimes billed as Karleman's II. It held its third-anniversary party in November 1988. The Miss Greater Miami Pageant was run out of this location.

This location has housed several queer clubs over the years including Bonfire, Cupid's Cabaret, Sandal Club, and Zippers (see listings).

Club Nu
245 22nd St., Miami
Circa: 1987-1991

This was a dance club that presented many live acts, including Flock of Seagulls, Bronski Beat, C&C Music Factory, Jesus and Mary Chain, and Nine Inch Nails. It was also home to Club 245, Heaven, and Onyx Room (see listings).

Club Sappho
6060 Miramar Pkwy., Miramar
Circa: 1977

A private bottle club. The membership fee was $5, and a $3 door charge included dinner. It featured a dance floor and a game room. This was also the location of Encounters (see listing).

Club Space
34 NE 11th St., Miami
Circa: 2000-present

One of Miami's top nightspots, not queer, but welcoming. Also has a performance space on the ground floor. Miami's Club Space is a Mecca for electronic music lovers craving marathon raves curated by acclaimed DJs. Even in a city known for its after-hours parties, Space has garnered widespread praise among audiences by regularly extending nighttime parties into mornings, afternoons, and subsequent evenings.

Space has been a mainstay in the Miami club scene for nearly two decades. *Miami Guide* describes it as "...a large nightclub located in the downtown area of Miami, Florida, owned by Louis Puig. The vast, arena-sized club Space keeps the progressive house and hip-hop pumping from Saturday night till way past Sunday morning when you're disgorged into the bright Miami light and the go-to venue for any nightlife enthusiast in Miami."

The vast, three-room, 25,000-square-foot complex consists of a large main room with a significant VIP area, an upstairs loft, as well as a rooftop patio.

The club's famous Terrace features a clear ceiling allowing dancers to watch starlight turn to sunrise as they dance the night away.

Club Sugar (see Azucar)

Club Therapy
60 NE 11th St., Miami Beach
Circa: 2013-2014

Its grand opening was on October 10, 2013. It was operated by Michael Brown, the former owner of Cupid's Cabaret (see listing).

Club Zen
1203 Washington Ave., Miami Beach
Circa: 1997-2000

Playing rap and "urban" music, it was a favorite of J Lo, P Diddy (as he was known in the day), and DJ Khalid. Luther Campbell of 2 Live Crew was in the club's VIP lounge and got into an altercation with another patron when he allegedly broke a bottle of Jack Daniel's over the youth's face. He was arrested at the club. It was later proved that the youth's claims were false.

Club Zen became one of the city's first smoke-free venues. This space was also home to Krave and Loverboy (see listings).

Cock
637 Washington Ave., Miami Beach
Circa: February-May 2014

An offshoot of the New York City club. This Cock didn't have much staying power, opening, and closing within a year. This space was also the home of KGB and Café con Leche (see listing).

Coco Palm Café
3430 Main Hwy., Coconut Grove
Circa: 1982-1984

Coliseum
3635 NW 78th Ave., Miami
Circa: 2005-2008

Bar guides mentioned its powerful sound system and dazzling light display and the décor, and Greco-Roman influenced décor.

Dustin F said, "South Florida's best and largest gay dance club—this probably would look like a club from (the television show) *Queer As Folk*."

THE COCK

MIAMI BEACH
637 WASHINGTON AVE.
WWW.COCKMIAMI.COM

Comedy Zone
1121 Washington Ave., Miami Beach
Circa: 1997

A straight comedy club—Tuesday was gay night.

Concorde Supper Club
2301 SW 32nd Ave., Miami
Circa: 2003-2010

New Times named it Miami's best lesbian bar in 2003, calling it "A spicy late-night dive on the edge of Coral Gables, with a knack for attracting single, fun-loving gay women with its mix of salsa, cumbia, merengue, rock en español, and American pop."

This was previously home to The Trip and would become home to the Azucar/Sugar (see listings).

Copacabana
3600 SW 8th St., Miami
Circa: 1983-1988 and 1991-1993

Manolo Godinez opened the club in Little Havana with a very Vegas-style production. But the expense overhead was unmanageable and soon Godinez was bouncing checks. By 1988 the building's owner had put padlocks on the doors, shutting down the club. After a brief re-opening after Godinez was bought out of his share of the club. The club shut down for good, three months later.

In 1991 the club was re-opened by Jesse Heydel, who immediately went after a younger demographic, advertising on Top 40 radio stations and formatting pop and dance music in favor of traditional Latin fare. He planned to offer the club's former customers their favorite performers on Sundays, booking big-name Latin acts. This is where *Miami Vice* filmed a segment and Gloria Estefan recorded her hit "Do the Conga." In the 1970s, this was home to The Little Spot (see listing).

Copa Cave
3690 SW 8th St., Miami
Circa: 1990

The bar featured male strippers.

Coral Gables Stables
1641 SW 32nd Ave., Miami
Circa: 1992-1995

A country dance bar.

Coral Room
1685 Alton Rd., Miami Beach
Circa: 1960s

A lesbian dance club, it adjoined the Onyx, a men's bar (see listing). This was the site of gay bars going back to the 1940s with Cas-bar. In 1962, a series of raids on gay bars led to the loss of its liquor license. This space was also home to The Alley (Room) Lounge, Cas-Bar, Delicate Frank's, and Freddie's Piano Bar (see listings).

Corner
1035 Miami Ave., Miami
Circa: 2012-present

A small neighborhood tavern has become a hipster hangout. It is a small, sit-and-chat kind of place, except for the third Sunday of the month, when Counter Corner took over for a once-monthly drag show, and things got wild. Counter Corner left the bar in 2017. Now, it is mostly straight folks sampling beer flights and smoked weenies.

Cos-Bar at Sea Shore Hotel
1390 Ocean Dr., Miami
Circa: 1960s

Crème Lounge
725 Lincoln Rd., Miami Beach
Circa: 2007-2013

You would enter Score's upstairs area through the back, on Lincoln Lane. They had a popular Thursday night party, and on some nights, there were dancers. On December 16, 2005, the club hosted the after-party for the Miami Gay & Lesbian Film Festival after the screening of *Brokeback Mountain*.

Paxton recalls visiting there. "The layout of this place was really cool! Saturdays were rocking because there were live bands on those nights. The decor is totally admirable: painted wooden floors, glass walls, and a sparkly blue ceiling. In the center, there were two grand bars with an excellent selection of wine and cocktails. Hot chicks, lesbians, and gay boys—this place had everything."

Crisco Disco
841 1st Ave., Miami
Circa: 1979

A private men's club that you entered through the parking lot on 8th St.

Crobar
1445 Washington Ave., Miami Beach
Circa: 2000-2006

The Cameo Theater was built in 1936, had a long history and was a major venue for punk acts beginning in 1985, when Richard Shelter struck a deal with owner Zori Hayon to book shows there. The first punk show was held in July 1985 and

Dante's
5950 S. Dixie Hwy., Miami
Circa: 1964

The building and business were purchased by Henry Leitson, who also owned the Candlelight Inn in Coconut Grove. He rechristened it Chez Pepe (see listings) and changed the cuisine from Italian to French. The building has since been torn down for an upscale strip mall.

featured the Canadian band D.O.A. Kristy O'Brien remembers, "Most of the great hardcore punk bands such as Black Flag, Ramones, and Dead Kennedys came to play in this tiny, decrepit hot pink and lime-green art deco throwback."

Ken Smith, owner of Crobar in Chicago, bought the building and opened the Florida outpost of his Chicago club when he made Miami his permanent home. It was known for its Sunday tea dance party. The official closing party was held on April 4, 2006. This became the site of Cameo (see listing).

Cupid's (Cabaret)
1060 NE 79th St., Miami
Circa: 2004-2005

A diverse crowd and naked dancers made Michael Brown's club a popular dance spot. Over the years, this location has housed several LGBTQ clubs, including Bonfire, Club Milord, Sandal Club, and Zippers (see listings).

Dek 23
655 Washington Ave., Miami Beach
Circa: 2007-2008

"Click" was the Sunday night gay party with Omar Gonzalez and Dustin Reffka as promoters. It had four stages for dancing, a silhouette box, and high-energy music in the main room, while the outside patio allowed patrons to dance under the stars while listening to international lounge music.

For a while, it was the club of the moment and attracted such celebrities as LeBron James and Lance Bass. Bash (see listing) was previously at this location.

Delicate Frank's
1685 Alton Rd., Miami Beach
Circa: 1939-1952

Advertised as the "Gayest Spot on the Beach," it was known for the variety of performers, many of whom were cross-dressers. Frank was said to weigh 500 pounds, however, looking at photographs, it is likely he was closer to 300 pounds. But his shows were unabashedly gay and quite open about it for a time. His ads boasted "Bedtime stories for adults," "novelty acts," "A Gay-lorious Show" and asked "Feeling Fagged? Relax and Delicate Frank's."

The bar was raided in 1952, not because of the cross-dressing performers or "gay" acts, but because Frank was running a bookie ring out of a back room and closed down shortly thereafter. This space later became home to The Alley (Room) Lounge, Cas-Bar, The Coral Room, Freddie's Piano Bar, and Onyx (see listings).

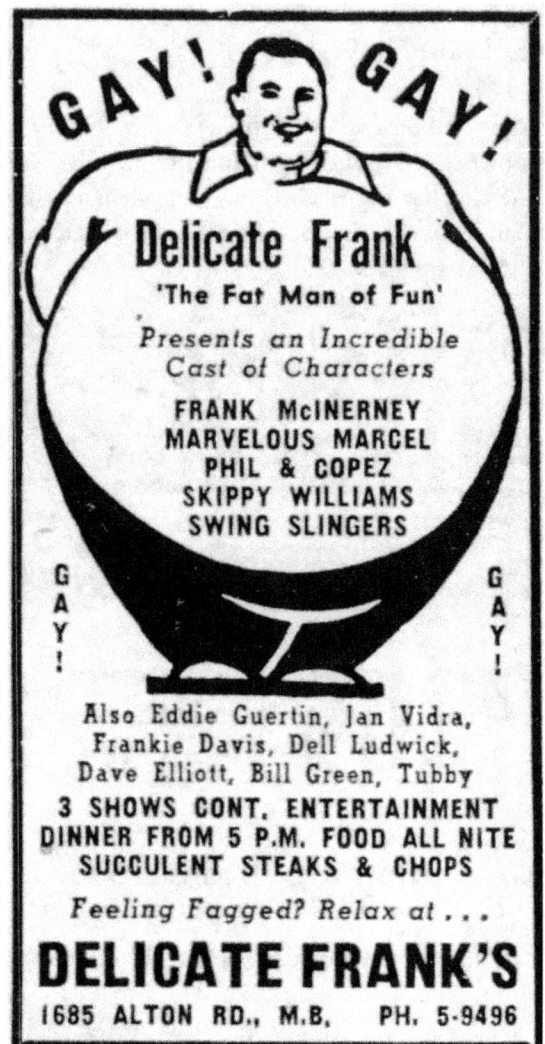

This has been a queer bar since the early 1970s, serving as home to BBC, Billy's Back Lounge, Billy's Backroom, Duck's Pastime, Groove Jet, Joseph's, Little Al's, Miss Kay's, Rain, Teran's, and WOW (see listings).

Discotekka at Mekka at Area 51
950 NE 2nd Ave., Miami
Circa: 2008-2014

Gay on Saturday nights only. A mostly Latino crowd populated this club, owned by Joe Marchello. Mekka was a huge complex (50,000 square feet). The website Culture Trip had this to say "One of the best gay bars in Miami, Discotekka is in Mekka, a location that houses six nightclubs. This vivacious joint offers live music on the weekends, a large area for dancing, and eclectic music to fit all tastes. Watch out for themed nights and drag shows. Discotekka is perfect for the more youthful LGBTQ community."

Dive
NW 79th St., Miami
Circa: 1957

The Miami-Dade County Sheriff's Office raided the bar and broadcast the raid live on TV, causing many people to lose their jobs.

Dolce
1501 Collins Ave., Miami Beach
Circa: 2010-2011

Alicia Keys once performed a set at this club which featured hip hop and Latin grooves. It originally opened as Billboard Live. Sky Bar (see listings) would take over this space.

Double R Bar/Café
1001 NE 2nd Ave., Miami
Circa: 1977-1987

A country and western/leather private membership club, owned by Michael Straight, who also owned Roxie's 5 & Dime (see listing). The Ramrod, another leather bar operated here previously (see listing).

Downtown
7th St. & 1st Ave., Miami Beach
Circa: 1992

Deluxe Club
2800 NW 27th Ave, Miami
Circa: 1962-1964

DeMarco's
701 S. Miami Ave., Miami
Circa: 1954

Raided by police in 1954, a part of a multi-bar crackdown by Miami-Dade County Sheriff Thomas J Kelly.

Diamante
1771 West Ave., Miami Beach
Circa: 2001-2002

The bar was located on the second floor. This space was also home to Maze, and Salvation (see listings).

Dinghy
323 23rd St., Miami Beach
Circa: 1975-1977

The bar attracted an older crowd and offered slow dancing. An ad in *Travel With Pride* from 1975 invited folks to "Dance to the latest beat on the shimmering dance floor, drink at the ship-shaped bar, and admire the nautical décor."

y. No need to dress up. Damn, there's not even a need to groom. It's that dark."

This location was once home to upscale vodka bar Vlada (see listing).

Dream Lounge
1534 Washington Ave., Miami Beach
Circa: 2009–2013

Mostly straight but hosted occasional LGBTQ events.

Duck's Den
22 Ocean Blvd., Miami Beach
Circa: 1984

Duck's Pastime
323 23rd St., Miami Beach
Circa: 1978

There was a buffet every Sunday at this neighborhood hangout. Happy hour from 4-7 p.m. featured beer for 50¢ and bar drinks for 90¢. This space has been a gay bar since the early 1970s, serving as home to BBC, Billy's Back Lounge, Billy's Backroom, Dinghy, Groove Jet, Joseph's, Little Al's, Miss Kay's, Rain, Teran's, and WOW (see listings).

Dugout
3215 NE 2nd Ave., Miami
Circa: 2012-2015

GayCities.com called it the gayest sports bar, or the sportiest gay bar. Ken D says, "The vibe is neighborhood, dark and dive-

Eclipse
1969 71st St., Miami Beach
Circa: 1992

Located in an isolated area, this became a popular after-hours dance club. This later became home to Lucky's (see listing) which continued in the same format.

El Carol
930 LeJeune Rd., Miami
Circa: 1954–1958

Miami police raided the bar many times. It is not clear if the later El Carol was affiliated with this bar. In a 1956 article titled "Profits in Perversion" in the *Miami Herald*, the writer describes the bar, "On successive Fridays and Saturdays it was packed three deep from the bar and the reporter was approached each time." Your Bar (see listing) later opened in this location.

El Carol
820 SW 42nd Ave., Miami
Circa: 1972-2000

Attracted a mixed crowd, men and women. Alan Dale Mobley owned the bar. Robert Fronner went there often, "It was a small, old, neighborhood gay bar. Very friendly crowd. Luis, the bartender, was very nice and gave you a generous pour for your cocktails. I would close this place many nights and help him clean up. Then we would go to the Steak and Egg restaurant for breakfast, and then back to the bar to open it again a couple hours after we closed it for the night. I was terribly smitten with Luis, but, alas, he already had a lover (Marc, who was also really nice and absolutely gorgeous)."

Earlier this was home to The Other Mother and The Stepmother (see listings).

Police Arrest 50 In Tavern Here

Metro police last night 'invaded' El Carol Bar and Grill, a suspected hangout for homosexuals at 920 LeJeune Rd., and **took** 50 persons to the County Jail.

El Morocco Bar
32nd St. and Collins Ave., Miami Beach
Circa: 1951-1954

It was in a hotel/apartment complex that included a restaurant. It was one of the many bars raided in 1954 by Miami-Dade County Sheriff Thomas J Kelly.

Equus
929 Washington Ave., Miami Beach
Circa: 1998-1999

Listed as a straight-friendly dance club, with Nasty Girls on Mondays. The Cabaret at Equus featured poetry and live acoustic music on Tuesday.

Eros Lounge
8201 Biscayne Blvd., Miami
Circa: 2011-2014

Owned by Peter Han, it was named "Best Gay Bar" by *New Times* in 2013, saying "A happy hour, tons of fun weekly events, and a local crowd." Those weekly events included Bingo Tuesday, Drag Fridays, fetish nights, and a monthly lesbian night.

Escuelita
220 NE Collins Ave., Miami Beach
Circa: 1997-1998

Just south of Lincoln Rd., it had two floors and a stage, it opened July 4th weekend, 1997, an outpost of the New York City club of the same name. Latin drag queens created their own characters rather than imitating known stars. A 1997 New Times article read, "The sweet boys of the beach converge for a drag show and dancing in the gay Latin showplace, with hostess Electra."

EVO
645 Washington Ave., Miami Beach
Circa: 2020

Held once-a-month parties for Black men on the down-low. Bambu (see listing) operated at this location earlier.

Falcon's Lair
1654 Meridian Ave., Miami Beach
Circa: 1992-1994

A combination bar and restaurant, the restaurant made news in 1994 for being one of the first in the nation to offer a special menu for those with a compromised immune system. It drew a mixed crowd of gays and lesbians, advertised as an "Alternative Club for Men AND Women." Friday was "Gay Teen Night," and in 1994, a group of Miami Beach lesbians hosted a Winter Solstice celebration as a benefit for the South Beach AIDS Resource Center.

Famous
671 Washington Ave., Miami Beach
Circa: 1984

Although it had been a landmark gathering place on Miami Beach for two decades, when The Famous re-opened in August 1984, the old-timers wouldn't have recognized it. The waiters wore high heels and bunny suits with bow ties, the waitresses wore men's tuxedoes. A delay in the liquor license meant that they couldn't charge for drinks, so there was a cover charge of $10 opening night, but unlimited free drinks, which turned some of the old timers off.

One person not turned off was community legend Miss Kay, who was known to knock back a few cocktails in her day. The Famous didn't last, but Gary Farmer used the rest of the space to create The Strand (see listing), one of the first places to draw a gay crowd to South Beach in 1985.

Fifth
1045 5th St. Miami Beach
Circa: 2009

Mostly straight, it hosted a few LGBTQ events. Every listing on Yelp cited how lousy the music was. It was short-lived, literally, from January to May.

Fire & Ice
3841 NE 2nd. Ave., Miami
Circa: 1985

Bill Mieldazis and Don Grier opened the club as the first of many planned venues. Unfortunately, not everyone was as impressed with the avant-garde characters and art installations as the owners were. One club reviewer stated that it was "full of posers and wannabes, and the so-called progressive music could be found on any radio station."

Black Flag lead singer Henry Rollins read his poetry at the club in 1986, in an event hosted by WLRN, Miami's public radio station.

According to Vivian Olivo, it was a fun place to go. "It was in the design district as the district was beginning to fade. It was mixed men and women, and it played the greatest progressive, new wave music."

This was also the location of Soho (see listing).

Five O'Clock Club
211 22nd St., Miami Beach
Circa: 1936-1962

The Club was opened on November 1, 1936, by the Barken Brothers. It was later purchased by comic and actor Martha Raye and was closed during the off-season. At five o'clock (a.m. and p.m.) drinks were on the house.

It featured many big-name entertainers, many of whom were gay, and friends of Martha's, who was also a lesbian. Belle Barth, the risqué singer performed at the club in the summer of 1954. Near the end of its run, the club was a notorious strip club and front for prostitution and was closed down by the state beverage agency in 1962. This was later the location of the Stonewall (see listing).

Floppy Rooster
7020 NW 72nd. Ave., Miami
Circa: 2014-2019

This was the original location near the airport. It highlighted male strippers who performed nude. After a few successful years, it expanded into a much larger space (see listing below).

Floppy Rooster
777 NE 79th St., Miami
Circa: 2019-2020

Male strippers who went totally nude. Daniel Gabriel said, "Most of the dancers weren't even gay. It's just straight guys who were hung who knew they could make money from gay guys. Half of them can't even keep a hard-on so it was basically a waste of money."

They moved to a new larger location just before the COVID pandemic hit. They closed less than a year later.

Florida Brewing Co.
1890 NE 4th Ave., Miami Beach
Circa: 1992

Mixed gay and some straight, it offered entertainment.

Fog Room
5779 8th St. Miami
Circa: 2009-2010

Fox Hole
2000 NE 2nd Ave., Miami
Circa: 1978-1981

A neighborhood bar that attracted an older crowd.

Frankie & Johnny's
1766 Bay Rd., Miami Beach
Circa: 2002–2003

It was a men's dance bar and cabaret that featured drag shows. Frank Scottolini and John Ormento opened it as the first gay bar in the Sunset Harbor section of Miami Beach on March 8, 2002. Frank and John had previously worked together for many years at Twist (see listing). It was billed as "Upscale, not up tight, gay but straight-friendly."

Shelley Novack had a show there called *Mangina*. It later became Jade Lounge and Madiba (see listings).

Freddie's Attic
809 SW 8th St., Miami
Circa: 1974

Kicked off with a four-day opening celebration beginning on November 21. This would later be home to Upstairs Bar/La Escalara (see listing).

Freddie's Piano Bar
323 23rd St., Miami Beach
Circa: 1972

It offered a buffet every Sunday at 9 p.m. This was the site of gay bars going back to the 1940s with The Alley (Room) Lounge, Cas-Bar, Delicate Frank's, Freddie's Piano Bar, and Onyx (see listings).

Frenchie's Pub
1614 Alton Rd. Miami Beach
Circa: 1964–1975

Friends
17032 Collins Ave., Aventura
Circa: 1999

It featured strippers every night.

Front Porch Café
1418 Ocean Dr., Miami Beach
Circa: 1990–2014

Originally located in the Penguin Hotel, the Front Porch Café was a favorite gathering spot for the LGBTQ community to have breakfast and Bloody Marys after partying all night. In 2014, when the Penguin was being renovated, the cafe moved up the street to 1458 Ocean Drive and is now more straight than gay.

Fruit Bar/Fruit Palace
12ᵗʰ & Ocean, Miami Beach
Circa: 1987

Original name and location of The Palace. The owner served fruit and added the word Bar, then Palace to the name of their place so as not to offend the gay folks who hung around the area.

Garden (of Earthly Delights)
37 NW 36ᵗʰ St., Miami
Circa: 1974-1979

A Levi and country and western private club, it hosted "The First Annual Mr. Earth Contest" in April 1974 with the mistress of ceremonies, Daphne Delight. By 1979, it was listed only as Garden, perhaps because there was a vegetarian restaurant by the same name located not far away at that time.

Garth's Annex Lounge
17490 Biscayne Blvd., Miami Beach
Circa: 1975

A dance bar for gay men.

Gertrude's
826 Lincoln Rd., Miami Beach
Circa: 1995

The bar hosted Beach Bingo with 100% of the $5 admission going to CRI, a non-profit AIDS research organization. It also hosted a packed-house poetry reading in honor of Jack Kerouac on the anniversary of his death on October 21.

Glam Slam
1235 Washington Ave., Miami Beach
Circa: 1994-1996

In 1994, rock icon Prince opened Glam Slam to coincide with his birthday and held an afterparty for one of his concerts. He soon lost interest in the club and left it to his management team to run. In 1996, after a drug raid, the Miami Beach Police shuttered the club, and it never fully rebounded. This space was also home to Club 1235, Icon, Mansion, Paragon, Level, and Z (see listings).

Glass Menagerie in the 8000 Resort
8000 Biscayne Blvd., Miami Beach
Circa: 1975-1976

Criss Cross and Rick Rivera starred in a female impersonation show in 1976. This space was also home to Mr. D's and Stonewall Too Disco (see listings). Classified ads for the resort stated "Private Men's Resort, Swinging Club! Pool, Nitely Disco, Deluxe Room TV $10 Nite!"

Gold Keg
93 NE 36ᵗʰ St., Miami
Circa: 1975-1979

Good Hotel Bar
4301 N. Collins Ave., Miami Beach
Circa: 1954

Raided by police in 1954, patrons were forced to be tested for syphilis. Hopefully, that did not apply to the ladies who attended the Hebrew Academy Women's annual scholarship luncheon on March 3, 1954.

Googie's (Inn)
5832 NW 27th St., Miami Beach
Circa: 1965–1975

Sometimes listed as Goo-Goo's. Googie's Inn was owned by Irene Cassin Naldi, a former stage performer whose claim to fame was creating the role of Little Orphan Annie on stage and dancing in many Oscar Hammerstein shows during her youth. She died in February 1966. In April 1965, the bar was robbed, and the robber ended up committing suicide.

Gracey's Tavern
8237-8239 NE 2nd Ave., Miami
Circa: 1990

Formerly Bit & Bridle, it tried to keep the same customers, but couldn't.

Gramps
176 NW 24th St., Miami
Circa: 2014-present

It looks like an old man's bar that was taken over by hipsters. It opened in 2014 and is mixed gay and straight, the percentage depends on the bands performing, many of which are queer, such as Man on Man. It hosts gay nights and drag shows but is always queer-friendly.

Gregory's
265 NE 79th St., Miami
Circa: 1987–1989

A neighborhood bar.

Groove Jet
323 23rd St., Miami Beach
Circa: 1998-2001

Gay-friendly, dancing, and entertainment billing itself as "the only club that matters," Groove Jet was one of the trendiest hot spots on the planet. Voted the best dance club in Miami, late-night revelers started pouring in around 2 a.m. Danny Tenaglia was the resident DJ. Just a block off the beach, it had three rooms with five bars, three dance floors, and the outdoor Crystal Lounge, named for the tiny mirror shards decorating every square inch. The celebrity clientele included Matt Dillon, Leonardo Di Caprio, and Marilyn Manson. This space has been a gay bar since the early 1970s, serving as home to BBC, Billy's Back Lounge, Billy's Backroom, Dinghy, Duck's Pastime, Joseph's, Little Al's, Miss Kay's, Rain, Teran's, and WOW (see listings).

Grove Village Pub
2624 NW 75th St., Miami
Circa: 1985

A cruisy neighborhood bar with a patio.

Gypsy's
7400 Bird Rd., Miami
Circa: 1977-1978

A restaurant with a sing-along piano bar and disco. It rebranded itself Studio 74 in July 1978 and then promptly closed.

Halo Lounge
1625 Michigan Ave., Miami Beach
Circa: early 2008-2018

Babak Movahedi opened Halo Lounge, with Jason Tamanin as the general manager. Edison Farrow recalls, "It was a beautiful, upscale lounge with DJs, a great happy hour, and a very attractive staff. I was the promoter for the Friday night party that became the busiest night of the week. On Fridays, we had DJ Bryan Zero, Pussila as hostess and performer, and guest drag performers."

New Times named Halo Lounge "Best Neighborhood Bar" in 2008. The newspaper said, "A must-stop on the gay and politico circuits, Halo Lounge is quickly becoming a favorite with straight locals looking for something a little out of the ordinary."

In 2019 it changed its name to MOVA (see listing).

Hamlet
3416 Main Hwy., Coconut Grove
Circa: 1971-1987

Cathy Johnson remembers, "In high school, my friends used to terrorize the people going in there and would throw stuff at the bar. But then, when I was older and came out, it was Hattie's, and I used to love going there." (see listing).

Hamlet
1663 Lenox Ave., Miami Beach
Circa: 1988-1994

In 1991 the bar hosted a reception for six local artists who created a mural saluting Miami's diverse community on the back exterior wall of the bar.

Hamlet's Hideaway
841 NE 1st Ave., Miami
Circa: 1977-1978

It was primarily a drag show bar, but a separate room housed Kockpitt (see listing), a leather Levi bar with a pool table.

Hattie's
3416 Main Hwy., Coconut Grove
Circa: 1988

It took over after Hamlet's (see listing). Vivian Olivio remembers, "The woman who ran it wore hats all the time; that's how it got its name. She was an elegant older woman. It was a wine bar. It was a place to meet before going out to the clubs. It didn't last long."

Hayloft
3673 Bird Rd., Miami
Circa: 1975-1978

A disco attracting a young, Latin crowd. It opened on January 8, 1975, and the ad promised "dining...disco...decadence." Gloria Gaynor appeared at the bar on February 22, 1975, as part of a tour of South Florida. Later, Uncle Charlie's (see listing) would open in this location.

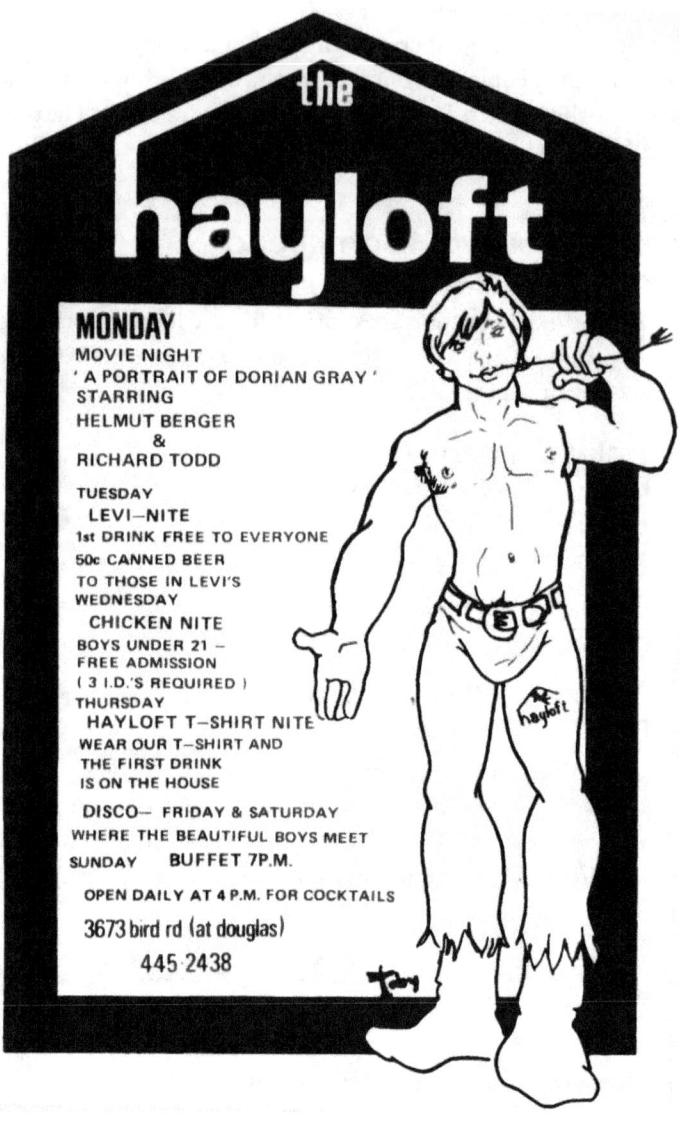

the **hayloft**

MONDAY
MOVIE NIGHT
' A PORTRAIT OF DORIAN GRAY '
STARRING
HELMUT BERGER
&
RICHARD TODD

TUESDAY
LEVI-NITE
1st DRINK FREE TO EVERYONE
50c CANNED BEER
TO THOSE IN LEVI'S
WEDNESDAY
CHICKEN NITE
BOYS UNDER 21 —
FREE ADMISSION
(3 I.D.'S REQUIRED)
THURSDAY
HAYLOFT T-SHIRT NITE
WEAR OUR T-SHIRT AND
THE FIRST DRINK
IS ON THE HOUSE

DISCO— FRIDAY & SATURDAY
WHERE THE BEAUTIFUL BOYS MEET
SUNDAY   BUFFET 7P.M.

OPEN DAILY AT 4 P.M. FOR COCKTAILS

3673 bird rd (at douglas)
445-2438

Heart
50 NE 11th St., Miami
Circa: 2015-2018

Mixed, but very LGBTQ friendly. Curtis F described it, "For the techno and house lovers out there, with a lust for the underground vibe!" It closed in 2018 as the entertainment district saw increased condo development in the area. Heart chief financial officer Michael Slyder attributed the end of the major downtown venue to its ongoing battles with the city and noise complaints from neighbors, "During this past year, the clubs in our 24-hour entertainment district have been constantly attacked by new condo developers, residents and the City of Miami," Slyder wrote in the statement. "We have fought a good fight and spent a great deal of money on lawyers but now it's time for us to throw in the towel."

Heaven
245 22nd St., Miami Beach
Circa: early 2000s

Known to be a very cruisy bar. An episode of the Spanish language television show *Que Pasa USA*, about a Cuban American family, filmed an episode where one of the characters, Joe Pena (actor Steven Bauer, born Esteban Ernesto Echevarría Samson), goes to the bar to research gay life. This was also home to Club 245, Club Nu and Onyx Room (see listings).

Helene's (see Rendezvous)

Hell
54 Ocean Dr., Miami Beach
Circa: 1992

Fittingly enough, the bar opened on October 29. Tuesday was its gay night. But Thomas Kramer and his management team just couldn't seem to get anything right. The neighbors complained, and people stayed away in droves, and by December, it was closed.

Hidden Sailor
3875 Shipping Ave., Miami
Circa: 1992

A grand opening ad in the July 2 issue of *David Magazine* promised "the ultimate gay club." According to an article in the November 2, 1992, edition of *The Miami Herald*, Esther Canseco, ex-wife of pro-baseball legend Jose Canseco, invested some of her divorce dollars into the bar, operated by her brother, Roberto Haddad. The bar was intended for older gay men in a higher income bracket looking for a sophisticated place to socialize. When it didn't draw the crowds they wanted, they changed the name to Canseco's in November and tried to draw a straight sports-oriented crowd.

Hi Room
Alton Rd., Miami Beach
Circa: 1960s

It was a lesbian bar that adjoined the Red Carpet, a men's bar (see listing). In the book *Lonely Hunters: An Oral History of Lesbian and Gay Southern Life, 1948-1968* by James Sears, Rose remembers, "The Hi Room was dark, with a velvety look, immaculate and cool."

Hole
1910 Red Rd., Miami
Circa: 1984-1994

Alonso R del Portillo-Leyva reminds us that, "Its actual name was 13th Hole, but no one referred to it anything other than The Hole. As one might assume by the name, it was a raunchy place with slings and other S&M accessories."

Hombre
925 Washington Ave., Miami Beach
Circa: 1993–1998

Bobby Guilmartin and Diane Iannucci owned this quasi-leather bar. Electra remembers, "They had a large patio, and at the back of the bar, they had a slide show (not videos) of naked guys."

Horizons
2054 NW 23rd Ave., Miami
Circa: 1986–1988

A late-night/after-hours club. Lori Tanner remembers the DJ was Alex Levene.

HQ Cabaret Club
8033 NW 36th St., Miami
Circa: 1989

A neighborhood bar.

Hurricane
250 NE 183rd St., Miami Gardens
Circa: 1977-1978

It had a happy hour from 2-5 a.m., with all drinks 75¢.

Icon
1235 Washington Ave., Miami Beach
Circa: 2015-2016

Miami nightlife promoters Louis Puig and Emi Guerra were partners in Icon. They named the club as a nod to acknowledge the days when the club's space was used as a theater that saw many "icons" perform. It was once owned by such well-known names as Al Capone and Prince. Puig and Guerra said in a statement announcing the opening, "The historic, 30,000-square-foot property will be respectfully redefined to offer a multi-sensory experience that pushes boundaries through the innovative use of technology but preserves the features that make the venue iconic."

This address was home to many other bars including Club 1235, Mansion, Paragon, Glam Slam, Level, and Z (see listings).

Il Libra
629 Lincoln Rd., Miami Beach
Circa: 1996

Indra Lounge (Wurk)
841 Washington Ave., Miami Beach
Circa: 2008-2012

A two-story mixed gay/straight lounge with lavish décor (a golden Buddha and Moroccan lamps), draped private suites, and hookahs. The music ranged from Latin to Middle Eastern beats to European House. This dance club was owned by Sammy Indra.

Janelle F said, "The best part about Indra Lounge is that you can get a hookah while listening to super chill music and drinking at a full bar. Most hookah places only serve beer and wine."

This was previously home to Stallions (see listing).

Jade Lounge
1766 Bay Rd., Miami
Circa: 2003-2009

Jade Lounge was in the former Frankie & Johnny's (see listing). Euphoria Fridays was the gay night. Edison Farrow was the promoter. There were three rooms. The front room had a DJ playing '80s music, drag shows, and sometimes live bands. The second room had Latin music, live drums, and a saxophone player. Upstairs was commercial hip-hop and dance music. Siren was its monthly women's night and was named *New Times'* "Best Lesbian Bar" in 2004.

Edison Farrow remembers, "There was always a line to get into the upstairs room. Many gay celebrities attended these nights including Rupert Everett, the cast of *Queer Eye for the Straight Guy*, and Janice Dickenson."

The venue later became Frankie & Johnny's, Madiba (see listing) and the party continued there for one more year.

Jade Show Lounge
192nd St. on the Ocean, Miami Beach
Circa: 1975

In the Marco Polo Hotel, "'The Gay Deceivers '75, America's Most Beautiful Boys with Pryce Williams, Carmen Terrell, and Frost Martin. Shows at 10 p.m. and midnight, nightly."

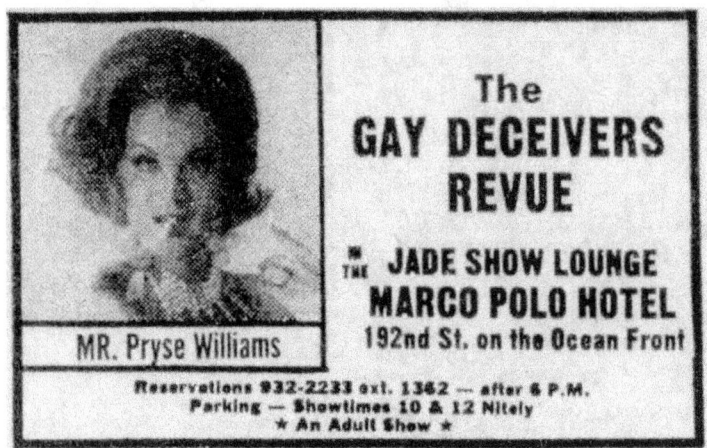

Jam's Tavern & Grill
1331 Washington Ave., Miami Beach
Circa: 1995-2000

A neighborhood hangout with multiple television screens turned to various games, dollar wings, and hot dogs.

Jamboree Lounge
7005 Biscayne Blvd., Miami
Circa: 2004-2020

Mostly men, a cruisy dive bar with dancing. The Elgeebee website described it as "Reputed to be Miami's oldest gay sleaze bar. The men's dive bar has beer and wine in the front, a back patio for cruising, and a stage for late-night drag shows."

In 2010, there was a contest for Miss Jamboree; by that time, the bar was primarily Latin. It closed in March 2020 due to the COVID pandemic.

Cheeks, Southpaw, and Stables (see listings) were previously at this location.

Jene's Barallery
1680 Coral Way, Miami
Circa: 1975

A men's bar.

Job Lounge
1795 Okeechobee Rd., Hialeah
Circa: 1975-1979

It did truncated productions of Broadway shows with a cast of drag queens and go-go boys, most notably, a production of "Funny Lady" with Jackie Jackson, Trixie Taylor, Tina Christie, and Camille St. Lawrence, and "Julio and Bobby." On February 29, 1976, it held a benefit for MCC Church with guest stars Jennifer Raquel, Rick Rivera, and Stacey Carlson. This space later became home to JP's and the Stonewall Lounge (see listings).

Johnny's Miami
63 NE 14th St., Miami
Circa: 2011-2013

The Miami location of Fort Lauderdale's famed stripper bar. It featured drag queens on Mondays.

Joseph's (on Miami Beach)
323 23rd St., Miami Beach
Circa: 1989

A small bar that played progressive and house music. In the "After Hours" column in *The Miami Herald* Juan Carlos Coto wrote, "If you want to see how popular Joseph's on the Beach is, stand outside on a weekend night. There's a long line at the door and you can watch it grow every night. Inside décor falls somewhere between New Wave and Ancient Greek. Patrons dance to progressive sounds as a Trojan soldier watches—there's a large mural of him on the wall."

135

This had been a gay bar since the early 1970s, serving as home to BBC, Billy's Back Lounge, Billy's Backroom, Dinghy, Duck's Pastime, Groove Jet, Little Al's, Miss Kay's, Rain, Teran's, and WOW (see listings). The building has since been demolished.

JP's (aka L'il JP's)
1795 Okeechobee Rd., Hialeah
Circa: 1976–1989

The ad announcing the opening of the disco/drag bar in the July 31, 1976, edition of *David Magazine* boasted, "The one and only Jackie Jackson from the original Jewel Box Revue, Julio Caesano, Mr. Aretha, Tiina Christi, and Trixie Taylor."

Robert Fronner recalls, "At one point, I worked here as a waiter, then as a backup bartender. They had a small stage with drag shows. The resident drag queens were Trixie Taylor, The Alluring Allison, and Mr. Aretha. Bobby LeMans was the male lead in some of the shows. There was also this old lady who would clog dance and show her big old boobies while she danced."

This was also the location of the Job Lounge and the Stonewall Lounge.

Kana Brava
1776 Coral Way, Coral Gables
Circa: 2006–2008

Owned by Teresa Martinez-Arroyo.

Kaos
6620 Red Rd., Miami
Circa: 1992–1994

Kaos took over the space formerly occupied by Club Manhattan, a straight club that had a lot of problems with gang shootings. The neighborhood and police were only too happy to see Alan Simpson and Richard Trainor take over the space as they were seasoned veterans at running gay clubs (13 Buttons and 2x2–see listings) which had little problems with the police or neighbors. The partners invested $200,000 in renovating the site, wrapping the pillars in galvanized metal and neon.

Friday was Boys' Night (18 and over). This was later home to Ozone and Patio (see listings).

Karleman's Bar
6822 Biscayne Blvd., Miami
Circa: 1978–1987

Paul Berger owned "Miami's Friendly Bar." The Miss Greater Miami Pageant was run out of the bar, which was earlier home to S&L Lounge (see listing).

136

Kelly's Torch Club
NW 37th St. and 38th Ave., Hialeah
Circa: 1938-1940

This bar advertised itself as "The Greenwich Village of the South," offering a "Bohemian Atmosphere," "Never a Dull Moment," and "female impersonation at its best."

Kelly's Torch Club opened on New Year's Eve, 1938. However, the club quickly became a hot point for guardians of Miami's morality.

In March, Jack Kofoed, an influential nightlife reviewer for *The Miami Herald*, wrote an acerbic column about the Torch Club and another club, La Paloma (see listing) featuring female impersonators. Describing the entertainers as "children of the moon," he argued, "They mark out something in the swampland and the jungle of the soul. To normal people, they arouse a revulsion that comes over one at the sight of a fetid, putrescent thing."

A few nights later, the county sheriff and a deputy, passing themselves off as "country hicks" and "gay men," went to the clubs and invited the performers to come to their table where they "engaged in highly sexualized and 'obscene' conversations." The next night both clubs were raided. Although the club continued operating, over the next ten months, the county waged a battle to close the club by trying to deny the liquor license, changing the zoning, and bringing to trial the performers on obscenity. Even a trip to the Florida Supreme Court and letters from the Florida governor were involved in the fight. Finally, in January 1940, the police closed the club.

KGB
637 Washington Ave., Miami Beach
Circa: 1998-2002

This was a club with an identity crisis. The name kept changing. It was KGB, then it was WOMB, then it was Mission, then it was KGB again. Before that it was Z. Through it all, Café Con Leche was the gay night at this dance club. This was later the home of Cock (see listing).

Kill Your Idol
222 Espanola Way, Miami Beach
Circa: 2012-present

A punk dive bar. The bar's website states "Your Idol opened in 2012 to provide an alternative to the local fair(sic) offered in the hustle and bustle of the tourism mecca known as South Beach. KYI offers a throwback to the emerging No Wave movement of the late '70s with emerging live local artists and musicians." Mondays are drag nights, and Shelley Novak hosts karaoke one night a week. In 2015, to celebrate its 3rd anniversary, it welcomed "Ru Paul Drag Race" star Bianca DelRio.

This was previously home to Blue (see listing).

King's First
1300 NE 1st Ave. Miami
Circa: 1978-1979

Its tagline was "Not a disco, more like Crisco." Thursday was bare chest night, half-priced drinks for bare-chested men. A later ad stated, "For men only! The King of Leather/Levi bars."

Kockpitt
841 NE 1st Ave., Miami
Circa: 1977-1978

A leather and Levi bar in Hamlet's Hideaway.

Krave
1203 Washington Ave., Miami Beach
Circa: 2004-2005

In 2004 porn star Heather Hunter was prowling the club in a black tank top and jeans. The music spanned the range from hip-hop to trance, to Brazilian, and special theme nights. This space was also home to Club Zen (see listings).

Krave X Miami
3890 NW 36th St. Miami
Circa: 2023

The women and LGBTQ-owned club, which opened amid a lot of fanfare and news coverage in September 2023, is advertised as. "A label-free, no-judgment space, inclusive to all, regardless of gender, race, or sexual orientation. A fully immersive fantasy world for the adventurous and open-minded." However, it appears it was all a scam because, after all the publicity, it just disappeared. The website is down, the web link to reserve "experiences" is no longer functioning, and the only presence on the Internet is all the hoopla about the opening.

Kremlin
727 Lincoln Rd., Miami Beach
Circa: 1995-1997

A dance club with shows. Advertised as "gay owned and operated." The layout was ingenious, making the place seem bigger than it was. At one end a large, stately bar sported all the elegance and mahogany ambiance of a drinking room inside an ornate old palace. At the other end, dancing go-go boys surrounded a loud, crowded dance floor.

Edison Farrow said, "Kremlin was a fantastic bar with one bar in the front and a main dance room in the back. There were DJs and dancers. The dancers would also perform in the showers that were high above the back wall on a catwalk."

Electra tells about a show she did there. "They had this chair that went across the dance floor, real high above, near the ceiling. So, I'm doing a number in it, and the chair gets stuck in the middle. All the queens under me moved away toward the wall. I guess they were thinking, 'If she's going to fall, I don't want her to fall on me.' So, I looked at the DJ and said, 'Just keep on going.' And I did the rest of the show from up there. I also saw the porn star Rick Donovan, the guy with the 14-inch dick, fuck somebody on the bar."

The Backdoor Bamby event, Score, and Tunnel 1437 (see listings) also called this location home.

La Cage
124 2nd St., Miami Beach
Circa: 1988

La Escalara
608 SW 8th St., Miami
Circa: 1996

It advertised, "The Upstairs Bar. Open seven days a week until 5 a.m. "Dancing! Shows! Entertainment! Go-Go Boys."

Las Lechuzas
21st St., one block west of Collins, Miami Beach
Circa: 1978-1982

Las Lechusas means "The Night Owls." It was a lesbian dive bar. Vivian Olivo remembers "It was owned by a trans couple. The bartender was Maria, but she presented as a man and was legally married to the entertainer Mario/Maria. He was going through a sex-reassignment surgery. That was the first person I ever met going through that in my life. They were truly in love with each other. Mario and Maria. You walked onto a dance floor with a bar to the left and pool tables down at the end of the room. It was mostly a lesbian bar, but men would come in for the drag shows when Maria would perform. She was known for imitating La Lupe, a Cuban performer."

La Madrague
1340 Collins Ave., Miami Beach
Circa: unknown

Located in the Shepley Hotel, once known for being the residence of such luminaries as Mr. and Mrs. Danny Kaye, in the 1930s, had fallen on hard times. In 1944-1945 it was sold four times in 18 months. By the 1960s, the single-room apartments were mostly home to Jewish retirees, and by 1980, most of those had been displaced by Cuban refugees, which was when La Madrague operated. It's speculated that La Madrague was in operation until the late 1980s when the South Beach Renaissance began.

La Paloma
2403 NW 79thSt., Miami
Circa: 1936-1941

Opened in a then-unincorporated section of Miami, it featured female strippers and drag queens. On November 15, 1937, the Ku Klux Klan raided the club. The Klan burned a cross on the lawn, made everyone leave the club, roughed up some employees, and choked three chorus girls. The sheriff closed the club, but it soon reopened, as Miami's tourist economy depended on the clubs. A newspaper at the time described it, as "A low ceiling main room presented shows filthy beyond words... (with) homosexuals in evening gowns, trousered lesbians and prostitutes."

INJUNCTION AGAINST PALOMA CLUB WAITS

Illness of County Solicitor Delays Suit To Prevent Alleged Lewd Act

George A. Worley, state attorney, will await the return of Robert R. Taylor, county solicitor, before asking for hearing on a motion for temporary injunction against La-Paloma Club, he said Friday. Taylor has been away from his office because of illness.

A suit filed by Worley and Taylor to close the club charges that men impersonating women sang lewd songs. The case is before Judge Paul D. Barns of Circuit court.

Judge Alto Adams after a hearing on a similar motion affecting Kelly's Torch Club enjoined dancing by nude women.

Worley said he will send to Taylor a transcript of evidence taken in his investigation of the Wine and Beer Retailers Association's effort to assess wholesalers 1 cent a case for operation of the association.

Las Olas Lounge
901 SW 8th St., Miami
Circa: 1976-1977

In 1976 the bar, located in a strip mall, was robbed by a regular customer. He stuck a gun in the back of the bar's owner, Mario Castro, and apologized, saying, "I'm sorry to do this, but I have to leave town, my life is in danger." He took $180.

An ad in *David Magazine* in 1977 read, "Your hosts Wilford & Freddy, we would like to welcome the customers who knew us at La Escalera."

On July 9, 1977, a father of five was dancing in the bar when he had a heart attack. He refused to let anyone call an ambulance (his friends suspected he didn't want to be found in a gay bar). His friends helped him out to the street, where he died.

Laundry Bar
721 Lincoln Rd., Miami Beach
Circa: 1999-2008

Karen Olen opened a real laundromat with a full bar, DJs, drag shows, and live bands. In April 2007 the bar hosted Queen Cabaret with a version of the musical "Chicago—en Espanol" and The Kinsey Sicks performed there in 2002.

Edison Farrow recalls, "You could do your laundry while having drinks and watching performances. Thursday night was the busiest night. It attracted a mixed crowd of men and women, queer and straight."

Vivian Olivo used to go to the bar, "But, what I didn't like was that people would smoke and your laundry would smell like smoke. So, I never did my laundry there."

Cathy Johnson adds, "I moved back from LA in 2000 and that became my spot because all sorts of people hung out there."

Bar 721 and Black Sheep (see listings) were also at this location.

Le Club Menage
8000 NE Biscayne Blvd., Miami
Circa: 1974–1975

It was a large complex with many rooms and billed itself as a "Non-Heterosexual Motel-Hotel." Rooms were $9 a night. The various public sections were Le Cabaret, Le Spa (a gym), Le Pool, and Le Bistro. The bar's tagline was "If you dig Bette Midler, wear Gucci's, and read *After Dark*, Le Club Menage will blow your mind."

Left Bank
829 Biscayne Blvd., Miami
Circa: 1940s–1950s

This bar is mentioned in an interview with playwright Merrill Mushroom in Dylan Foley's blog, "The Last Bohemians," on February 10, 2021. However, this is the only citation of the bar that has been found.

This address was the location of Leon & Eddie's (see listing).

Leprechaun Bar (Michael's)
7305 Bird Rd., Miami
Circa: 1965–1992

A piano bar and patio, popular since the mid-'60s. It was known as a "wrinkle room" because it attracted an older crowd. In June 1966, the bar was robbed just before closing, and the bar's owner David Andersen, who was in the office, slipped out the back and followed the thieves' home, called their location to the police, and they were arrested. An ad for the first-anniversary party ran in the LGBTQ press in September 1987, although "gay guide" listings go back to 1965. Perhaps it was the first anniversary under Michael's ownership?

Les Girls
1622 Ponce de Leon, Coral Gables
Circa: 1984

A women's bar.

Les Violins
1751 Biscayne Blvd., Miami
Circa: 1992–1998

A former Latin cabaret revived its customer base by switching to an Americanized drag show. Producers Lou Paccioco, Michael Gruber, and Ray Sarlot offered a local version of the La Cage drag show with drag legend James "Gypsy" Haake that also ran in Las Vegas, Atlantic City, Los Angeles, and San Francisco. In 1993 the show title changed to "Bedazzled" without the big names star performers, but kept the same format. By 1997 the shine had begun to fade, and the owners were shopping for a buyer. The club closed in 1998, and the building was razed to make way for a shopping mall.

Level
1235 Washington Ave., Miami Beach
Circa: 1999–2004

Opened by Rick Lazes and Gerry Kelly on November 11, 1999. It had four dance floors with state-of-the-art sound and lighting equipment, nine service bars, and six VIP areas.

It would have a Sunday morning party starting at 8 a.m. In 2000 it was White Party headquarters. In August 2001 it hosted a hip-hop's Source Music Awards with Rick Ross, Trick Daddy, and Trina presented by WEDR 99 Jamz, and in 2002 Poppa Dizzom's Birthday Bash. In 2003, it hosted a production of "Hedwig and the Angry Inch."

Originally opened in April 1935 as The French Casino, it was built as a supper and vaudeville club, featuring cabaret acts and showgirls. This space was also home to Club 1235, Mansion, Paragon, Glam Slam, and Z (see listings).

Lime (see Maze)

Lion's Den
7140 SW 8th St., Miami
Circa: 1977

A piano bar and cabaret, it was sometimes called Chez Vivian. In *David Magazine*, April 1972, the This Week With David column raved, "Superb dining and Live Entertainment Nitely featuring our own Chuck Lyons, Walter Lena, John Vance, Juan Alonsi, and special surprise guests weekly!"

Liquid
1439 Washington Ave., Miami Beach
Circa: 1995–2004

Club Liquid was opened in late November 1995 by Chris Paciello, a reputed member of the Mafia, with local celebrity Ingrid Casares (best known as Madonna's girlfriend) as a partner, it was usually just referred to as Liquid. Friday nights and Sunday tea dances were popular times for this trendy club housed in an old art deco building with two music rooms and a large VIP room. It was synonymous with Washington Avenue's glam heyday of the late nineties. It was a favorite of Madonna and Versace and was written up in *Vanity Fair, The*

Village Voice, and *Women's Wear Daily*, as well as several important NYC society publications.

L'il JP's (see JP's)

Little Al's
323 23rd St., Miami Beach
Circa: 1979

This was a disco that attracted a Latin crowd. It has been a gay bar since the early 1970s, serving as home to BBC, Billy's Back Lounge, Billy's Backroom, Dinghy, Duck's Pastime, Groove Jet, Joseph's, Miss Kay's, Rain, Teran's, and WOW (see listings).

Little Spot
3600 SW 8th St., Miami
Circa: 1975

This was later home to the Copacabana (see listing) where Gloria Estefan filmed her music video for "Do the Conga."

Little Tiki
SW 27th Ave. & 28th Ln., Miami
Circa: 1971–1972

It featured go-go girls and offered a buffet on Saturdays.

LIV
4441 Collins Ave., Miami Beach
Circa: 2008–present

Located in The Fontainebleau Hotel, it is a mixed club, queer and straight. Listed as one of the top clubs in the world. The performers range from rapper L'il Jon to Free the People, to DJ Kaskade, to an event for the Miami Hurricanes using the venue to reveal its new uniform designs. It closed for a brief time in 2018 for a complete remodel and re-opened after the COVID pandemic. As if to cement its place in celebrity-dom, Kim Kardashian was spied hanging out at the club after catching soccer star Messi's game in July 2023.

The website boasts, "LIV at Fontainebleau, consistently ranked one of the top nightlife venues in the world, reopened after a $10 million renovation to kick off the nightclub's tenth season. With over 18,000 square feet of striking architecture, soaring ceilings, vibrant lighting, and its iconic dome. LIV will continue to set the stage for the ultimate nightlife experience."

Living Room
671 Washington Ave., Miami Beach
Circa: 1999–2002

Located in the Strand Hotel, it was a lounge with a sexy atmosphere, for dining, and dancing with DJs Cedric Gervais, Stephan Luke, Top Cat, Ivano Bellini, Radimus, and Sugar. The Sunday tea dance was held in the Moroccan VIP room with DJ David Solero. Wednesdays were uber-fashion industry nights. In November 1999 the club held the official anniversary party for *Penthouse* magazine hosted by Bob Guccione.

Loading Zone
1426 Alton Rd., Miami
Circa: 1993–1997

A leather bar that you entered through the back alley on 14th Court. It hosted monthly sex parties; it also hosted numerous discussion groups and workshops presented by The South Beach AIDS Project on safer sex practices, including an event for the deaf community.

The bar closed during the COVID pandemic.

Loft
1053 Washington Ave., Miami Beach
Circa: 2002

A leather bar, it's part of the space now occupied by Twist (see listing).

Lua
409 Espanola Way, Miami Beach
Circa: 1997–1998

Lua was a members-only club, an intimate affair where the in-crowd went to relax and chit-chat. Overstuffed couches and chairs, discreet lighting, and candlelight lent this spot the air of an exclusive retreat, and there was usually a famous face or two among the patrons.

Lucky's
1969 71st St., Miami Beach
Circa: 1995–1996

A neighborhood bar. This was also home to Eclipse (see listing).

Lucky Cheng's
1414 Ocean Dr., Miami Beach
Circa: 1995–1996

A drag performance restaurant opened by Hayne Suthon, the owner of the NYC location. It featured nightly performances by drag queens who doubled as the restaurant's servers. *The Miami Herald* described the decor as "Oriental Cliché" and said "Unlike other drag nights, Lucky Cheng's gets lots of first timers who aren't necessarily into the art form—people who just think it's funny to see a man in a dress and a big wig delivering spring rolls. Perhaps because they sense this lack of appreciation for their craft, Lucky Cheng's servers...tend to walk about robotically...."

Lucky Cheng's
600 Lincoln Rd, Miami Beach
Circa: 1997

Hayne Suthon, the owner of the NYC location, opened a drag performance restaurant on Ocean Dr. and later moved to Lincoln Rd. It closed soon after the move.

Lunna (or Luna)
3470 SW 8th St., Miami
Circa: 1999–2000

Ads and listings in the LGBTQ press spell the name both ways. This space was later home to the Miami Eagle (see listing).

Madame Restaurant & Cabaret Lounge
239 NE 163rd St., Sunny Isles
Circa: 2002–2007

The grand opening was held on July 23, 2002. It was a show bar and restaurant and was presided over and starred the drag queen Electra. The place fits right into the neighborhood hosting the Greater North Miami Beach Chamber of Commerce for a "Business After Hours" networking event in March 2003. Among the acts were twins Sheri and Stasea Rosenblum's "Stripomedy," a vaudeville-type act.

Electra recalls, "It was wonderful, but I was always battling with one of my partners, Reuben Perez. It got to be too much, so I convinced my other partners to sell our shares to him. He turned it into Ruby J's (see listing), and it closed almost immediately afterward."

Madiba
1766 Bay Rd., Miami
Circa: 2009

This club, which started as an event at Jade Lounge (see listing) before taking over the venue, was earlier home to Frankie & Johnny's (see listing).

Magnum
709 NE 79th St., Miami
Circa: 2005–2015

A neighborhood piano bar owned by Jeffrey Landsman, it had lots of Liza and Judy on the playlist, making it comfy for older gay men. Landsman said, "No matter what stage of my life, as a young man, even today, I've always loved piano bars. They have such phenomenal energy. You can come around and enjoy the music and never be disappointed."

Cathy Johnson recalls, "It was also a restaurant. Jeffrey was the owner—he also had a place on South Beach. And he was very nice. When they banned smoking in the bars, he set up a covered patio area outside."

Mansion
1235 Washington Ave., Miami Beach
Circa: 2009–2016

Mostly straight, it hosted occasional LGBTQ parties. In a true blending of cultures, it held a guava rugelach festival in August of 2012. Other events over the years included a week-long residence by DJ Irie capped off by a party hosted by Jamie Foxx, a concert by electro-rocker Peaches, and DJ Clockwork. This address was home to several other bars including Club 1235, Icon, Paragon, Glam Slam, Level, and Z (see listings).

Martini Bar
5701 Sunset Dr., Miami
Circa: 2009–2010

Mostly straight, it held occasional LGBTQ events.

Mayflower Lounge
1716 Alton Rd., Miami Beach
Circa: 1948–1978

In 1948, Billie Lee opened Billie's Backroom at the Mayflower. It was one of the first bars in Miami Beach where same-sex couples could dance. Gay men and lesbians, while both there, rarely socialized with each other. An ad in *David Magazine* from June 1976 notes, "Your hosts Tony Rinaldo, Roger and Julio."

The Stonewall Archives has notes from Robin Bodiford in which she writes about The Mayflower Lounge, "...the women were served by a butch woman bartender named Lou. Ethel Merman once propositioned a woman at the bar."

By 1977, the bar had changed its approach, advertising for topless go-go dancers and "bunny-type" barmaids. In April 1977, two police, supposedly undercover, started a fight at the bar and were suspended, when all the patrons, including a former police officer, testified that they did not identify themselves as police, according to *The Miami Herald* of August 16, 1977.

This space would later house The Atlantic House (see listing).

Maze
1771 West Ave., Miami Beach
Circa: 2003-2004

Lime was the upscale lounge inside of Maze, offering a variety of DJs in three different lounge areas. The design was sleek and modern. A gay-friendly dance bar—Saturday was Gay Day.

Salvation and Diamante (see listings) also occupied this space.

Meet Rack
231 SE 1st Ave., Miami
Circa: 1973-1976

A cruisy, leather bar.

Mermaid (Room)
102 NE 2nd Ave, Miami Beach
Circa: 1965-1977

Located in the back room at Vick's Restaurant.

Miami Eagle
3470 SW 8th St., Miami
Circa: 2002

The dance club attracted a diverse crowd. Fridays were women's nights. This space was earlier home to Luna/Lunna (see listing).

Miami Eagle
1252 Coral Way, Miami
Circa: 1996-2001

Sometimes listed as just The Eagle, it was a leather bar.

Middle Room
2232 Park Ave., Miami Beach
Circa: mid-1960s-1973

The neighborhood hangout featured pool tables and pinball games. It shared the space with The Pin-Up Lounge and The Nite Owl (see listings). It advertised "Three bars under one roof." One of Miss Kay's numerous bars (see listing) was located here for a brief period.

Midway
2322 NE 2nd Ave., Miami
Circa: 1976-1977

A small club, it attracted an older crowd.

Mimi's
2847 Coral Way, Miami
Circa: 1985

A women's bar. This space was also home to Chez Louise, Blackie's Hideaway, and Womyn's Town. Downstairs housed the men's bar Bachelor's II (see listings).

Mineshaft
112 S. Miami Ave., Miami
Circa: 1977-1990

A leather and western bar.

Jesse Monteagudo, "Shortly after I graduated, I ran into one of my high school teachers in the backroom."

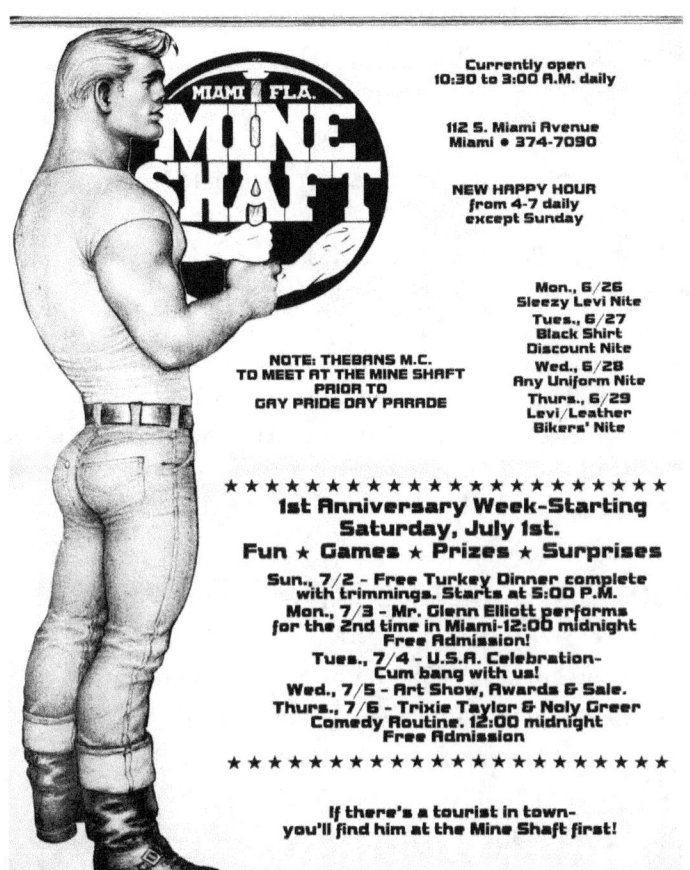

The bar moved from the location on 23rd St. Wednesday. There was a free buffet, but Kay didn't stay at this location for long, and her crowd moved with her. This was previously home to the Middle Room, Nite Owl, and Pin-Up Lounge (see listings).

Miss Kay's 71 Bar
1220 Normandie Dr., Miami Beach
Circa: 1975

An ad in April 1975 read, "Grand opening soon! Your hostesses: Annie (days) Miss Kay (nights)." Miss Kay was a popular bartender from the late 1960s through the early 1990s. She had a mixed following of men and women.

Lori Tanner reports that Miss Kay ended up living in the abandoned Carillon Hotel. "Miss Kay was quite the character. She had a big white bouffant and used to drink Crown Royal. Nobody ever knew if she was a lesbian or not. I don't think anyone ever wanted to sleep with her. We never found out. I think she was married to Crown Royal."

Miss Kay's (& Marie's) Hideaway
323 23rd St., Miami Beach
Circa: 1971–1974

The bar later changed its name to Miss Kay's in 1972. Miss Kay was later at the Blue Waters Hotel Lounge on Collins and 74th (see listing) and several other locations (see listings below.) This location served as home to BBC, Billy's Back Lounge, Billy's Backroom, Dinghy, Duck's Pastime, Groove Jet, Joseph's, Little Al's, Rain, Teran's, and WOW (see listings).

Miss Kay's Lounge
2232 Park Ave., Miami Beach
Circa: 1974

Miss Kay's Lounge
1137 Washington Ave., Miami Beach
Circa: 1977

Another of Miss Kay's bars, this one featured Bernie Randall's Follies every Friday and Saturday. In 1977 it advertised "New show starts Friday, May 13: "Boys A La Carte" starring Jan Britton." Monday nights were "69 Nights-all bar drinks are 69¢." Later this would become the location of 8½ and Calypso Lounge (see listings).

Miss Kay's Lounge
6901 N. Collins Ave., Miami Beach
Circa: 1992

Miss Kay's Zoo Lounge
2457 Collins Ave., Miami Beach
Circa: 1979

A bar with a pool. Freddie was a popular bartender.

Mixers
2490 NW 17th St., Miami
Circa: 1987

It was mixed men and women, and it had a small dance floor and a pool table. This was also home to Sappho's, Sebastian's, and Cheers (see listings), all primarily women's bars but male-friendly.

It's all happening at...
Miss Kay's
ZOO
2457 Collins Ave., Miami Beach
(In the Surfside Plaza)
531-0801

This Friday & Saturday
February 16th and 17th

THE BERNIE BRANDALL REVIEW

With TWO Special Guest Stars on Fri.
SHOWTIME 11:30 P.M.

Miss Kay's Pool Bar
Open 11 A.M. - 6 P.M.,
The Inside Bar is
Open 6 P.M. - 2 A.M.

Mon Petite Lounge
Miami
Circa: 1975

You entered by a side entrance and went upstairs.

Mother's
133 NW 1st Ave., Miami
Circa: 1980-1983

A multiple-bar complex, including a leather bar. Randy Clark remembers, "On the first floor it was a regular bar, then you went upstairs, and they had a bathtub. You could get in that bathtub, and all kinds of things could happen. ALL kinds of things. It was a raunchy bar."

Mother Kelly's
1405 Dade Blvd., Miami Beach
Circa: 1932-1940s

One of the popular bars of the era. Owner Robert A. Kelly, aka Mother Kelly, appeared in drag, doing an impression of actress and personality, Tex Guinan. In 1941, *Time Magazine* described him as, "...fat male, Mother Kelly dishes up steaks, drinks and hermaphroditic comedy."

Mother's Old Village Pub
2824 SW 27th Ave., Miami
Circa: 1983

Mova
1625 Michigan Ave., Miami Beach
Circa: 2010-2014

A late-night club, it was formerly known as Halo (see listing). Both clubs were owned by Babak Movahedi. As *Time Out* said, "If you like your gay bars slick, posey, and full of pretty boys, your prayers have been answered. MOVA—formerly known as Halo—embodies stark South Beach minimalism with its white walls, shiny black bar, and red leather banquettes. Pink and blue lighting notch up the glitz factor. Needless to say, cocktails are more prevalent than brewskis." By May 2014 it was closed.

Mr. D's
8000 Biscayne Blvd., Miami
Circa: 1975

This nightclub in the 8000 Resort was also home to The Glass Menagerie and the Stonewall Club (see listings).

Mug
9th Ave., Miami
Circa: 1960s

3058 N.W. 79th Street, Miami, Florida
691-9727
Things to do Today
Open: 12 P.M. — 1 A.M.
7 Days a Week
Beer • Wine • Pool Tables • Pinball

"A women's bar with a very butch/femme aesthetic," recalled Robin Bodiford in papers in the Stonewall Museum & Archives.

Mug Bar
3058 NW 79th St., Miami
Circa: 1960s

Twenty-three women were arrested in a raid in 1960, according to an article in the *Miami News*. The article stated that the raid was held to "put the lid on reported homosexual nightspots." The names, addresses, and occupations of the women were listed in the newspaper article. It was a quiet, neighborhood bar with pool tables and pinball. A reunion party for the old Mug Bar was held on June 10, 1979.

23 Women Held After Vice Raid

Twenty-three women and a Hialeah businessman were charged with vagrancy yesterday after Metro vice raiders found them gathered in a Northwest 79th Street bar described as a "hangout for homosexual women."

The officers said they entered the Mug Bar, 3080 NW 79th St., after neighbors complained about it.

Three plainclothes vice detectives started the round-up late Friday. The raid was the fourth recent attempt by Metro to put the lid on reported homosexual night spots.

The 23 women and the man were loaded into three squad cars by uniform officers who answered a call for more help.

Joe Gorman, who heads the vice squad, said the beer and wie bar had a normal one o'clock a.m. closing but that his men locked up the place early because of the raid.

The Beevrage Department has promised an investigation of any licensed establishments where homosexual activity is suspected.

Gorman said his report would be forwarded to George O. Davis, new local head of the State Beverage Department.

Gorman identified Charles Joseph Headley, 33, a food process man, of 233 E. 38th St., Hialeah, as the lone male patron of the Mug.

His bond was set at $250.

The following women were jailed and released under $250:

Phylis N. Durham, 31, 461 E. 13th St., Hialeah, statistician.
Betty Alderman, 34, 3565 NW 36th St., clerk typist, and Marjoire Wimmer, 24, factory worker, of the same address.
Belva V. Mcakleroy, 28, meat packer, and Atta Gault Gee, 24, bookkeeper, both of 7600 NW 27th Ave.
Hattie E. Morrell, 34, 1917 NW 85th St., barmaid.
Dorothy F. Snyder, 29, 631 E. 14th Pl., Hialeah, clerk typist.
Mary M. Bellman, 36, 233 E. 38th St., Hialeah, food manager.
Virginia G. Burton, 47, 9245 NW 33rd Ave. Rd., screen maker.
Norma J. McCartney, 32, meat packer, and Ruth Richardson, 38, meatpacker, both of 2550 NW 26th St.
Carol S. LaMay, 22, and Lillie Marie Beagle, 33, lab technician, both of 1300 NW 86th St.
Bernice Van Brunt, 38, 3700 NW 79th St., caterer.
Jane M. Elliot, 32, 265 NW 133 St., telephone operator.
Jackie A. Riley, 26, factory worker, and Thelma J. Dinsmore, 28, clerk typist, 3380 NW 79th St.
Ann S. McLeod, 45, set typer, Louise L. Craig, 46, sales manager, both of 3063 NW 75th St.
Sandra B. Sandler, 21, buyers clerk, Pelican Hotel, Miami Beach.
Mae Marie Morella, 30, 2980 NW 79th St., factory worker.
Marion A. Busch, 29, 631 E. 14th Pl., bartender at the Mug.
Shirley Ann Nichols, 23, 2543 SW 13 St., sales agent.

Mynt Ultra Lounge
1921 Collins Ave., Miami Beach
Circa: 2005–2008

A mixed gay/straight dance club, with DJs Chico Secci, Rob Dino, Tom La Roc, Karim, Tony G, and Julian.

Nathan's
1216 Washington Ave., Miami Beach
Circa: 2020–2022

It was a popular video bar with drag shows. Edison Farrow recalls, "Nathan Smith joined forces with the owners of Pilo's Taco, which was previously in this venue. They later expanded and took over a former tattoo parlor next door. They added a dance room with a DJ booth and couches on the new side, along with a small bar in a second room."

This was previously home to WaterLOO (see listing).

Neil's Hideaway
1675 Alton Rd., Miami Beach
Circa: 1972

New Stables Club
71st and N. Miami Ave., Miami
Circa: 1936–1944

This was a female impersonator show bar. An entertainment column in *The Miami Herald* on December 21, 1938, stated, "Sid White presents 10 variety acts new to this area. Also guest star Lou Gordon, master of ceremonies. Featuring Gloria

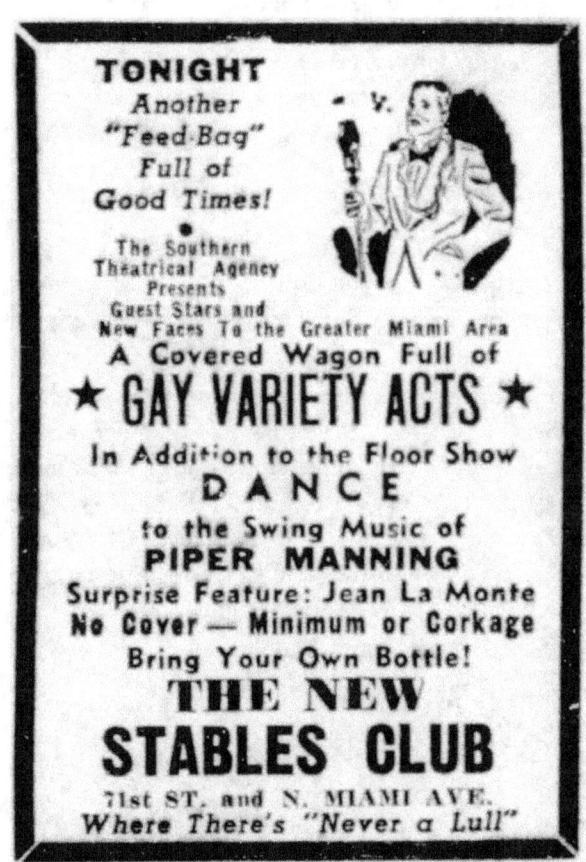

Stoddard and Bonnie Lee, comic Jean La Monte, and Piper Manning and his Orchestra.

Advertisements promised that it was "Gay and Daring!" and "Gay Boys! Daring Girls!"

Nite Owl
2228 Park Ave., Miami Beach
Circa: 1965–1977

On October 1, 1977, it invited everyone to "Celebrate Sally's birthday and first anniversary at the Nite Owl." It shared the space with The Pin-Up Lounge and The Middle Room (see listings) and advertised itself as "Three bars under one roof. Something for guys and gals."

This was also the location of one of many of Miss Kay's bars (see listings) and is now the location of the upscale boutique Kayak Hotel.

Nook
255 Minorca Ave., Coral Gables
Circa: 1971–1979

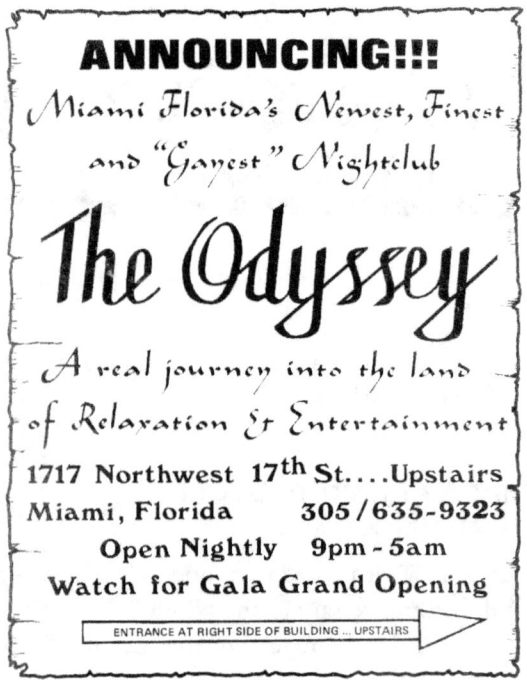

The grand opening (under new ownership) was held on November 16, 1974, with the premiere performance of The Nookettes. It attracted an older crowd and closed at midnight. It advertised, "Your love for tomorrow is at The Nook today." The bar featured drag shows with Trixie Taylor and Jackie Jackson. According to Robin Bodiford's notes in the Stonewall Archives, Wednesday was women's night.

OJ's
2305 NW 107th St., Miami Beach
Circa: 1989

Odyssey
1717 NW 17th St., Miami
Circa: 1972

OLA!
5061 N. Biscayne Blvd., Miami
Circa: 2004–2005

This was more of a restaurant than a bar, focusing on South American cuisine. However, after the dinner hour, the tables were moved aside, and dancing took over. It hosted many events, including a 4th of July summer pig roast, a Halloween costume contest, and a dance party. In 2004, they held a torch run up Biscayne Boulevard in honor of the Olympics.

Old Town
343 SW North River Dr., Miami
Circa: 1983

This was earlier home to Cattle Co. (see listing), a leather and Levi's bar. It was demolished to make way for a highway overpass.

On the Waterfront
3615 NW South River Dr., Miami
Circa: 1985-2010

Popular with the Latin crowd. It would hold outrageous drag contests, such as "Prostitutes on Parade." It was owned by Abdan Grau who built the entire thing without any permitting or licenses. He was eventually shut down by the city.

Electra says, "It was a shady, seedy place. You could score in the parking lot before you even entered the club. Whatever you wanted, sex or drugs." It is now a straight stripper bar called The Booby Trap.

Cathy Johnson remembers, "It was a dance club. We only went once a week."

Lori Tanner agrees, "It was a scary place in a scary location. It was a huge late-night Latin disco. It would get raided all the time. Let me tell you, in that area, you waited in your car until the manager showed up. You did not get out of your car till then. I think I lasted two weeks there. It was too much."

Onyx
1685 Alton Rd., Miami Beach
Circa: 1960s

"Lonely Hunters: An Oral History of Lesbian and Gay Southern Life, 1948-1968" by James Sears called it "A swank, hot, touristy club that featured nationally known female impersonators such as Charles Pierce..." It adjoined the Coral Bar, a lesbian club (see listing). It lost its liquor license after a series of raids on gay bars in 1962. This space was also home to Alley (Room) Lounge, Cas-Bar, Delicate Frank's, and Freddie's Piano Bar, (see listings).

Onyx Room
245 22nd St., Miami Beach
Circa: 1998-1999

Onyx Room
245 22nd. St., Miami Beach
Circa: 1998-1999

This was a dance club, gay on Fridays only, known for hip-hop, and reggae. Tuesdays were taken over by Cuban music, Busta Rhymes performed in February 1998. Ron Gibbs, of The Sugarhill Gang, held a talent contest at the club to sign artists to his label on May 24, 1999. It was also the location of Club 245, Club Nu and Heaven (see listings).

Other Mother
820 SW 42nd Ave., Miami
Circa: 1971-72

A private key club downstairs from Stepmother's (see listing). This would later become El Carol (see listing).

Oxygen
2911 Grand Ave., Miami
Circa: 2003-2004

A mixed straight/gay club, it occasionally hosted LGBTQ events and was only open from June 2003 to January 2004.

Oz Miami
3470 SW 5th St., Miami
Circa: 2001

A restaurant and dance club. Wednesday was male strippers, Thursday salsa dancing, and Friday was women's night.

Ozone
6620 Red Rd., Miami
Circa: 1994-1998

It attracted a Latin crowd and was sometimes listed as Club Ozone. It was owned by Eddie O'Reilly, who also owned 13 Buttons. One of its big parties was New Year's Night (not New Year's Eve). They also had a monthly birthday party for all the people with the horoscope sign for that month. This was in a dangerous area—there were numerous police reports of people being robbed and beaten in the parking lot, including one man who was punched in the face while he was standing in line waiting to get in the club and another of the club's doorman being stabbed and having a gold chain ripped from his neck. It still managed to draw some big-name acts. Kristine W performed there in 1994.

Nikki Adams recalls, "I was performing, and I leaned forward to take a tip, and someone took me, and I crowd-surfed all around the club, taking tips all the time."

This was previously home to Kaos (see listing) and later became the second location of Patio (see listing).

NUDE MARDI GRAS DANCE MARATHON
Tuesday, February 27th
Starting 5 P.M. till?
EVERYONE IS WELCOME TO ENTER
★ CASH PRIZES ★
Judging at 1 A.M.

PAGE 36 DISCO

NOW
Two Different Shows Fri. & Sat.
One at 11:00P.M., One at 1:00A.M.
Plus...
One BIG SHOW at 11:30P.M. an Sundays

NUDE DANCERS	SHOW STARS
Dale	Diana Drake
Ray	Kelly Thomas
Mike	Julio Casano
Iggy	and the
Chico	Pagettes

Special added attraction
Bobby La Mans, male lead!
4591 N.W. 36th Street, Miami Springs 887-0733
(Across from Miami International Airport)

Page 36 Disco
4591 NW 36th St., Miami
Circa: 1978–1980

BRING YOUR FRIENDS TO

The PALACE
BAR & GRILL

**1200 OCEAN DRIVE
MIAMI BEACH**

OCEANFRONT DINING & COCKTAILS
Breakfast • Lunch • Dinner

The Damron Guide called it a "hot bar—but future uncertain." The grand opening was held August 11, 1978, "With your host, Julio Cassano." It featured "Nude Go-Go Boys" and "Free Munchies 'til 2 A.M.," and was affiliated with Doc Watson's next door, which featured "X-Rated Show with All Nude Girl Dancers."

Palace
1200 Ocean Dr., Miami Beach
Circa: 1988–2017

Originally it opened as a juice bar called Fruit Palace (see listing). Edison Farrow recalls his time working for the bar, "The Palace was a restaurant on Ocean Drive across from the gay beach. They had drag shows and a popular Sunday afternoon party. It closed and then reopened as another restaurant that only lasted for a few months. Henry and Douglas re-opened The Palace and owned it for a few years—Thomas Donall later bought it from them. I was the promoter for the Sunday tea dances with DJs and drag shows. We would stop traffic on Ocean Drive with dancers performing in the street."

Vivian Olivo recalls, "It really wasn't a bar, it was a place to eat, watch the drag shows, and be seen."

It closed in its original location in 2017 when the building was sold, and it moved two blocks away to its current locale (see listing below).

Palace
1052 Ocean Dr., Miami Beach
Circa: 2018–present

The only gay bar left on Ocean Dr., it is a landmark and a tourist attraction famous for its drag shows that spill out onto the street—with drag queens rolling about on the pavement. It is somewhat of an institution now and attracts mostly tourists, some gay, many straight. It stages drag shows every evening and drag brunches on Friday, Saturday, Sunday, and Monday—many of its performers have competed on "RuPaul's Drag Race."

Pandora's Box
79th St. near Ocean Dr., Miami Beach
Circa: 1980

A lesbian bar.

Paragon
1235 Washington Ave., Miami Beach
Circa: 1992–1994

A dance club, it was the place to go on the weekend. How hot was it? In 1992, during The Winter Music Conference, Frankie Knuckles was the headline DJ, and a few weeks later, Debbie Harry appeared at the club. They also taped an episode of the HBO comedy special *One Night Stand* with Gilbert Gottfried there. Paragon was also into holding community events, such as the annual high school AIDS dance-a-thon, and a benefit for LA's earthquake victims in 1994 with an all-star line-up that included Sylvester Stallone, Sharon Stone, Eric Roberts, and James Woods (before he went all Repulicrazy). Even as late as 1994, it was able to draw acts like New Kids on the Block.

Miami beach icon Kitty Meow recalls, "When Paragon opened, they had this big cattle call. They said, 'Okay, you all get out there and dance.' At Torpedo, I'd met James St. James, part of New York's club scene, and he told me 'If you really want to work the clubs, you have to work the door.' So, I said, 'I'm not here for that, I *want* to work at the door.' They gave me a little text, and I used to look at all these celebrities in magazines...and they gave me the door. Comes the grand opening and I'm working the door. That gave me so much notoriety in South Florida, it offered me the opportunity to...travel all over the world, and I'm so grateful for it."

The space was home to many other bars including Club 1235, Icon, Glam Slam, Level, Mansion, and Z (see listings).

Paris Modern
550 Washington Ave, Miami Beach
Circa: 1988–1989

A late-night spot, open until 5 a.m., that held its opening night party on July 29, 1988. It was known for its ultra-modern décor and dedication to the community. It hosted many benefits including a cut-a-thon to raise funds for The Community Alliance Against AIDS, a food drive for Feeding Miami, and "A Midsummer Night's Masquerade Ball" to raise money for Partners for Youth. It was not all fundraisers, though, Pilar Gatto's club held a circus-themed "Moulin Rouge" party in August 1988, with chanteuse Zizi crooning "La Vie en Rose" and welcomed the Colombian musical group Las Perlas Negras. In July of 1988.

Park Place
17932 Collins Ave., Sunny Isles
Circa: 1994–1998

Victor Zepka's video bar affiliated with Boardwalk (also owned by Zepka), it was right behind The Boardwalk in Sunny Isles.

Park West Nightclub
30 NE 11th St., Miami
Circa: 2011–2012

Stereo and TWILO (see listings) were previously at this location.

Patio
5949 SW 8th St., Miami
Circa: 1992-1998

Popular with the Latin crowd, it closed and moved to Red Rd. (see listing below).

Patio
6620 Red Rd., Miami
Circa: 1998-2000

A popular Latin bar, its original location was on 8th. St. (see listing above). This was previously home to Kaos and Ozone (see listings).

Patsy's Club 79
766 E. 25th St., Hialeah
Circa: 1970-1976

In gay guides of the time, it was listed as a women's bar, but an ad in *Michael's of Florida* (undated) boasts, "The greatest gay show bar, featuring the Criss Cross Review," however, most ads we found, from the 1970 and 1971, list "The Sensational Four Bits."

Peacock Alley
821 Lincoln Rd., Miami Beach
Circa: 1994

A very short-lived club that started as a piano bar in October of 1993, It morphed into the "Sophisticated Ladies" drag show with Lola St. James as Diana Ross, David Allen as Judy Garland and Dolly Parton, Joseph Perotta as Liza Minnelli and Cher, and Chico Starr as emcee. By March 1994, it was Snap, then 821, and Bulldog's (see listings).

Peg's Place
1049 Washington Pl., Miami Beach
Circa: 1999

A restaurant and bar owned by Bill Adams and Norm Savoie, that was known for its late-night weekend service and Sunday tea dance. It opened in January and was out of business by September.

Peter's
1717 NW 17th Ave., Miami
Circa: 1979-1980

It called itself "Miami's Most Beautiful Disco." It had three dance floors and a light show "ready for the 21st century." This was also home to Club El Patio, Pier 17, and Womyn's Town (see listings).

Phillis's Place
248 Sunny Isles Blvd., North Miami
Circa: 1987

A women's bar. Its grand opening was on December 4, 1987.

Phoenix
1125 Washington Ave., Miami Beach
Circa: 1994-1995

A dance club, Mondays were two-for-one drinks and Adora hosted "Out of the Fire."

For the Discriminating...
A Very, Very Private, Private Club.

11 PM - 4AM
7 Days

Phoenix One Comes Alive

Free membership to approved applicants thru Feb. 22, 1979
Cocktails at popular prices
Open 7 days
Hours: 11PM - 4AM
Food service until 4AM
Restaurant & Lounge open to public 11:30AM-10PM
PIANO BAR

17450 Biscayne Blvd. 940-5292
(Between 163rd St. & Miami Gardens Dr.)
All major credit cards accepted.

Phoenix One
17450 Biscayne Blvd., North Miami Beach
Circa: 1979-1981

It was a restaurant with a lively piano bar that attracted a young crowd. Later, it was home to Swinging Richards (see listing).

Piano Lounge
113 Lincoln Rd., Miami Beach
Circa: 2010-2012

It opened as Crescendos Piano Lounge, then dropped Crescendos for a year and just went by Piano Lounge, then started using it again, but misspelled it as Cresendos. All the while it attracted a mixed gay/straight crowd, as most piano bars do. In 2013, it closed and auctioned off all of its equipment.

Pickwick Lounge
5525 NE 2nd Ave., Miami Beach
Circa: 1987

2228 PARK AVE.
MIAMI BEACH, FLORIDA

PIN UP
LOUNGE

OPEN 1 P.M. TO 5 A.M.

DICK & BOB   531-9301

Pin-Up Lounge
2228 Park Ave., Miami Beach
Circa: 1969-1982

A neighborhood bar. In 1971, Dick and Bob were the hosts. It celebrated its 6th anniversary on October 7, 1975. "Bobby, Wayne, Walter, and the crew invite you to join the fun." It changed locations in 1982 reopening as Pin-Up II (see listing).

This was also the location of the Nite Owl (see listing) and is now the location of the upscale boutique Kayak Hotel.

Pin-Up II
22 Ocean Dr.,Miami
Circa: 1982-1983

After the original Pin-Up Lounge (see listing above) closed in 1982, it reopened for a brief time at this location.

Pink Elephant
13705 Biscayne Blvd., Miami
Circa: 1977-1980

This would become Sugar's (see listing).

THERE'S ALWAYS SOMETHING HAPPENING AT THE
Pink Elephant LOUNGE
945-9465
13705 BISCAYNE BLVD. MIAMI
OPEN DAILY 2P.M. to **4am**

SUNDAY - PENNY NIGHT
Buy one, get the next drink for one cent, excluding beer
MONDAY - SIXTY NINER NIGHT
Drinks 69c all night long, call your own brand
TUESDAY - DRAFT BEER BUST - 25c ALL NIGHT
WEDNESDAY - "LITTLE BROTHER NIGHT:"
Two for one for dudes 18-21 years old. "BIG BROTHERS" WELCOME
THURSDAY - GET YOUR COOKIES NIGHT
Bloopers - Fun - Prizes - Fortunes

CRUISE ON IN...

Try the P.E. for a delightful pick-me-up The pool is cool

Polly's Cage
2900 NW 54th St., unincorporated Dade County
Circa: 1935-1936

According to *Welcome to Fairyland Queer Miami Before 1940*, by Julio Capo, it served "intoxicating drinks," even though it had no liquor license. In January 1936, a fire destroyed the club; passing motorists discovered two watchmen asleep and rescued them from the blazing building. The building was owned by Charles Leffler and the club was operated by George Parrott.

Pub
365 N. Poinciana Blvd., Miami Springs
Circa: 1964-1975

It was previously known as Fritz's Pub, although it is not known whether it had a queer following then. In 1966 Miami City Council member William Donina and his friend Richard Scott were attacked outside the bar, according to a November 12, 1966, article in *The Miami Herald*. Soon thereafter it changed its name to The Pub.

Purdy Lounge
1811 Purdy Ave., Miami
Circa: 2007-2020

The bar, which opened in 2000, saw its neighborhood and surroundings evolve over the years, with the area transforming into a high-end destination filled with restaurants, boutique gyms, and grocery chains. Very different from its beginnings when the area was mainly populated with tow yards and gas stations. One of its owners, Dan Binkiewicz, said that the lease was up, and it would have been too expensive to renew.

Cathy Johnson remembers, "Lou Purdu owned it. I never considered it a gay place, but it was a place you could go late at night, and it had a 'live and let live' feeling."

Purple Parrot
2890 SW 27th St. Miami
Circa: 1984-1985

A dance club.

Rack Bar in Dallas Park Hotel
231 SW 1st Ave., Miami
Circa: 1974-1978

A leather and Levi bar. In 1974 a fundraiser for Variety Children's Hospital raised $66, which was donated in the name of Miami's Gay Community. On November 17, 1975, the bar hosted a "Trash and Treasure Auction" sponsored by Thebans Motorcycle Club.

Rain
323 23rd St., Miami Beach
Circa: 2007-2008

The dance club included an outdoor patio, a 108-foot high glass suspended ceiling, and a tropical resort vibe. In May 2007, it hosted "Afterglow" the closing party with music by DJs Kaprah, Rae Rae, and Sugahill.

This location has been home to gay bars since the early 1970s, including BBC, Billy's Backroom, Billy's Back Lounge, Dinghy, Duck's Pastime, Groove Jet, Joseph's, Little Al's, Miss Kay's, Teran's, and WOW (see listings).

Rainbow
201 NE 2nd Ave., Miami
Circa: 1965-1973

A classified ad in *The Miami News* had this bar for sale in 1973. This was the site of Roman Room, 2x2, and Uncle Charlie's Downtown (see listings).

Rainbow Bar
66 NE 54th St., Miami
Circa: 1964-1975

In 1974, *The Miami Herald* reported that Carole King, Elton John, and Ringo Starr were spotted at the bar.

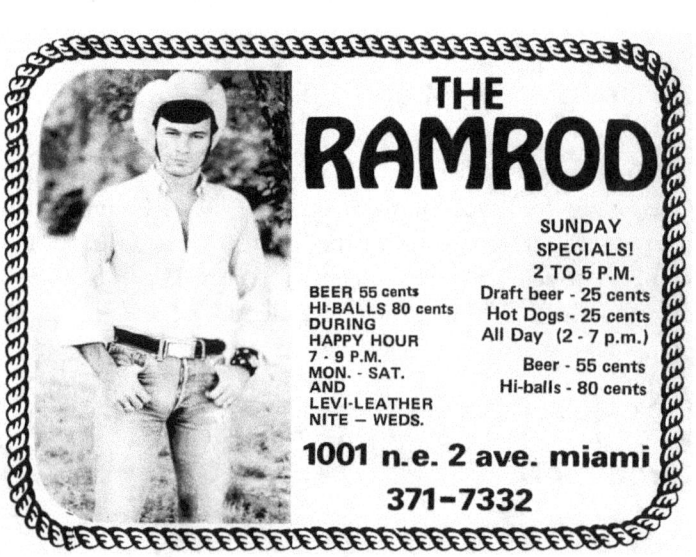

Ramrod
1001 NE 2nd Ave., Miami
Circa: 1974-1976

A leather bar. *This Week in David* from October 1974 reported that "Two super-sharp-looking dudes are opening The Ramrod, a groovy western-style bar just before Halloween." It held its grand opening on November 15 and 16 of that year. The Double R leather bar opened at this location shortly after Ramrod closed (see listing).

Ready Bar
560 Washington Ave., Miami Beach
Circa: 1996-1997

New Times reported in December 1996 that the club's Sunday night Mulberry Party featured, "Special guest drag queens Adora, Taffy, and Marvella both perform at and host the all-out extravaganza with a special performer each week—anything from a fire eater to a contortionist—adding to the gaiety. But why stop there? Stick around for Ready's late-night Sunday party 'Recycle,' with lounge-y tunes by DJ Top Cat."

It filed Chapter 11 in November 1997 and closed after a New Year's Eve fundraiser for the American Cancer Society.

Red Carpet Lounge
1610 Alton Rd., Miami Beach
Circa: 1957-1960s

A newspaper at the time reported that, on April 6, 1957, "35 patrons of the Red Carpet Lounge on Alton Road were arrested for vagrancy by Miami Beach deputy Joe Gorman. Local TV stations were present filming the raid." There was also a Red Carpet Lounge in Hollywood, Florida, just up Federal Highway a few miles that booked the likes of Lawrence Welk, Steve Lawrence, and Eydie Gorme, which often caused some confusion.

This was formerly the location of Basin Street and Club Benni (see listings.)

Rug Pulled From 'Red Carpet'
Deviates' Hangout And Bookies Raided

The Red Carpet Lounge, 1610 Alton Rd., Miami Beach, a notorious homosexual hangout, has had the rug pulled from under it by sheriff's deputies.

Pressing a recently stepped-up campaign against "pervert palaces," deputies raided the club last night. Earlier they smashed two Miami horse-betting parlors.

Patrons — mostly male — at the Red Carpet were caught unawares when the raiders under Deputy Joe Gorman swept into the club and cleaned it out, arresting 35 men on charges of vagrancy.

The night spot is the former Club Benni, a popular gathering spot for deviates now under new management.

Manager Nabbed

Also nabbed in the vice net was manager Robert Shulman, charged with selling alcoholic drinks to minors.

Shulman provided some extra excitement to the raid when he smashed a television cameraman's flashbulb with a broken whisky glass.

The cameraman, Dick Pitschke, 24, of WTVJ, said he would confer with his employers about the possibility of filing charges of assault against the club operator.

"I was wrong," Shulman commented after cooling off, "but I've got two kids and I try to raise them right — I just didn't want my picture taken."

The club was the third meeting place for homosexuals raided by deputies in the last two weeks.

WORKING FROM BEHIND
Deputy Al Molina Handcuffs Robert Shulman
— Miami News Photo by Charlie Trainor

ISADORE BECK
Headache?

HARRY KATZ
Sweating It Out

Red Neck's
2500 Biscayne Blvd., Miami
Circa: 1984

A disco in a hotel

Red Rooster
2404 NE 2nd Ave., Miami
Circa: 1978-1988

Attracted an older crowd.

Red Square
411 Washington Ave., Miami Beach
Circa: 1998-2002

Very dark and very upscale, the cabaret was decorated in dark red velvet, and Cold War propaganda posters decorated the walls.

Vodka was the house specialty with 120 offerings between brands and flavors. DJs spun high-energy music and Elaine Lancaster, Chyna Girl, and Taffy performed. Will and Jada Pinkett Smith had been known to hang out in the VIP room, On July 19, 1998, the cabaret hosted "Toast Toward a Cure" a fundraiser for CAresource, an AIDS service agency

Rendezvous
751 NW 79th St., Miami
Circa: 1959–1960

After having swastikas painted on the door on January 8, and then being raided by police on January 10, 1960, it closed.

(Helene's) Rendezvous
6835 Bird Rd., Miami
Circa: 1992–1996

A neighborhood men's bar, owned by Helene Miller.

Rendezvous on the Lakes
6685 Eagle Nest Ln., Miami Lakes
Circa: 2009–2011

A dance bar that was gay on Sundays only, for "Rainbow Nights." It mostly attracted Latin men.

R House
2727 NW 2nd Ave., Miami
Circa: 2014–present

It started as an art gallery and morphed into one of the most popular restaurants in Miami's trendy Wynwood neighborhood. Edison Farrow explains its metamorphosis: "They started a Sunday drag brunch which became extremely popular. They later added drag shows throughout the week and are now best known as a drag performance restaurant. Athena Dion is the main hostess along with a large cast of performers."

The popular weekend Drag Queen Brunch raised the ire of Governor Ron DeSantis. Following that, Ana Novarro praised the show and bar on the television show *The View*, which had some of the queens perform. This increased the brunch's exposure, which only made it more popular.

Rise
1230 18th St., Miami Beach
Circa: 2000

A dance club.

Rocks on the Nile
96 Miracle Mile, Coral Gables
Circa: 2008

The crowd was both gay men and lesbians. It had a small dance floor.

Roderick's
7500 Biscayne Blvd., Miami
Circa: 1980

A disco in the Aloha Hotel, which at one time was home to a gay bookstore and was known for waterbeds and X-rated movies, then converted to senior citizen's housing in 1980—the building was demolished in 1984.

Roger's (see Vagabond Inn)

Rok
1905 Collins Ave., Miami Beach
Circa: 2004-2005

Owned by the great unwashed Tommy Lee, it was at the time of its opening in April 2004, one of the hottest clubs in town. On any given night you could spot an Olsen twin, Mary J. Blige, Karen O of the Yeah Yeahs, Naomi Campbell, or Lenny Kravitz. DJs Rob Dinero and Midas would blow out punk and '80s jams at Thursday's "Wasteland" party. Tuesday was rap night.

Roman Room
201 NE 2nd Ave., Miami
Circa: 1964-1965

This was later the site of 2x2, Rainbow, and Uncle Charlie's Downtown (see listings).

Roxie's 5 & Dime
125 NW 1st Ave., Miami
Circa: 1984

A large complex with hotel rooms and four bars, including dance and leather-oriented rooms. It was owned by Michael Straight, who also owned the Double R (see listing).

Ruby J's Restaurant & Lounge
2389 Sunny Isles Blvd., North Miami Beach
Circa: 2008-2009

Attracted a mixed crowd of gay and straight people. This was previously Madame Restaurant & Cabaret Lounge (see listings) before a dispute between owner Reuben Perez and his partners led him to buy them out. He then changed the name to Ruby J's and took over as the headliner from Madame Electra.

Rumpus Room
22nd and Park Ave., Miami Beach
Circa: 1942

Famed female impersonator Ray Bourbon appeared at the supper club, which promised "Havoc from dusk 'til dawn."

Runway Inn
656 East Dr., Miami Springs
Circa: 1976

A bar in a hotel near the airport catering to divorced men. There were often shootings involving ex-wives and girlfriends (and boyfriends). An ad in an issue of *David Magazine* dated

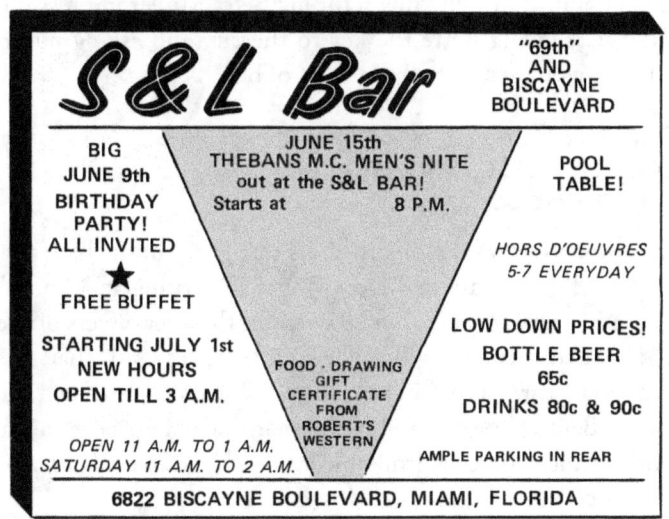

January 24, 1976, boasted, "Another Larry Goss Spectacular with Julio Cassano and Dynamite '76 with Tina Christi, Jackie Jackson, and Bobby Lamans."

S & L Lounge
6822 Biscayne Blvd., Miami
Circa: 1977–1979

It was a Levi-Western bar that hosted a party for the Thebans, a gay motorcycle club, on August 15, 1977. The bar would later be home to Karleman's Bar (see listing).

Sabado Calientes
LeJeune & NW 19th St., Miami
Circa: 2000

A Saturday night dance party, held in Howard Johnson's banquet hall.

Salvation
49 NW 5th St., Miami
Circa: 1980

The multi-level disco opened in May 1980 in an old Salvation Army headquarters building in downtown Miami. Vivian Olivio says, "To this day, it is my favorite club ever. The lights when you came in were breathtaking. The guest DJs came in from New York; the music was fabulous. There were draperies all around. It was one of those legendary big nightclubs, two to three stories tall. It was an old Salvation Army building."

Salvation
1771 West Ave., Miami Beach
Circa: 1996–2001

Open only Friday through Monday, it was one of the leading dance palaces in the early 1990s, often referred to as the Versace era. Hilton Wolman co-owned it, producing many fundraising events in South Florida. This space was also home to Maze (see listings). Randy Clark recalls, "Our apartment was in the building next door, and the whole building would shake with the music from Salvation."

Electra said, "I'm well known for my Bette Midler impression. They were giving Bette the key to the city and asking me to emcee. I wouldn't do Bette in front of her."

Samba Bar
249 NE 1st. St., Miami
Circa: 1950s

The Samba Bar was among the bars caught up in the bar raids of 1954. Bob Hardin and Dom Bonafede writing an "expose" in *The Miami Daily News* in 1956 about the after-effects of the raid, stated that they had negligible effect and that the "perverts returned to the same places." The piece described the Samba Bar. "A wavy-haired blond man walked up next to the reporter and ordered a drink. He made a suggestive remark and introduced another man as 'Mother.'"

Silver Lounge/The Grill (see listing) were also located in this building.

San Francisco
2810 NW 27th Ave., Coconut Grove
Circa: 1980–1990

A local guidebook described it as "A cruise bar with fine food."

Sandal Club
1060 NE 79th St., Miami
Circa: 2008–2012

A diverse crowd, of mostly Spanish-speaking folks cheered on drag queens and strippers. The bar featured women's nights. This location housed several queer clubs over the years including Club Milord, Cupid's Cabaret, Bonfire, and Zippers (see listings).

Sappho's
2490 NW 17th St., Miami
Circa: 1984–1985

A neighborhood lesbian bar, it had a pool table and a decent-sized dance floor. This was also home to Mixers, Sebastian's, and Cheers (see listings) primarily a women's bar, but male-friendly.

Score
727 Lincoln Rd., Miami Beach
Circa: 1994–2013

The club featured cabaret on Mondays. Randy Clark remembers, "It was the place to go. They spent a fortune on that place, it was even featured in *Architectural Digest*. It was really hot." In 2013, it expanded to fill the entire space with the main entrance on Washington Ave. (see listing below).

Edison Farrow reports, "Score was very popular, with big-name DJs and a dance party on the weekends. Planeta Macho was the Tuesday night party which was started by Rafael Defalco and Raul. Outside was a large area of outdoor seating, great for people watching on Lincoln Rd."

Score
1437 Washington Ave., Miami Beach
Circa: 2013–2020

Elaine Lancaster ruled the roost at Score, a bar owned by Andrew Delaplaine and his sister, Rene Delaplaine, who also owned Warsaw and Scratch (see listings). *New Times* reported, "Since its inception, Score has been the epicenter of the well-coiffed and tightly muscled set."

Cathy Johnson adds, "They were also very supportive of the lesbian community. They held benefits. They also had a karaoke night."

Suite and Tunnel 1437 (see listings) also called this location home, specifically the back room with an entrance at 727

Lincoln Rd. where Backdoor Bamby's parties were held. After closing, many of the folks involved began producing roving parties, many in the Wynwood neighborhood, which continue until the present day.

Scratch
427 Jefferson Ave., Miami Beach
Circa: 1990–1991

Originally opened as Clayton's (see listing), the bar changed its name to Scratch a month later. It was owned by Andrew Delaplaine and his sister, Rene Delaplaine, who also owned Warsaw (see listing). Scratch was a restaurant and dance club that billed itself as a "gay theatre bar."

Sea Gull
100 21st St, Miami Beach
Circa: 1987

A hotel and bar with drag shows and a popular tea dance on Sunday. Cathy Johnson recalls, "It was right next to the gay beach (21st. St. Beach), and we'd all go there after a day at the beach for drinks."

Nikki Adams said, "We called it 'The Dirty Bird.' It was skeevy, but a good time."

Sebastian's
2490 NW 17th St., Miami
Circa: 1974–1983

When it first opened, Sebastian's was a women's disco and restaurant that became popular with gays and lesbians. Its tagline was, "Where spirits flow and friendships grow." By 1975, it was primarily men, and Tuesday night was "Round-Up" night. Bar drinks and beer were 75¢ for folks in Levi's. This was also home to Sappho's. Mixers, and later, Cheers.

Second Landing
820 S. LeJeune Rd., Miami
Circa: 1975–1991

The address was sometimes listed as 820 SW 2nd Ave. (LeJeune Rd. is also 2nd Ave.). Bachelor's (see listing) had previously occupied this space. Second Landing was a dance club on the second floor, and it was mostly Latin men looking for papis. On January 30th, 1976, it held a "Mr. Hot Pants" contest. On

February 24, 1976, the bar held a Mr. Chicken contest emceed by Noly Greer. A Mr. Levi Western contest was held on June 9, 1977, with a first prize of $750.

THE SECOND LANDING

SUNDAY - Free Hors D' Oeuvres

MONDAY - ½ Price 9 - 11 PM

TUESDAY & THURSDAY - 2 for 1, 9 - 12 Midnight

FRIDAY & SATURDAY - NO COVER CHARGE

820 S.W. LEJEUNE ROAD, MIAMI, FLORIDA • 446-9412

Nikki Adams remembers doing a show there. "The dressing room was a stairwell to the ground floor (it was an emergency exit). I was gathering up my clothes at the end of the night and, suddenly, the door to the stairwell opened. A guy ran down the stairs and people were throwing glasses and beer bottles at him. I hid behind my clothes."

Semper's Underground
860 Ocean Dr., Miami Beach
Circa: 1990s-2000

Located in the basement of the deteriorating Waldorf Towers Hotel, it was a popular spot to stop in for karaoke with Kitty Meow. It was organized by Mykel Stevens and Carmel Ophir, the duo responsible for the popular Backdoor Bamby club events.

Club owner John Becker would also let theater groups produce shows there for free, just taking a percentage for the house, including a production of *Vampire Lesbians of Sodom.* Comedians Rich Purpura, Tom Ryan, Sal D'Elia, and Jody Weiner all performed there. The building was declared unsafe in 1995.

Seven
685 Washington Ave., Miami Beach
Circa: 2008

A multi-racial group of men frequented this dance bar opened by Dan Sehres and Jefferey Sanker and designed by Madonna's brother, Christopher Ciccone. It was a restaurant and lounge.

Shack Bar
709 E. 79th St., Miami
Circa: 2009-2010

A piano bar that attracted a mixed crowd of gay and straight patrons.

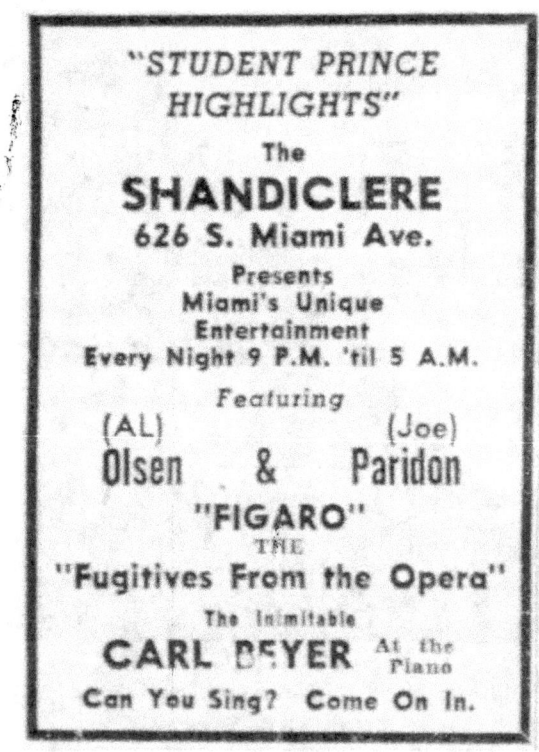

Shandiclere
626 S. Miami Ave., Miami
Circa: 1950s

One of the bars that was raided in 1954 by Miami-Dade County Sheriff Thomas J Kelly.

Shore Club
1901 Collins Ave., Miami Beach
Circa: 1994-1995

Patrick Reilly and Dennis Doheney, formerly of The Copa and Paragon (see listings), leased the property from the Berkowitz family, kicked out the elderly Jews who lived in the building and remodeled the residential hotel into a resort and nightclub.

Its grand opening was on Columbus Day weekend, 1994. It was closed by the end of the year, although it was operating again for a brief time in 1995 under different management.

Silhouette
21440 Biscayne Blvd., Aventura
Circa: 1987

Held its grand opening on May 22, 1987. It was a three-bar complex, which featured male strippers.

Silver Lounge and The Grill
249 NE 1st St., Miami
Circa: 1953

Two bars were in the same building. Both catered to "perverts," according to an article in *The Miami News* dated January 13, 1953. Samba Bar was also located in this building (see listing).

Singapore Lounge
Miami
Circa: 1950-1954

The bar opened on July 28, 1950, by Jack Sable in his steak house building, working with Barnie Barnett as manager. Freddie Jefferson was the pianist. The club offered a variety of musical entertainment over the years, without any interference from law enforcement. It was raided by police in 1954 as part of a multi-bar crackdown.

Singing Bar
235 NE 1st St., Miami
Circa: 1930-1953

The club was known for entertainment and sing-alongs, *The Miami News* described it as," Where one can hear his favorite songs and join in if he likes, Jimmy Broach, Phil Clark, and Jim Hamilton lead the singing. Always the friendliest atmosphere around." It sometimes featured drag shows. In 1953 two men took another man and threw him into the bay after he made advances. He drowned. The two men later told a Marine captain about the incident.

Sky Bar
1500 Collins Ave., Miami Beach
Circa: 2020-present

Unlike the 1950s, when gays had to be on the down low in downtown hotel bars, the Axel Hotel hosts a proudly LGBTQ bar. The rooftop pool, deck, and restaurant are LGBTQ-dominated. The hotel previously operated as Billboard Live and Dolce (see listings).

Soho
3841 NE 2nd Ave., Miami
Circa: 1983

A very short-lived (less than six months) weekend-only dance club that attracted a young crowd. It then converted to a new wave kind of place, called Fire & Ice, but the actual new wave

people got tired of being gawked at by the suburban types, and stopped coming, so it turned very suburban and then it closed.

This was also the location of Fire & Ice (see listing).

Solutions
1115 NW 22nd Ave., Miami
Circa: early 2000s.

Formerly cheeks

Southpaw Saloon
CRUISE BAR

(SORRY, PARDON OUR DUST, REMODELING)
NOW THRU MAY

OPEN NOON till 3 A.M.

EVERYDAY
DOM. BEER & WINE
ONLY A $ BUCK $ 12 p.m.-8 p.m.

WEDNESDAY
• Amateur Strippers 2-5 p.m.
• Date Nite - Surprises & Drink Specials

FRIDAY
• Amateur Strippers 2-5 p.m.
• Strip Show 11 p.m.-2 a.m.

SATURDAY
• After The Beach Special 4-6 p.m.
• Strip Show 11 p.m.-2 a.m.

SUNDAY
• Cold Buffet At 6 p.m.

COME ON DOWN...
7005 BISCAYNE BLVD., MIAMI
758-9362

Southpaw Saloon
7005 Biscayne Blvd., Miami
Circa: 1988-2002

Nude go-go boys and Western music were the attractions at this bar, the former location of Cheeks (see listing) and would become the location of Stables and later Jamboree (see listings).

Splash
5922 S. Dixie Hwy., South Miami
Circa: 1996-1999

It was a men's dance bar with videos, and being in South Florida, of course, it featured at least one Latin night a week. Tony Stefanelli was the original owner. When the bar opened, the Country and Western dance craze hadn't died down, so Tuesdays were Down Home night, Thursdays were Men's

Cruise bar nights, 'Friday Fantazia' with guest DJs, and Sundays were a Tropical Co-Ed Tea Dance.

Taylor Dayne dusted off her repertoire of platinum pop as a benefit for the United Foundation for AIDS (before she decided to sing for Trump) and was just one of the many stars who performed at the club.

The place has been home to many bars, including Cheers (the World), Climax, Club 5922, and Steel (see listings), but nothing equaled the impact of Splash.

Stables
1631 SW 32nd Ave., Miami Beach
Circa: 1987–1992

A country and western bar open at 9 a.m.

Stables
7005 Biscayne Blvd., Miami
Circa: 1994

A neighborhood bar, most likely with a country theme. It was previously home to Cheeks and Southpaw and later to Jamboree Lounge (see listings).

Stallions
841 Washington Ave., Miami Beach
Circa: 2005

The club lasted for a month, tops! But the ad caused many to scream, "Papi!" at the top of their lungs. It promised hot Latin men, dancing, videos, and...hot Latin men! This would later become home to Indra Lounge and Steel (see listings).

Steel
5922 S. Dixie Hwy., Miami
Circa: 2003–2004

Sometimes listed as Club Steel, it attracted both men and women and country dancing and had nights when lessons were offered. Some of the nights included Tease, Ultra, and Pandora (gay women's night). On weekends, the music tended toward dance, synth, 80s, and hip-hop and there were male dancers.

The place has been home to many bars, including Cheers (the World), Climax, Club 5922, and Splash (see listings.)

Stepmother
820 SW 42nd Ave., Miami
Circa: 1971–1972

A second-floor dance club, above Mother's (see listing). It would later become the location of El Carol (see listing).

Steps (See Warehouse VIII complex).

Stereo
30 NE 11th St., Miami
Circa: 2009–2010

Owned by Space's Louis Puig, Stereo sat adjacent to Space like a malnourished conjoined twin in what is now a vacant lot behind the venue. A 2009 *New Times* article described it as follows, "At first it seemed like it wanted to compete with the Studio A and Pawn Shop set, but when that didn't work out, it changed more to traditional house, and after that, it just went straight up hip-hop." It never did find its footing, and after a few months, it quietly died. TWILO and Park West (see listings) also occupied this space.

Stockade Bar
5731 NW 2nd Ave., Miami
Circa: 1954

During a bar raid in October 1954, Detective C.E. Hall complained to Judge Cecil Curry that Stockade's bartender Rose Wesser, "Used a cuss word" at him. The judge ruled that using profanity does not make a person guilty of disorderly conduct and dismissed the charges.

Stonewall
211 22nd. St., Miami Beach
Circa: 1971-1974

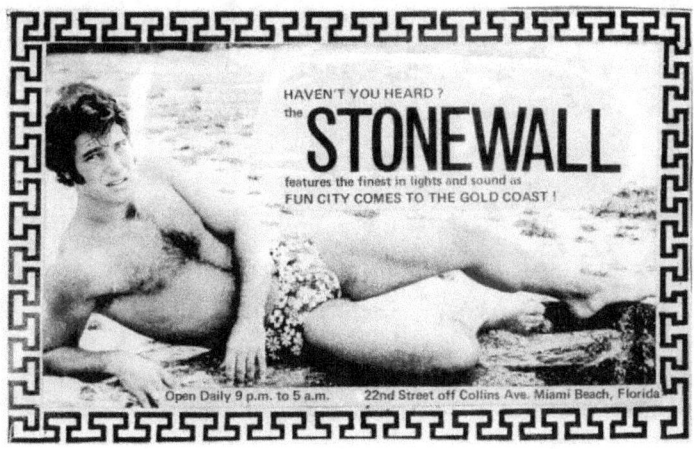

In 1972, the Stonewall completed an extensive expansion, boasting four different parts, including the Cockpit and the Fishbowl, a women's bar. *The Miami Herald* reported on March 3, 1974, "A fire destroyed the Stonewall Discotheque in Miami Beach Saturday, injuring three firemen before it was brought under control. 'It seems like arson. There were too many separate fires going at once,' Fire Captain Barry Rice said. Owner Larry Bochner said he closed the night spot and went home at 5:45 a.m. Years earlier, this was home to the Five O'Clock Club (see listing).

Stonewall Lounge
1795 Okeechobee Rd., Hialeah
Circa: 1990

This bar used to be the location of JP's and Job Lounge (see listings,) both gay bars that featured male go-go boys and drag shows. However, Jim Tunididor then decided to turn it into a straight bar, bringing in female strippers and showing football games to make it a "manly" bar. Ironically, he names this new straight bar The Stonewall Lounge.

Stonewall Too Disco
8000 Biscayne Blvd., Miami Beach
Circa: 1975

A popular disco in the 8000 Resort, it opened on July 3, 1975. This space was also home to Mr. D's and The Glass Menagerie (see listings).

Strand
671 Washington Ave., Miami Beach
Circa: 1984-1996

Gary Farmer, one of the original owners of The Strand, took the old Kosher restaurant and worked to preserve the art deco beauty of it. The original dining room The Famous Restaurant (see listing) was dark. When he changed it to The Strand, he opened up the space and used mirrors and pastels to make the environment seem even bigger, so that there was a feeling of openness, but also intimacy.

He spent a year promoting it as a "mixed crowd restaurant" at parties, in gay clubs, and with hairdressers. Cheryl Cook, a bartender at the Strand for many years, invented the Cosmopolitan drink there. She was given a proclamation for that cocktail from the City in 2015, as part of their 100-year celebration.

The Strand soon became the place to be seen in South Beach. The papers would list sightings daily; Whoopi Goldberg, Lauren Hutton, Rod Stewart, Julian Schnabel. It soon became more like who wasn't at The Strand this week!

Studio
2340 SW 32nd Ave., Miami
Circa: 1981-1988

The bar and restaurant featured entertainment. This is in the same building as Sugar/Azucar (see listing).

Studio 74 (see Gypsy's)

Sugar (see Azucar)

Sugar's
13705 Biscayne Blvd., Miami
Circa: 1982-1994

A young, mostly Black crowd favored this dance club, formerly known as The Pink Elephant (see listing). On September 18, 1993, friends Dennis Kelley and Robert Marshall Tinsley got into an argument after an evening at the bar. *The Miami Herald* made it a point to note that Tinsley's friends called him "Marlo." In the parking lot, Kelly pulled out a handgun and shot Tinsley in the face, killing him, just days after his 29th birthday. There were numerous police reports of crimes surrounding this bar.

Suite
1437 Washington Ave., Miami Beach
Circa: 2006

"For a short time, this was celebrity central, with Paris Hilton holding her album release party at the club. Fergie and Venus Williams were also spied at the club. "Sleaze Sundays" was a popular night. Score and Tunnel 1437 (see listings) also called this location home—the rear entrance was 727 Lincoln Rd. where Backdoor Bamby parties were held.

Surfcomber Hotel
1717 Collins Ave., Miami Beach
Circa: 1975

Known for its Sunday tea dance.

Swinging Richards
17450 Biscayne Blvd., North Miami Beach
Circa: 2010-2013

Opened by the owners of Swinging Richards in Atlanta. For the short time it was open, it was visited by Dennis Rodman and caused the City Manager of Miami to lose his job after he was pulled over by the police shortly after leaving the club when he was arrested for driving while intoxicated. After harassment from the city, the strip club which featured nude men, moved to Pompano (see listing in Broward County.)

Swirl
1047 Washington Ave., Miami Beach
Circa: 1995-1997

Digby Liebovitz's high camp club was a favorite dance spot, attracting men and women, but just didn't attract a strong enough following to support the costs. Then the city hit him with a bunch of code violations, and he couldn't afford to fix them, so he shut down.

Tambourine
3600 SW 28th St., Miami
Circa: 1965-1978

Along with Steps (see listing) one of the bars in the Warehouse VIII complex (see listing). In 1973 an article in *The Miami Herald* described it as, "...young men, clad in bathing suits, dance as go-go boys."

Tantra
1445 Pennsylvania Ave., Miami Beach
Circa: 2009-2014

Ultra-trendy restaurant/club, mostly straight, with a sprinkling of LGBT folks here and there. Fridays featured vocal house music by DJ Scarab, The Filthy Rick party featured hip-hop, house, and rock. Dr. Dre was spotted at the club in 2010. Owned by Tim Hogle, Monday nights were the hot nights to attend this restaurant and nightclub, which also offered hookahs.

Tavern on the Beach
1799 Collins Ave., Miami
Circa: 1989-1995

Popular for its Sunday tea dance.

Ted's Hideaway
124 2nd St., Miami Beach
Circa: 1977-present

Still open, but no longer a gay bar.

Teran's
323 23rd St., Miami Beach
Circa: 1984-1988

Announcing
the Grand Opening of
Terans Disco Club and Lounge
December 31st, 1984
Free Champagne, Hors d'oeuvres,
and Party Favors at Midnight
323 23rd St., Miami Beach
Call for Reservations Now!
673-0228   673-9520
The Terans wish you a Happy New Year.

A late-night bar with strippers and dancing. This has been a gay bar since the early 1970s, serving as home to BBC, Billy's Back Lounge, Billy's Backroom, Dinghy, Duck's Pastime, Groove Jet, Joseph's, Little Al's, Miss Kay's, Rain, and WOW (see listings).

Terminal Bar
45 NE 3rd Ave., Miami
Circa: 1965-1975

Known for rough trade and hustlers, it was in the Greyhound Bus Terminal.

Tobacco Road
626 S. Miami Ave., Miami
Circa: 1941-2015

The history of this club goes back to 1912 when it was the first bar to get a liquor license in Dade County. During Prohibition, it operated as a speakeasy located above a bakery shop and featured gambling. It opened as Tobacco Road in October 1941, advertising as "Miami's Gayest and Newest Nite Club" featuring female impersonators and male strippers. Opening night featured Ray Bourbon, a female impersonator who appeared in clubs throughout the U.S. and was noted for his outrageous material, a "professional vulgarian." He performed "Mr. Wong Has Got the Biggest Tong In China," a song specially written for him.

It became one of the pre-eminent gay bars in the Southeast. With its many military bases during World War II, Miami was filled with soldiers and sailors, and Tobacco Road was a favorite night spot. Eventually, the military declared it off-limits, and in October 1944, the city took away its liquor license. Over the next decades, with new owners getting its license back, and being located in an increasingly run-down neighborhood, it operated as an iconic dive bar. It was even featured in the 1985 movie *Mean Streets*. However, as gentrification changed the neighborhood, the bar, no longer a "gay bar" became the site of a popular music scene. The building was demolished in 2015 as part of neighborhood renewal.

Tony Pastor's
634 Collins Ave., Miami Beach
Circa: 1930-1950

Drag shows were part of the nightclub act for a primarily straight audience in the bar front by the band leader and radio star. In the 1990s Torpedo Bar (see listing) would open in this spot.

Tops
238 Sunny Isles Blvd., North Miami Beach
Circa: 1988

This was a women's bar. It was also the location of After Dark (see listing). Julie McGowan and Sandy Lockwood were popular bartenders.

Torch Club
62nd St. & 25th Ave., Miami
Circa: 1933-1939

With the opening of the Torch Club in north Miami in November 1933, one month before the end of Prohibition, female impersonators became a fixed part of the Miami nightclub scene. Featuring "an mazing cast of female impersonators recruited from clubs in New York, Atlantic City and Chicago, the Torch Club, promised an evening of "constant, continuous (and) convulsive entertainment." One of the first reviews noted that one of the "boys' will come to your table and sing you a nice song or a naughty one according to your wishes...A sensitive person should stay away, but if your moral prejudices are not too strict, you'll get many a laugh out of it, and have an excellent opportunity to make some pertinent observations concerning the seamy side of life."

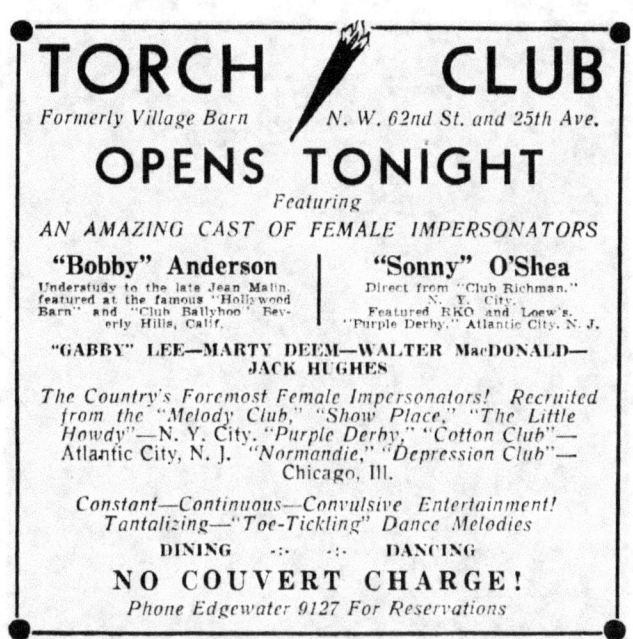

Some of the customers found the entertainment a bit raw. One threw a punch at one of the entertainers who allegedly made a sexual pass. The scene erupted into a brawl with other female impersonators trying to restrain the guest and take him outside. The customer's wife filed charges of assault, later dropped, against those involved. A few days later the county sheriff threatened to close the club as "a menace to the moral welfare of Miami."

One reviewer in *The Miami Herald* argued that the "female impersonations (were) coloured with abnormality and that the 'quips and cracks boldly suggested homosexuality," making the whole thing "disgusting and disgraceful."

Even though *The Herald* stopped running ads for the club, it remained popular, featuring female impersonators and a "bohemian atmosphere." The county, contending the entertainers there exerted "immoral influences," continued to try to close it, but was unsuccessful.

In April 1935, a benefit was held for a local emcee, Charlie Miller, arranged by the bar's manager, Stanley Jabin—performers from all over the city volunteered to participate. Miller was listed as having a debilitating illness. Only in January

1936 when the board of county commissioners, contending that the club's "entertainers exerted 'immoral influences' and that the nature of the entertainment constituted a 'public nuisance,' denied to renew its liquor license, the club closed. In March 1936 the club was destroyed by fire.

Torpedo Bar
634 Collins Ave., Miami Beach
Circa: 1990–2005

The club opened on April 28, 1990, with the Del Rubio Triplets performing. It was known as a cruisy bar. Performer Kitty Meow, aka Shaun Palacious, recalls starting his career at Torpedo, "I got my start there. A friend brought me to them and said, 'You've got to hire him for your club.' It was such a great Bohemian scene there at the time." In the 1930s and 1940s, this was a popular show lounge known as Tony Pastor's (see listing).

Trip
2301 SW 32nd Ave., Miami
Circa: 1979–1981

A dance club with a young crowd, it had a Sunday tea dance and barbecue and featured rock music on Mondays. This was

also home to the Concorde Lounge and Azucar/Sugar (see listings).

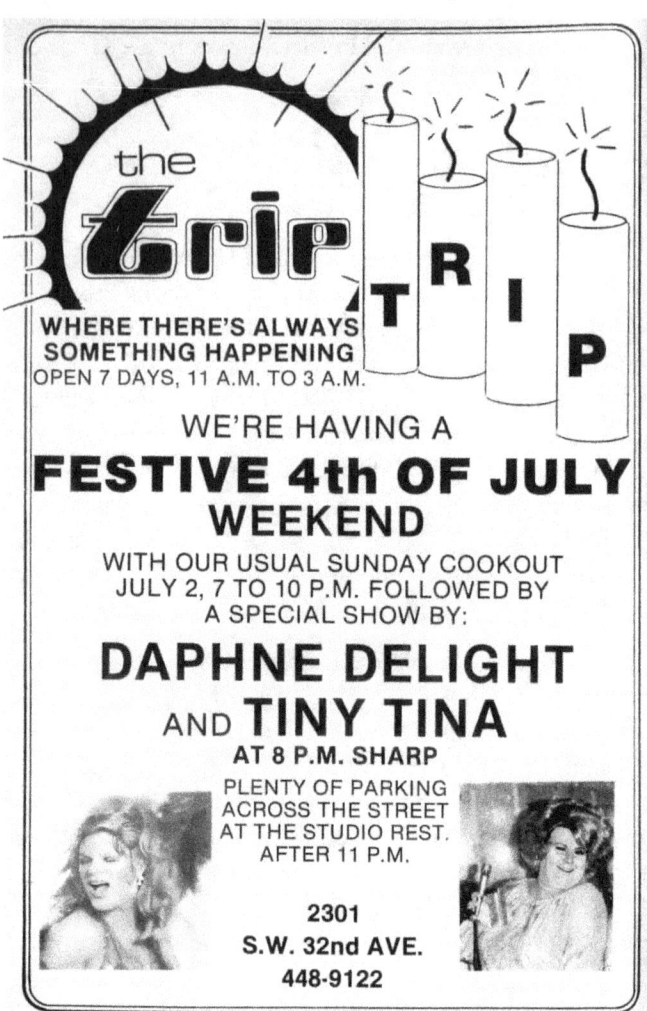

Tunnel 1437
1437 Washington Ave., Miami Beach
Circa: 1999–early 2000s

Score and Suite (see listings) also called this location home, the rear entrance was on Lincoln Rd., where the legendary Backdoor Bamby parties were held.

TWILO
30 NE 11th St., Miami
Circa: 2006–2008

Known for its state-of-the-art light and sound system, it held its grand opening on July 22, 2006. An article in *New Times* citing the five biggest nightlife failures in Miami said, "TWILO, a once prosperous and now defunct New York nightclub that sought to relocate to the Miami market in 2006, had drive in spades...But despite being 'equipped with a custom Phazon sound system' and possessing 'state-of-the-art lighting walls,' TWILO suffered the humiliation of closing yet again." Stereo and Park West (see listings) both occupied this space.

Twist
1057 Washington Ave., Miami Beach
Circa: 1993-present

The club started as a single storefront and as it became more popular, it expanded into neighboring spaces. Loft, a leather bar (see listing) used to occupy a portion of this space. The complex now features seven bars and three dance floors. Male dancers and drag queens enliven the scene. After 30 years, it is a Miami institution. It has consistently been named the best gay club in Miami Beach. As the bar states on its website, "Twist was founded in 1993 by Richard Trainor as a friendly and welcoming environment where people from around the world could meet and have a wonderful time. From its first day, appreciation of the customer and exceptional service has been central to Twist's concept. Professional bartenders, world-class DJs, and the absolute hottest dancers you'll find anywhere make Twist a 'must do' in South Beach."

The music was so loud here that *The Miami Herald* once famously wrote, "The sound system here would make even Helen Keller shout 'Turn it down!'"

Edison Farrows remembers its transformation, "Twist opened in 1993 with a downstairs bar and a dance room upstairs. They later added the patio bar behind the dance room. In 1999, they expanded and took over the former Lulu's next door which added the Latin room, the upstairs video bar, the garden bar, and the Bungalow bar."

Uncle Charlie's
3673 Bird Rd., Miami
Circa: 1983-1994

One location of the Charlie's chain of bars featuring dancing and videos, popular with a young crowd. Nikki Adams produced their turnabout nights. The bar hosted the official after-party for the 1989 White Party. Monday nights were airline nights and many flight attendants arranged their schedules so they could be there.

Cathy Johnson recalls, "On some nights, women had to get there by a certain time, or they weren't allowed in. If you were one minute past the time, they turned you away. But we loved to go because it was so much fun."

In December 1991, the police raided it. An article in *The Miami Herald* quoted a customer, Jonathan Runge as saying, "I think it's really harassment. People don't buy drugs in the bar." The police impounded forty plastic bags containing a half gram each of cocaine which were found strewn across the dance floor. Near the end of its run, it dropped the Uncle and the apostrophe and just went by Charlie's. Earlier, this was the location of the Hayloft (see listing).

Uncle Charlie's Downtown
201 NE 2nd Ave., Miami
Circa: 1979-1995

Perhaps as a sign of the times, the review of Uncle Charlie's, when it opened in December 1979 that ran in *The Miami News*, wasn't at all sensational. Nightlife columnist Dary

Matera, who appeared to have been to more than a few gay bars in his career, was surprised at the dreariness of it all and found the place boring. "Where is the flash, the style?" he asked. He seemed to wonder why Charlie's was like any other neighborhood bar.

Uncle Charlie's Downtown was the first Miami location to open (there were already four in New York City), and it started as a private club. In an interview, the owner Bob Sloate, stated it was "... a gay establishment, run by a gay businessman, for the distinguishing [sic] gay male. We want to keep it that way."

Vivian Olivo remembers, "The neighborhood around it was scary—I almost got mugged, but once you got inside, it was

Coming Very Soon!

Uncle Charlie's Downtown

"A beautiful Place for beautiful People!"

201 N. E. 2nd Avenue,
Miami, Fla. 371-8237

fun. They didn't allow women in on certain nights, but I was always able to get in. You walked in; there was a large U-shaped bar and then a stage at the back. It was a lot of fun. There was a dance bar, a second-floor piano bar, and drag shows."

This location had been the site of gay bars going as far back as the 1960s, including the 2x2, Roman Room, and Rainbow (see listings).

Upstairs Bar/La Escalara
809 SW 8th St., Miami
Circa: 1975

This was previously Freddie's Attic (see listing).

Uranus
55 NE 24th St., Miami
Circa: 2004-2005

A neighborhood men's bar, with leather nights, and dancing.

Vagabond
30 NE 14th St. Miami
Circa: 2008-2014

In 2008 *Miami New Times* named it the best new bar, citing its low-key vibe and cheap drinks and quoting the club's official slogan: "You are no one. You are everyone." In 2011 it hosted the official opening party of the Winter Music Conference, one of the biggest events of the season with legendary DJs Def Mix and one of the last appearances by Frankie Knuckles.

SATURDAY APRIL 5TH 2014
THE VAGABOND
THE LAST DANCE...
A TRIBUTE TO THE GODFATHER OF HOUSE MUSIC
FRANKIE KNUCKLES
JANUARY 18, 1955 - MARCH 31, 2014
A CELEBRATION OF THE MAN AND HIS MUSIC
WITH VERY SPECIAL GUEST
DAVID MORALES
DEF MIX

DOORS OPEN 10PM
PROCEEDS TO BENEFIT THE AMERICAN DIABETES ASSOCIATION IN HONOR OF FRANKIE KNUCKLES

American Diabetes Association.

THE VAGABOND
30 NE 14TH STREET
DOWNTOWN MIAMI
305-379-0508
THEVAGABONDMIAMI.COM

One of its legendary parties was the Shameless Burlesque, it would also feature live performances by a range of artists such as Rub and Tug, The Juan MacLean, Manthraxx, Marcus Blake, and a spoken word night.

In April 2014, co-owner Carmel Ophir announced the bar was closing.

HAP HAPPY
RETURNS
DEC. 16th   9 P.M.
VAGABOND MOTEL LOUNGE
7301 BISCAYNE BLVD.

Vagabond Inn (Roger's)
7301 Biscayne Blvd., Miami
Circa: 1971-1988

Vick's Bar & Restaurant
101 NE 2nd Ave., Miami
Circa: 1950-1959

OPENS TONITE
GARY GRAHAM
"KING OF RISQUE"
VICK'S BAR
101 N.E. 2nd AVE., MIAMI

More restaurant than bar, it hosted a weekly variety show. The Mermaid Room was its backroom bar. Part of the bar raids of 1954. In an article in the February 25, 1956, edition of *The Miami Herald* on Miami's gay bars titled "Profits in Perversion," Vick's was the place to go after the Samba bar closed and it was noted that the homosexuals there were more discrete, but that the reporter was still propositioned twice. According to *The Lavender Guide,* it was still open in 1975, but in 1959 there was an ad in *The Miami Herald* stating that it had lost its lease. There are no news reports for the bar beyond 1959.

Vivid
743 Washington Ave., Miami Beach
Circa: 2000

Attracted a mostly Latin crowd. One notable event was a "Fashion show with host Ernesto Arambatzis and house DJs Dean Drake and Tracy Young." Sayra Moto was the club's events promoter.

Vlada
3215 NE 2nd Ave., Miami
Circa: 2010-2012

Opened by Vlada Von Shats, the owner of Vlada in Hell's Kitchen in New York. It featured a bar covered in ice and offered in-house-made infused vodkas. It billed itself in the *Gay*

& Lesbian Directory as, "A stylish, sophisticated and romantic new gay lounge, where artists, actors, models and freaks alike can all gather and be comfortable just being themselves."

It would later become home to The Dugout, a gay sports bar (see listing).

Wagon Wheel Pub
1211 17th St., Miami Beach
Circa: 1976

The grand opening was held on May 22, 1976, with the return of Donnie Jay the queen of high camp and the original Great Pretenders.

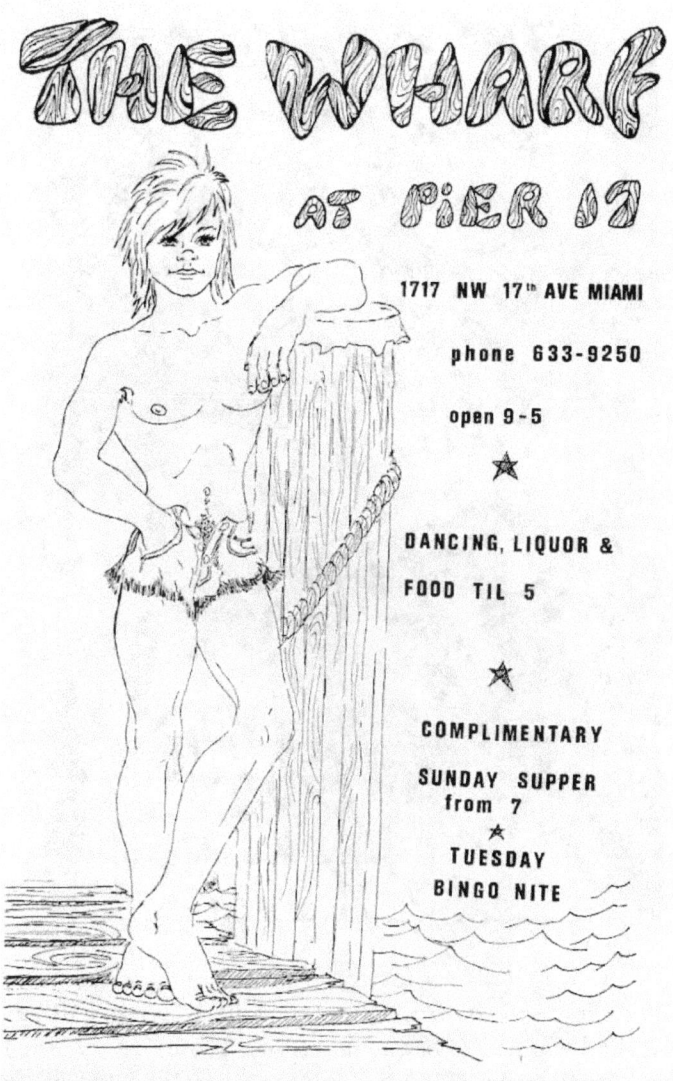

THE WHARF AT PIER 17
1717 NW 17th AVE MIAMI
phone 633-9250
open 9-5
DANCING, LIQUOR & FOOD TIL 5
COMPLIMENTARY SUNDAY SUPPER from 7
TUESDAY BINGO NITE

Wharf at Pier 17
1717 NW 17th Ave., Miami
Circa: 1984-1985

Attracted a Latin crowd. This space was also home to Club El Patio, Peter's, and Womyn's Town (see listings).

Warehouse VIII
3604 SW 8th St., Miami
Circa: 1974-1978

It was a large complex filling a warehouse, with numerous bars—it was popular with Latin, Black, and leather folks. In 1974 the bar welcomed Craig Russell for a week of shows. In 1975 it held the "Missed America Pageant and Bake Sale" with performances by Rosemary and the Warehouse staff. It was owned by Bob Stickney, who also owned the Candlelight Club in Coconut Grove. In 1977 it hosted a meeting for the Dade Human Rights Coalition and a group of Minnesota Human Rights organizations.

Robert Fronner describes the bar as, "It was a huge warehouse building, with a massive dance floor. Also, there was a bar upstairs and an outdoor area on the roof."

Vivian Olivo recalls her first visit, "This is the first bar I ever went to. It was a catty-corner from Versailles Restaurant. It was seedy and you had to be careful because people were waiting outside to beat you up or try to run you over when you left."

On July 22, 1974, *The Miami News* reported on a patron of the bar, 17-year-old William Canet, who was followed walking home from the club at 1:30 a.m. He was captured by three men who doused him with lighter fluid and set him on fire; his cries were heard by a passerby, who chased the trio off and took Canet to the hospital, where he was treated for second-degree burns.

Warsaw (Ballroom)
1450 Collins Ave., Miami Beach
Circa: 1989–2012

This was a very large dance club. In 1989, Andrew Delaplaine took over the lease on what had been the China Club (see listing) and renamed the club the "Warsaw Ballroom." Warsaw transformed itself into the center of the buff-boy universe in 1989. George Tamsitt redesigned the interior in 1991 for Warsaw's second anniversary. Cathy Johnson remembers, "It had a big dance floor and a seating area in the back, and Sunday was a special night."

Celebrities such as Suzanne Bartsch, Louis Canales, and Gianni Versace came to the club attracted by artistic pseudo-S&M performances that degenerated into the real thing being performed on-stage, requiring the owners to kill the lights and separate the performers, to strippers whose act consisted

primarily of allowing patrons to extricate 30-foot ribbons from various orifices—all generating an unending list of warnings, citations, and fines from the city.

In 1995 it held a "Mr. Hard-On Pageant and later that weekend, a Red-Hot Ball with Electra and a cast of Marilyns for "Some Like It Hot" and a Marilyn Look-A-like contest.

Boy George was the featured performer on New Year's Eve. Electra says, "Boy George saw me at Warsaw and took me to London to open for him. Versace also saw me there. He and his lover used to go there all the time. He hired me to perform as Elton John for Elton John's birthday."

WaterLOO
1216 Washington Ave., Miami Beach
Circa: 2019–2020

Ahmed Labib and Tony Ferro, business partners, and co-owners, decided to open WaterLoo to offer an inclusive space. It was a small bar with a dance floor and occasional big-name drag performers. This would later become home to Nathan's (see listing).

Weekend Club
924 Lincoln Rd., Miami Beach
Circa: 1997–1998

A neighborhood hangout.

West End
942 Lincoln Rd., Miami Beach
Circa: 1993–2020

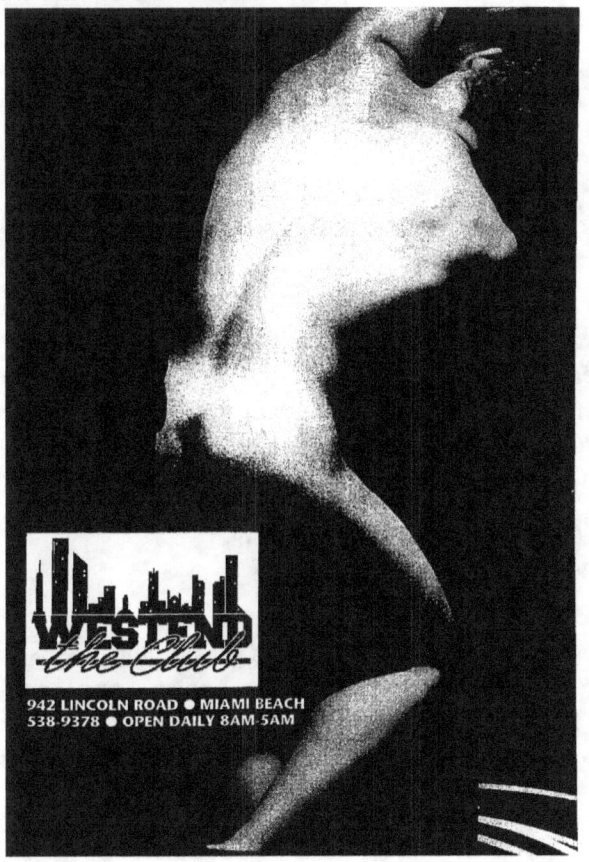

MEET YOUR BEST END AT WEST END

942 LINCOLN ROAD ● MIAMI BEACH
538-9378 ● OPEN DAILY 8AM-5AM

The bar hosted exhibits of the art of Tomata du Plenty. In December 1979, the show was called "Tipsy with Tallulah," and half of the proceeds went towards Women of Miami Beach, a local nonprofit for victims of domestic abuse. Another show was called "Tomato Loves Lucy." The bar would also host what it called "Old-time drag cabaret shows on Fridays and Saturdays.

Nikki Adams said, "At one time, it was the place for tea dances. They had a very small stage behind the bar, so performers would have to jump from the stage to the bar and then walk the bar to connect with customers."

Electra remembers performing at the bar, "I bent down to take a tip, and my dress was over one of the candles, and it caught on fire. Somebody threw a drink on me and put it out."

Edison Farrow recalls, "They had a 3-for-1 happy hour. There were dancers on the bar that you could see as you walked down Lincoln Road."

Wet
1728 SW 8th St., Miami
Circa: 2009–2015

A club popular with Latin men was in the Latin district known as Calle Ocho. *Time Out* wrote, "Hispanic go-go boys provide the eye candy, DJs spinning bilingual dance tunes will tickle your ears and bang at your hips, and drag queens with accents will guide you through the wildest of Miami's Latin nights."

Willy's Neighborhood Bar
356 NW 24th St., Miami
Circa: 2024–present

"We want this bar to feel like it's been in the neighborhood for decades, and that the current Wynwood [Pride Festival], with all its growth and gentrification, has been built around it," says José Atencio, who co-founded the bar along with Jor-El Garcia and Scott Bernardez. The bar is trying to help to recenter Miami's gay community, by placing a stronger emphasis on locals. "This has been a dream of ours since we started producing LGBTQ+ events in Miami," Atencio told *Time Out*. "After years of being asked to do gay nights at straight bars on the least desirable days of the week, it became apparent that the community needed its own, full-time LGBTQ venue. We strategically turned them down because the offers didn't feel authentic or fair. We took the features we love most from our favorite gay bars around the world and brought them to Willy's. Because no one is more deserving of the best than this Miami community."

The team has years of experience running the Wynwood Pride Festival and plans a stellar lineup of local queer talent. Guests can look forward to dance parties, themed nights, RuPaul watch parties, and album release nights. And save the occasional special event, there won't ever be a cover charge.

Windjammer Lounge
16051 Collins Ave., Miami
Circa: 1974–1978

Located in the Windward Resort, it was a piano bar and cabaret. It also hosted drag shows, including The Jewel Box Revue. Wayland Flowers and Madam appeared in 1974. The resort had other bars, the names of which changed from time to time but included The Buccaneer, Stowaway, and Tahitian pool bar.

Nikki Adams remembers working there, "We had a cast of fourteen and we all lived in the hotel. The show director would sometimes call a rehearsal at 4 a.m. after the bar closed. It was my first job, it was rough, but great training. We had a South American customer who would tip $100 bills. He always had a bodyguard around. I think he was from a wealthy South American family who paid for him to stay away from home. One night they had just pulled out of the parking lot when the driver shot him right between the eyes. We all went out to see the dead body."

Womyn's Town
1717 NW 17th Ave., Miami
Circa: 1972

"Dancing food and liquor 'til 5" This was also home to Peter's, Pier 17, and Club El Patio (see listings).

Womyn's Town
2847 Coral Way, Miami
Circa: 1984

A women's bar, located on the second floor. This space was also home to many women's bars, including Louise, Mimi's, and Blackie's Hideaway, but it also housed the men's bar, Bachelor's II (see listings).

Woody's on the Beach
455 Ocean Dr., Miami Beach
Circa: 1984–1989

Mostly a straight music rock club, located in the Arlington Hotel and owned by Ron Wood of the Rolling Stones, but it was gay-friendly. How gay-friendly? Melissa Etheridge played there numerous times. Other performers include Paul Shaffer and Ray Charles. Woods closed the club after too many noise complaints from neighbors in the surrounding high condos.

WOW (aka World of Women)
323 23rd St., Miami Beach
Circa: 1994

The bar was geared towards women's parties and events. It lasted two months. This has been the location of a gay bar since the early 1970s, serving as home to BBC, Billy's Back Lounge, Billy's Backroom, Dinghy, Duck's Pastime, Groove Jet, Joseph's, Little Al's, Miss Kay's, Rain, and Teran's (see listings).

Y
8099 NE 5th Ct., Miami
Circa: 1975

The grand opening was held on Friday, October 11, 1975. Admission was $2 and you got two free drink tickets. It billed itself as "South Florida's cruisiest bar," and Wednesdays were "Chicken Night." Drinks were half-priced for those between 18 and 21.

Yancy's
10755 Sunset, Kendall
Circa: 1990-1992

A cabaret bar.

Your Bar
930 Lejeune Rd., Miami
Circa: 1965

El Carol (see listing) was previously at this location.

Your Father's Moustache
7232 SW 59th Ave., South Miami
Circa: 1974-1979

The bar showed football games, featured a pool table, pinball machines, and four English tournament dart boards—and they were serious about their darts, playing every day. Just to keep things gay enough, they'd have an occasional drag show. It billed itself as "A bit of Greenwich Village in South Miami."

Yuca Lounge
501 Lincoln Rd., Miami Beach
Circa: 2009-2010

A straight bar, but it hosted occasional LGBTQ events. Popular with salsa dancers.

Z
1235 Washington Ave., Miami Beach
Circa: 1986

Originally opened in 1935 as The French Casino, it was a supper and vaudeville club, featuring cabaret acts and showgirls. By 1937, the interior was converted to a movie theater by adding 1,000 seats. It was re-designed by noted architect Thomas Lamb, at a staggering cost of $3 million for that era and renamed the Cinema Casino Theatre. When Miami Beach went through a low period in the 1960s and 1970s, the building's owners wished to demolish the lobby and convert it into three separate stores. Local preservationists stepped in and convinced the owners to close off the entire auditorium and upper lobby mezzanine and turn the lobby into storefronts.

In the 1980s, as Miami Beach began to experience its renaissance, the management team of Z took over the space to open a club. When they took down the drywall separating the old ballroom from the lobby/storefronts, they found an art deco jewel of a design and had only to tweak it to accommodate modern lighting standards.

This address was home to several other bars including 1235 Club Icon, Glam Slam, Level, and Paragon (see listings).

Zep Tepi
1532 Washington Ave., Miami Beach
Circa: 1997

Someone once described Tim Kelly's club as "a disco theme park with gothic overtones." Soon after it opened, established parties from defunct clubs were resurrected under its roof, including Mykel Steven's Backdoor Bamby events on Mondays, Frankie Morales and Carmel Ophir's Church on Sundays, and "Boy Band Tuesdays. One-off parties included "King—a night for men, with Kitty Meow" and a Studio 43 party This would later become the location of Temptations (see listing).

Zipper's Cabaret
1060 NE 79th St., Miami
Circa: 2002

Nude male strippers, men only. Attracted a diverse crowd. An 18+private club. This location has housed several queer clubs over the years including Club Milord, Cupid's Cabaret, Sandal Club, and Bonfire (see listings).

Zissen's Bowery
1749 N. Miami Ave., Miami
Circa: 1940-1956

The club hosted drag shows. It was raided in 1947, the same night as the Jewel Box Revue raid. A guide to *Miami After Dark* in 1956 said, "A longtime Miami favorite that has sawdust on the floor, insulting waiters, bowls of pretzels, peanuts, and big steins of beer. Here everyone gets into the act."

Zorita's Show Bar
17604 N. Collins Ave., Miami Beach
Circa: 1969–1975

A lesbian bar with drag shows. Zorita, whose real name was Ada Petillo, a lesbian, had been a stripper who had performed with a boa constrictor at several clubs in Miami, including the Five O'Clock Club (see listing) before opening her own bar.

Zorita was a trendsetter and savvy businesswoman. Although appearing very straight, she was, in fact, a lesbian and liked very butch women. She raised her daughter with her partner and became a well-respected leader in Miami's business community.

Her bar was raided many times, and her dancers were charged with public indecency but never with prostitution, which was unusual for a strip club. Zorita made sure there was none of that in her bar.

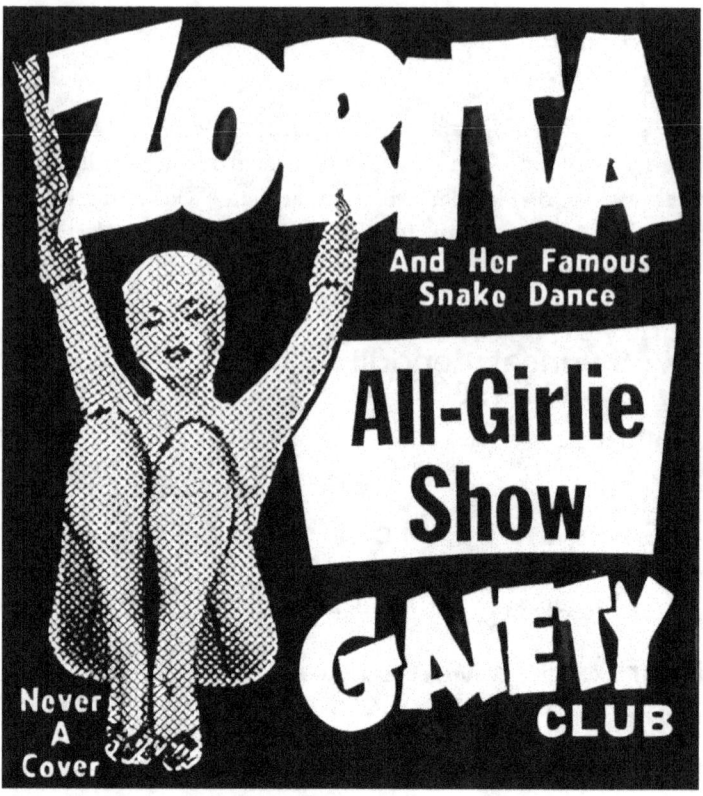

STREET SCENE IN DOWNTOWN MIAMI

A pretty girl leading a poisonous snake on a leash—which must come under the heading of "things that can't happen here"—blocked traffic in busy Flagler st. shortly before noon today, resulting in arrest of the woman on a charge of disorderly conduct. Police debated what charge should be lodged against her for quite a spell, but agreed finally that was the statute which covered such episodes. The woman gave her name as Zorita, but withheld the name of the snake. Veteran members of the police department said it had all the appearance of a publicity gag, but admitted it was a new twist.

Zorita, 1939

MONROE COUNTY
A QUEER PLAYGROUND
AT THE END OF THE EARTH

In many ways, Monroe County is unlike other counties in South Florida. It was founded in 1830 to combat piracy. It's made up of a chain of many little islands with a large swamp on the mainland. At one time the city of Key West, at the end of the island chain, was one of the wealthiest cities in America per capita. It has a tumultuous history of economic difficulties, with salt production, salvaging sunken ships, fishing, turtling, sponge fishing, cigar manufacturing, and providing docking for navy ships being the high points, and hurricanes and national depressions being the low points.

As with other South Florida counties, Henry Flagler and his railroad played a key role, connecting the city of Key West to the rest of the state with a series of bridges between the islands in 1912. However, in 1935 a hurricane destroyed many of the bridges. The Federal Government replaced the bridges with a narrow, non-passing, two-lane highway in 1938, which to this day, has been the main access route to Key West.

With its semi-isolation, tropical gardens, sleepy sun-drenched streets, and late 1800s Victorian gingerbread homes, it was a paradise waiting to be discovered. Unlike the other counties in this book, it was not the land speculators and retirees from South Florida who settled there. It was more artistic and adventurous spirits such as Ernest Hemingway, Tennessee Williams, and Leonard Bernstein. Indeed, because it was such a hard place to get to, it was particularly attractive to the emerging post-war queer community.

As Guy Ross, a 25-year resident noted, "Back when gay life existed in a parallel universe separate from jobs, birth families, and a harshly intolerant mainstream society, the LGBTQ community opted to vacation in out-of-the-way destinations like Key West. By the 1970s the stream of gay visitors to the island had turned into a torrent, with more than 30 same-sex guest houses on the small island catering to gay men."

A few guest houses also catered to lesbians. In 1967, the city elected its first openly gay mayor, Richard Heyman, and the first resort hotel was built. Shortly after that, floods of gay men bought up many of the old, deshabille gingerbread houses and restored them to their former glory.

Truman Capote, James Leo Herlihy, Pulitzer Prize-winning poet James Merrill, and gay literati, such as Christopher Cox, Edmund White, and Terrence McNally, all spent considerable time and creative energy in Key West during those years.

Long-time resident Gordon Ross (no relation to Guy Ross) explains part of the appeal of Key West for celebrities in the early days, "They could come down here and just be (themselves). Nobody bothered them. It was, "'Do you like rum? Got some weed? Okay, sit down and have a drink.' I used to hang out with Tennessee Williams, Jamie Herlihy who wrote *Midnight Cowboy*, and Jimmy Kirkwood. I didn't even know Jimmy was famous until I saw his picture in *People Magazine*."

The island's reputation as a center of creative writing was sealed in 1983 when David Kaufelt established the Key West Literary Seminar, an annual sold-out event that has become a significant economic boost for the island. Like everything else in Florida, the city lives on tourism (around five million tourists visit annually, and Fantasy Fest in October brings in 75,000 visitors).

Too much tourism can also be a terrible thing (just look at Orlando). The residents of Key West like its unhomogenized atmosphere and work hard to keep it that way. The city has limited the number of cruise ships stopping and dumping off hundreds of day-tripping tourists. The city recently set limits on the number of boats that can dock in any given week. The building of large hotels and apartment complexes is strictly controlled. The bars and restaurants have worked hard to keep their quirky atmosphere.

Long-time Key West resident Rikki Regretto-Fessler recalls, "Down Duval from Fleming used to be Pier House, then they began opening strip clubs and hippie shops, but now it's the kind of place you get when cruise ships come in."

Gordon Ross added, "When Copa opened, everybody went up there (north of Fleming) and that became the more desirable part of town, from Fleming on up to La-Ti-Da. We really haven't had any 'new' places for quite a while. Bars and clubs get bought and renovated but it's all basically the same places."

Calling Key West a "gay" paradise undervalues the place, and the residents feel it. As out-lesbian County Mayor Heather Carruthers noted when first elected, "Labels work fine for clothes. Down here in Key West, not so much for people."

They take pride in the motto of the city: "One Human Family." Gay bars line Duval Street, the city's main thoroughfare, but all are "straight welcoming." It is second only to Wilton Manors as the gayest city in Florida and it shows no signs of changing.

Truman Capote, Tennessee Williams and James Kirkwood in Key West, 1970s

22 & Company
705 Duval St., Key West Circa: 2019-present

Is it a store? Is it a bar? Is it a tutu factory? It seems to be all the above. Glitter abounds at this tiny store and bar, which is co-owned by Jenn Stefenacci. It is part of the Aqua Complex (see listing).

416
416 Appelrouth Ln., Key West
Circa: 1992

Mixed men and women, but primarily a men's bar on a small side street off Duvall St. Cathy Johnson, who was once a resident of Key West, recalls, "For a while, this was the only women's bar in town. They only sold beer and wine, but folks would bring in their own hard liquor and pour it into soft drinks. It was built around a tree. Stretch worked there—she was a bartender."

This tiny space was also home to Annabelle's (see listing) a decade earlier and would later become home to Mary Ellen's (see listing).

801 (Piano) Bar
801 Duval St., Key West
Circa: 1989-1997

It dropped Piano from its name after the first year (see listing below).

801 Bourbon Bar
801 Duval St., Key West
Circa: 1997-present

Not to be confused with Bourbon Street Pub at 724 Duval, but both are owned by Joey Schroeder. It is known for its drag shows. Sky T said, "One of the staple gay bars of Key West. The downstairs bar area is a good watering hole." Cathy Johnson points out, "It has the longest-running drag show in Key West and Sushi runs the shows there. She is infamous for being in the high heel that is dropped every New Year's Eve." (Sushi retired from the high heel drop, which takes place at Bourbon St. Pub, in 2024, but not from the shows at 801). Christopher Peterson now sits in the high heel on New Year's Eve). The bar is also connected to One Saloon (see listing) which is way more uncensored and intimate. 801 Piano Bar (see listing above) was also in this location.

Annabelle's
416 Appelrouth Ln., Key West
Circa: 1980s

A small bar on a side street from Duval, it was also home to the 416 and Mary Ellen's (see listings).

Aqua Complex
711 Duval St., Key West
Circa: 2003-present

A popular dance bar with drag shows. There are numerous bars throughout the complex, which include 22 & Company. (see listing), and a restaurant, Poke in the Rear, each with its own atmosphere. The various rooms are constantly being changed and renamed. It has one entrance on Duval and annexes through to another building with an entrance on Angela St. It has a mostly male clientele, though women are welcome. Jonathan and Michael Barrett purchased Aquaplex in May of 2023 and did extensive renovations. The Angela St. entrance has been home to Sidebar (see listing), which was a drag showcase and in early 2024, was renamed The Birdcage (see listing). This space also used to be home to KWEST, with Diva's on one side, and Dude's on the other (see listings).

Atlantic Shores Beach Club
511 South St., Key West
Circa: 1997-2005

There were numerous bars and food was available, all surrounding a pool. "Tea By the Sea," its Sunday and Wednesday tea dances poolside, were a big draw. Cathy Johnson remembers, "We went to La-Ti-Da and headed right over to Atlantic Shores. The party just kept on going."

This was a clothing-optional resort with lots of nude sunbathing by the pool. *The Guardian* wrote, "The official dress code there appears to be butt-naked (it is optional, thankfully), and a mixed crowd starts the party at sunset and continues in the same mad vein through the night."

Back Bar
711 Duval St., Key West
Circa: 2018-2021

One of the many bars to have occupied the Aqua the same space as the Aqua complex, along with Diva's, Dude's, and KWEST (see listings). It is currently Poke in the Rear, a poke restaurant.

Backstreet
700 Duval St., Key West
Circa: 1987-1992

This was later home to Club Tropic (see listing).

Bamboo Room
422 Appelrouth Ln., Key West
Circa: 1994-1997

Bamboo Room

This has been a bar going back as far as 1965 (if not earlier) when it was a jazz club. Pianist Coffee Butler remembers playing for Tennessee Williams and Tallulah Bankhead one night. Blu Room and Spurs (see listings) would later open at this location.

Birdcage Cabaret
504 Angela St., Key West
Circa: 2024-present

The Birdcage Cabaret, formerly Sidebar (see listing), is the home for drag performers singing live. It is part of the Aqua complex (see listing) and is a showcase for Christopher Peterson and The Aquanettes, who dance and sing live, rather than lip sync. Gerry Butcher says, "Best show in the Keys!"

Blu/Blue Room
422 Appelrouth Ln., Key West
Circa: 2006

A dance bar, owned by Catherine Simonton, which catered to a young crowd. Bamboo (see listing) was at this location earlier and Spurs (see listing) would open there a year later.

Bobby's Monkey Bar
900 Simonton St., Key West
2004–present

Mostly men, a favorite with locals and a refreshing hangout away from the hustle and bustle of Duval Street. Dana Manchester headlined there for quite a while. Fans flock there for karaoke and cheap drinks, both of which are found in abundance, as is echoed by Jacob's comment, "It's a nice little gay dive bar. They do karaoke every night."

(Donnie's) Club International/Peacock (see listings) also occupied this space.

Boca Chica
US Hwy. 1, Boca Chica Key
Circa: 1977–1989

A working-class bar with go-go boys, dancing, and a primarily Black clientele. Hunter S. Thompson supposedly liked to hang out there. Richard and Robert Berard owned it. Gordon Ross remembers, "I had a customer, a gay Vietnam War vet, who used to come in every afternoon and sit at the bar and drink until closing. After closing he'd drive over to Boca Chica, which is off Key West, and because of that was able to be open 24 hours. It was sailors, shrimpers, and conchs (locals). He'd drink there until morning, and then the next afternoon he'd be back at my bar. One night a bunch of us went with him to the bar and the locals weren't very happy about it. But the two women who worked as barmaids defused the situation. They announced, 'We've made more money tonight from these gay boys than we've ever made from you. Leave them alone.' And they did. Ever after that, it was like there were two parts of the bar. The shrimpers and the gay boys."

Bogart's
904 Duval St. Key West
Circa: 1995–2011

Some people raved about this place, while others found it disgusting. It no longer appears to be primarily LGBTQ, but in Key West, everything's a little bit queer.

Bootleggers
410 Petronia St., Key West
Circa: 2008

It was a men's bar with country dancing, karaoke, and occasional drag shows.

Bourbon Street Pub
724 Duval St., Key West
Circa: 1997–present

Probably the most popular and well-known bar in Key West. Famous for its high heel drop on NYE with the drag queen Sushi. (Sushi retired in 2024 and Christopher Peterson now rides the pump at midnight). It is a large complex that includes several bars including a cabaret, a "male only-clothing optional"

garden bar with a pool and hot tub, a leather bar, and the main bar, all located in the New Orleans Guest House.

Owner Joey Schroeder also owns 801 Bourbon (see listing). It once used the 730 Duval entrance in the same building and some guides listed that address.

Brooklyn Boys Inc.
610 Green St., Key West
Circa: 1997

A short-lived New York City-themed bar with a pool table and food service.

Brown Derby Bar
601 Whitehead St., Key West
Circa: 1940s–1965

Originally opened as a grocery store in 1890, Cuban and Bahamian transplants often hung out and played music in the back room. During the Great Depression, the grocery store became Brown Derby Bar, visited by submarine sailors stationed at the nearby Navy base. As such, it attracted many gay men. It is now the location of the Green Parrot, a straight bar for locals.

Buttery
1206 Simonton St., Key West
Circa: 1986–1989

More restaurant than bar, it attracted a mixed gay/straight crowd and was renowned for its southern cuisine. The building has been torn down and replaced by a bank.

Captain Tony's
428 Greene St., Key West
Circa: 1968-present

In 1968, Tony Tarracino (called Captain Tony), a local charter boat captain, purchased the well-known Sloppy Joe's bar and renamed it Captain Tony's Saloon. It was always open to all sorts of people, including the growing gay and lesbian community in Key West. Jimmy Buffett got his start at Captain Tony's in the early 1970s. Bob Dylan, who released the song "Key West" has frequented the place over the years, resulting in his name being painted on a bar stool. Which started a tradition of painting the names of famous patrons on bar stools.

Gordon Ross recalls when Wayland Flowers first performed at Captain Tony's. "This was before cell phones. The word was flying up and down the street, saying, 'You have to get down there to see this guy. He's got the most foul-mouthed puppet, but it's hysterical.' By the end of the night, the street was blocked with folks watching the show from the street."

Tarracino was so popular, that he was elected mayor. He sold the bar in 1989 but continued to appear there most Thursdays to greet customers and fans until his death in November 2008. It's more of a tourist stop now.

Carmen Miranda Veranda
418 United St., Key West
Circa: 1982

A lesbian bar and guesthouse.

Cecil's
613 Duval St., Key West
Circa: 1968

Cecil's is the only listing in the 1968 *Damron Guide* for Key West and is identified as a men's bar.

Claire
900 Duval St., Key West
Circa: 1985–1994

Primarily a restaurant, but the front porch bar was a popular gathering place.

Club 504 (see Aqua listing)

Carmen Miranda Veranda

A tropical guest house... for women.

418 United St., Key West 33040   (305) 294-8345

Club Chameleon
524 Eaton St., Key West
Circa: 2000

A church that was converted into a dance hall, then into a bar, and is now a theater. It is most famous because it is reputed to be haunted. Soon after the church was built in the 1800's, the minister discovered his wife having an affair with the deacon. Supposedly he boarded up all the doors and windows and set the church on fire. His wife and the deacon were both caught inside the church when it burned, and fourteen children ended up dying in the fire. Many visitors to the pink and turquoise club said that they could smell smoke constantly, while some say that it was the smell of flesh.

In 1995 the bar staged "Flamingo Follies," an ongoing musical satire of Key West tourist attractions. *Good Morning America* featured the cast doing a number on the air.

Club International (Donnie's)
900 Simonton St., Key West
Circa: 1993–2002

A video bar, it briefly changed ownership and name to Peacock (see listing), but it only lasted a few months before reverting. It was a neighborhood hangout offering pool tournaments and karaoke. Not long after it closed, Bobby's Monkey Bar (see listing) took over the space.

Club Key West
621 Truman Ave., Key West
Circa: 1976

Club Tropic
700 Duval St., Key West
Circa: 1992–1994

A mixed bar (men and women) that offered dancing. This was earlier home to Backstreet (see listing).

Copa Key West
623 Duval St., Key West
Circa: 1986–1993

An outpost of the popular Fort Lauderdale club (see listing), it attracted a young crowd who enjoyed dancing. Madonna

performed there in the '80s. Katrina Klein remembers, "I was crowned Miss Copa Key West on February 26, 1992."

Cathy Johnson recalls her days and nights at the Copa, "It was an old theater, so when you walked in from the lobby, there were bars lining both walls and the dance floor was the entire room in the middle. Near the back was a stage. The balcony had seating. There was a patio off to the side. Sylvester appeared there. It was the place to be. A lot of good-looking shirtless guys, and good-looking girls. It was so much bigger and better than the one in Fort Lauderdale."

After it closed, Epoch and Cabaret Key West (see listings) opened in this location.

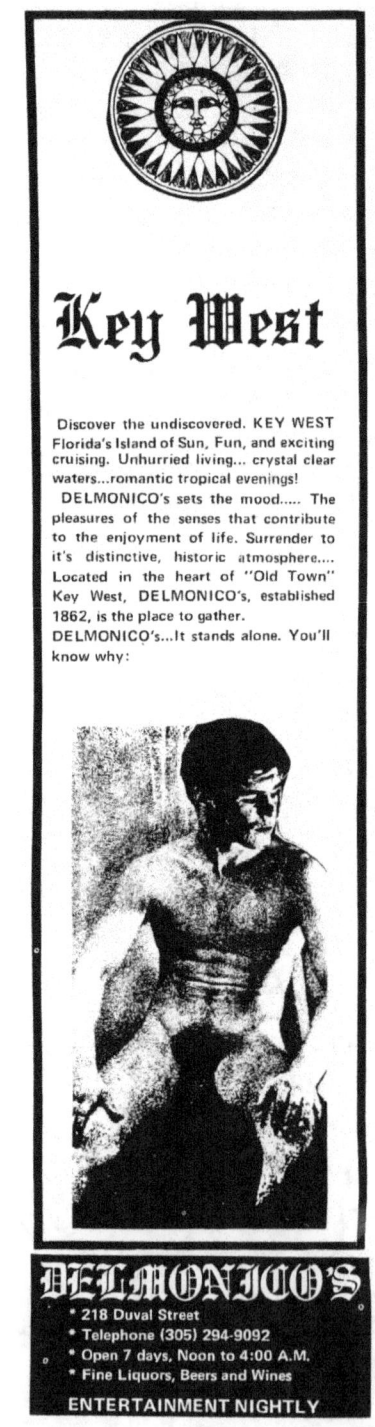

Delmonico's
218 Duval St., Key West
Circa: 1970-1982

A dance bar and restaurant, Delmonico was the first recognized bar on the island to advertise as a "gay bar." It hosted the first drag shows, although the shows were not exactly the choreographed masterpieces we think of today. Longtime Key West resident Rikki Fessler recalls, "Back in the early '70s before I came down here, Delmonico's brought down a show called 'Broad Minded Men.' Delmonico's was the only fully recognized gay bar in the city at the time."

Delmonico's opened in 1862 as a restaurant. In the intervening years, it was a gambling casino and a whorehouse before re-opening as a gay bar in 1970. This space also housed Michael's, Foley Square, and Jimmy Kirkwood's (see listings).

Diva's
711 Duval St., Key West
Circa: 1999-2001

A drag show bar, also home to Dude's (see listing). It was sold and became KWEST, and later, combined with Dude's. Now home to the Aqua complex (see listings).

Donnie's (Cocktails)
618 Duval St., Key West
Circa: 1994-2004

Donnie's was a favorite hang-out for locals no matter where he was, and he moved around a lot, but his clientele always seemed to find him. We were able to find at least two addresses attributed to him in addition to the one listed above. 900 Simonton St. (1998), 618 Duval, and 900 Simonton (see listings), as well as one we could not document at 422 Appelrouth Lane.

Dude's
711 Duval St., Key West
Circa: 2001

"A Gay Man's Bar" with drag shows, dancing, and underwear contests. It was combined with Diva's when it became Aqua. It was also home to KWEST (see listings).

Epoch
623 Duval St., Key West
Circa: 1997-2003

After Copa Key West (see listing) was destroyed by a fire, Epoch took the place of the large dance club. The DJ booth was suspended above the dance floor. This was the location of Cabaret Key West (see listing).

Equator Resort
818 Fleming St., Key West
Circa: 1996-2018

Primarily a guest house but was known for its tea dances

Foley Square
218 Duval St., Key West
Circa: 1989

A piano bar, Tom Luna was a popular bartender. This was also home to Michael's, Delmonico's, and Jimmy Kirkwood's Cabaret (see listings).

Gallery Lounge
224 Duval St., Key West
Circa: 1965

Hog's Breath Saloon
400 Front St., Key West
Circa: 1995-present

Randy Clark remembers, "In the mid-'90s it was very gay. On Sundays, you could hear the music for miles. Most places were predominately gay in the '90s." Before that, this space was home to The Monster (see listing), the Key West outpost of the popular New York City disco. In the early 2000s, it was sold to David Siegel, CEO of Westgate Resorts, and his business associate Jim Gissy. Now it is primarily filled with straight tourists (next to Ripley's Believe or Not Museum of Oddities!) and is no longer considered as gay-friendly as it was before.

Island House Café & Bar
1129 Fleming St., Key West
Circa: 1976-present

A full-service guest house with a restaurant and bar open to the public. Originally it just had a wine and beer license, in 2001 it got a full-service liquor license. It serves food 24 hours a day, seven days a week. Liquor during legally designated hours. Island House is a clothing-optional resort and has become a legend in the LGBT community for its wild parties! It was named "The Best Gay Resort In The World" by OUTTraveler. com.

Jimmy Kirkwood's Broadway Piano Bar
218 Duval St., Key West
Circa: 1988

The famed Broadway playwright of the book for the musical *A Chorus Line* fronted this bar for a year. Kirkwood described his adopted hometown as, "... a crazy little island. It's not Florida or even America, but a country and a state of mind. It's the end of the line, even the world." He lived in Key West for 10 years before he died from HIV complications. This space was also home to Foley Square, Michael's, and Delmonico's (see listings).

Kelly's Caribbean Bar
301 Whitehead St., Key West
Circa: 2000-2005

Located in an old Pan American Airlines building. It is most notable for having once been owned by actor Kelly McGillis. Earlier it had been home to Pigeonhouse Patio (see listing).

Keys Piano Bar
1114 Duval St., Key West
Circa: 2010

A short-lived bar. The only mention I could find of this was in a newspaper called Southern Exposure.

Key West Cabaret
623 Duval St., Key West
Circa: 1994

Once the location for Epoch and Copa Key West (see listings).

The Cabaret

and

Women's Week!

Schedule Of Events:

Live Music & drink specials all week

Monday, Sept. 13
6pm-Midnight
Meet & Greet
Welcome to Key West
Live Music with:
Leslie Kille

Wednesday, Sept. 15
Doors open at 7pm
Live Music with:
Leslie Kille
8pm till 10pm

Saturday, Sept. 18
Live Music with:
Leslie Kille
2pm till 4pm
Afternoon Street Fair
Appelrouth
Lane

Look For Our Suprise Guest Bartenders

Key West Cabaret

416 Appelrouth Lane

Kokomo's
600 Truman Ave., Key West
Circa: 1992

There was a mixed crowd. Some are gay but mostly straight. It is also a restaurant. It was named after the Beach Boys song that became a hit, possibly to capitalize on the name recognition.

KWEST
711 Duval St., Key West
Circa: 2003-2010

A dance club catering to a mixed crowd of men and women, KWEST was once home to Diva's and Dude's and is now home to Aqua (see listings).

KWEST Men
705 Duval St., Key West
Circa: 2003-2010

A cruisy bar. Now home to Aqua's 22 & Co. (see listing).

La-Te-Da
1125 Duvall St., Key West
Circa: 1982-present

La-Te-Da has a long and glorious history, dating back to Cuba's fight for independence from Spain in the late 1800s. The name is short for "La Terraza de Marti" or "The Balcony of Marti," named after Cuban revolutionary Jose Marti who delivered speeches from the second-floor terrace overlooking Duval

Street. Its Sunday tea dance is a big draw. Upstairs was a piano bar once called the Treetop Lounge, now the complex's piano bar and cabaret room, and a big tourist draw for drag performers who impersonate stars and sing with their own voices, such as Christopher Peterson and Randy Roberts.

Gordon Ross remembers, "If you climbed to the top, up three flights of stairs, there was a sun deck and during tea dance, I would bartend up there."

Cathy Johnson recalls, "Larry Formica was the owner. We'd start with tea dance there and then head over to Atlantic Shores."

Lighthouse Court
902 Whitehead, Key West
Circa: 1970-1996

A very popular guest house with a historic Lighthouse, especially with Europeans. It had a bar and weekend tea dance. In the early 1990s, it was sold to one of the major hotel chains and has since been operated under several major hotel brands, primarily catering to straight tourists.

An exquisitely relaxed compound of apartments, suites, rooms and cottages with private guest accommodations. Pool, Jacuzzi, Health Club, Restaurant and Bar. Across from the Hemingway House.
902 Whitehead, Key West, FL 33040 (305) 294-9588

Lou's
Duval St., Key West
Circa: 1972

Lou's is listed in the 1975 *Damron Guide* as "hip and unisex, with a young crowd."

Mary Ellen's
416 Appelrouth Ln., Key West
Circa: 1994-present

Mary Ellen's is a friendly neighborhood bar with comfort food. There are nine versions of grilled cheese. It is known for events such as the drunken spelling bee and its weekly vibrator races

(for charity!). Annabelle's and 416 (see listings) were formerly located in this space.

Mermaid Lounge
430 Duval St., Key West
Circa: 1984

A multi-story Crowne Plaza hotel occupies this site now.

Michael's
218 Duval St., Key West
Circa: 1984-1987

Disco with a patio bar, the garden bar was for women. This location was also home to Jimmy Kirkwood's Cabaret, Foley Square, and Delmonico's (see listings).

TROPICAL GARDEN BAR • DISCO • GRAND PIANO BAR
218 Duval Street • Key West • 294-4383

Michelle's
218 Duval St., Key West
Circa: 1985

An intimate women's spot featuring slow dancing, a pool table, and a quiet atmosphere.

Monster
400 Front St., Key West
Circa: 1977–1978

The Key West outpost of the popular New York City disco also had a piano bar area. Rikki Regretto-Fessler worked there, and he recalled, "In the winter season they had a cabaret behind the piano bar. They brought in Linda Eder, Betty Carter, and Pat Carrol did a comedy act there. Divine did a show there. It was only for three months. The cabaret used to be the storeroom for the liquor, but the owners got tired of opening the door and always finding people having sex in there. So, Sven, the owner, added another backspace to store the liquor and he converted the room. They called the cabaret BJ Flat's, because of all the

blow jobs that had been given in that room."

Gordon Ross remembers, "My friend Bobby Nesmith played piano there. He's sitting there and one night who should come in, because they ALL came into the Monster, but Leonard Bernstein, who said, 'Do you mind if I sit down and play with

you?' And Bobby's thinking, 'What am I gonna say? No, no you can't!?'"

That story reminded Rikki, "One time Bernstein came in and played the entire score of *West Side Story*."

Gordon added, "Jimmy Kirkwood would come in with him and sit there and listen. Oh, and Christine Jorgensen, and Eartha Kitt."

Rikki adds, "And Paul Lynde, the most obnoxious man in the world. He had a great sense of humor, but when he got drunk, we had to throw him out. The Monster also had these Sunday $1 dinners that had people lined up waiting to get in. They also did drag shows. Each of the bars had a little troupe of performers. We were the Monsterettes."

Gordon added, "The La-Te-Dettes and the White Glove Girls who worked at Atlantic Shores. We all did shows and on our off nights, we'd go to the other groups' shows."

Numbers
1023 Truman Ave., Key West
Circa: 1993–2001

A dance club with shows and male strippers, it was sort of an outrageous place. It is now a straight stripper bar called Bare Assets.

Ocean Key House
0 Duval St., Key West
Circa: 1997

Home to Zero's Café, with jazz music. Most notable because it is the site where David Wolkowsky, a gay native of Key West, opened Pier House, the first true resort on the island in the 1960s.

Old Plantation
300 Southard St., Key West
Circa: 1983–1985

Dancing, strippers, and wet jockey shorts contests were the main draws of this bar. Gordon Ross remembers, "It used to be called the Gate Bar because it was right across the street from the naval base gate, and it was a straight stripper bar. When the navy left, the bar closed. Then someone opened it as a gay dance club. I did some shows there."

Old Plantation Too
700 Southard St., Key West
Circa: 1983–1987

The Old Plantation (see listing above) moved to this location before closing two years later.

Orchid Bar
1004 Duval St., Key West
Circa: 2008–present

Located in the Orchid Key Inn, an adults-only resort motel, the bar was opened in 2008 after a complete renovation of the mid-century modern property. General manager Trudy Bowden says, "It has steadily become recognized as a popular local spot with a great reputation for its craft cocktails and revolving doors wine list with some of the best mixologists on the island." It is quite popular with LGBTQ locals.

Papillion
510 South St., Key West
Circa: 1981–1994

It was the bar in the Atlantic Shores guest house and was known for its cruisy cocktail hour.

Peacock Club
900 Simonton St., Key West
Circa: 1996–2000

Opened as (Donnie's) Club International (see listing). When that didn't work, it changed its name to Peacock Club. That didn't draw a crowd either, so it reverted to just International Club before eventually closing. This location later became home to Bobby's Monkey Bar (see listing).

Pearl's Patio Bar
Key West
Circa: 2003–2014

The Patio bar was in Pearl's Rainbow Guesthouse, which originated as a women-only space. Cathy Johnson recalls, "It was a women's hotel and patio bar, one of the few lesbian guesthouses. They would do some special events during Women's Week."

In 2011, the guesthouse decided to allow men on the property. Owner Heather Carruthers said it was a business decision based on tough economic realities. However, the business soon dissipated. The building was demolished, and a large resort was built on it and surrounding properties.

301 WHITEHEAD ST. 296-9600
KEY WEST, FLORIDA 33040

Pier House
1 Duval St., Key West
Circa: 1992–1995

Built in 1967 as a small 50-room motel, at one time it played host to Hemingway and Truman Capote. Bob Marley and Jimmy Buffett started their careers in the hotel's funky Chart Room Bar. Gordon Ross says, "It was gay-friendly, but all the local gays and lesbians used to hang out on its beach during the day. Now it's so corporate you can't do that. They lost a lot of local support."

By the 1990s it was a shadow of its former self, but its location proved to be popular with gays and lesbians. It closed in the late 1990s and is now home to a very upscale, luxurious, and definitively hetero-oriented resort.

Pigeonhouse Patio
301 Whitehead St., Key West
Circa: 1970–1994

A piano bar, it later was bought by actor Kelly McGillis and opened as Kelly's Caribbean Bar (see listing).

Rooftop Café
310 Front St., Key West
Circa: 1992–2020

As a cabaret and restaurant, it attracted many tourists. The following depended on who was in the cabaret. During its final years, there was no longer a cabaret, and it lived off its reputation and the gorgeous view, and only tourists went there.

Rudy's
124 Duval St., Key West
Circa: 1964

It was a hole-in-the-wall bar and the smallest bar in town, measuring no more than ten feet across.

Saloon 1
524 Duval St., Key West
Circa: 1984–1994

The original location of Saloon 1 (see listing below) was later home to Virgilio's (see listings).

There's NEVER a Cover Charge at 1 Saloon!

SUMMER SPECIALS

HAPPY HOUR 4 - 8 PM
75¢ Happy Well Drinks / $1.50 Top Well Drinks

EVERY NIGHT 10 - 4 AM
50¢ Happy Well Drinks

WED. & THURS. 12 - 2 AM
Country & Western Night $1.25 Top Well Drinks

SUNDAY
SUNDAY T-DANCE from 4 - 8 PM plus
DOUBLE DOLLAR DINNER 6 - 8 PM, with
75¢ Happy Well Drinks / $1.50 Top Well Drinks

DAY & NIGHT
75¢ Draft Beers / $1.00 Schnapps

HOT MEN 7 DAYS A WEEK . . . TILL 4:00 A.M.
524 DUVAL ST. (Side Entrance) KEY WEST

Saloon 1
504 Petronia St., Key West
Circa: 1994–present

The only leather and Levi's bar in Key West. Marqus R. said, "Though the location has changed in the past, Saloon 1 has been around Key West since the early '80s and has pretty much always been its only gay leather bar. Though the main entrance is off Petronia St., you can also enter through 801 Duval, a small hallway located inside the 801 Bourbon Bar (editor's note: It's the same management for both bars). It's dark, somewhat dingy, and divey but that is what a gay leather bar is supposed to look like. The patrons here tend to be older but pretty much dress the part with leather harnesses, and biker hats. It's definitely not the twinkie or disco swim-suited go-go boy crowd."

Samoa Club
Located on the water at the Yacht Basin, Key West
Circa: 1941 - 1942

In 1941, Club Cayo Hueso became the Samoa Club and featured female impersonators, including the world-renowned

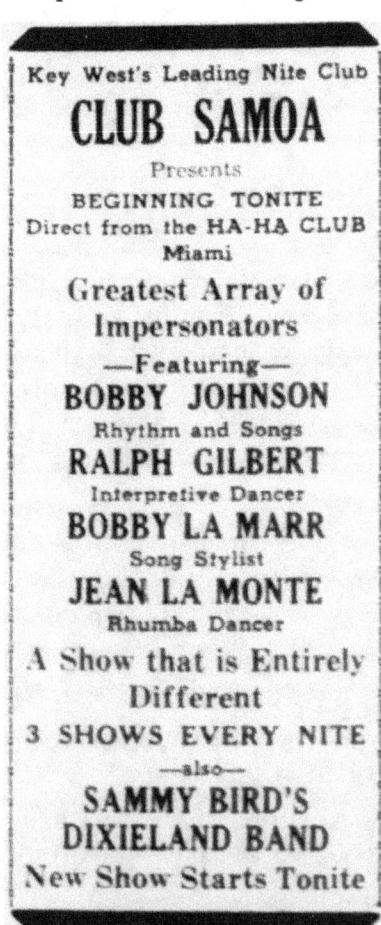

Jean La Monte, among its entertainment. The bar also advertised, "Penny cocktail hour daily 5:00 to 6:00 P.M." The club closed in 1942 when it became a club for enlisted men.

Female Impersonator

MR. JEAN LA MONTE shows the ladies of Key West how to dress at the Samoa.

Sidebar
504 Angela St., Key West
Circa: 2010–2024

A nightclub and party venue with a large dance floor, part of the Aqua complex (see listing) with an entrance around the

Sea Isle
915 Windsor Lane, Key West
Circa: 1979–1990

The resort had a nude deck and was known for its weekend tea dances. The original owners, Randy and Jim, sold the place in the late 1980s, and the new owners were not well-liked or very welcoming to the gay community. They eventually sold the property, and it was bulldozed in the early 2000s to make way for condominiums that now bear the Sea Isle name.

corner from the main bar on Duval St. In 2018 it started going by the name Club 504/Sidebar, but that was soon dropped. In 2023 it was completely renovated and went by Sidebar and was known for its over-the-top drag shows. It was recently renovated and renamed The Birdcage (see listing).

Stables
423 Caroline St., Key West
Circa: 1984

A very butch leather/Levi bar, with a pool table and erotic videos.

Spurs
422 Appelrouth Ln., Key West
Circa: 1997-2000

A country and western bar on a small side street off Duval is now home to a leather apparel shop. Bamboo Room and Blu (see listings) both preceded Spurs at this location.

Treetop Lounge (see La-Te-Da)

Virgilio's
524 Duval St., Key West
Circa: 2003-present

Virgilio's (named after the founder of the restaurant) is an elegant indoor/outdoor cocktail bar, adorned with huge photos of gay icons (Monroe, Hepburn, etc.) tucked behind La Trattoria restaurant. It became so popular and well-known (especially for its Key Lime martinis) that it ended up taking over the entire space. It is now more of a restaurant than a bar. This was the original location of Saloon 1 (see listing).

Voodoo Lounge
200 Duval St., Key West
Circa: 1993-1995

It is now a tourist souvenir shop.

INDEX

ACKNOWLEDGEMENTS

It takes a village to create a book of this scope and the authors gratefully acknowledge those who shared their experiences and resources with us; Nikki Adams, Charles Apers (aka Melissa St. John), Toni Armstrong, Jr., Graham Brunk, Randy Clark, Electra, Edison Farrow, Mark Foley, Pam Folsom, GayBarchives.com, Gayle Greene, Rand Hoch, Houstonlgbthistory.org, Judy Ireland, Cathy Johnson, Penny Johnson, Andy Martin, Tim Miller, Newspapers.com, Cheryl O'Bryan, QueerMusicHeritage.com, Rikki Regretto-Fessler, Gordon Ross, Walter Silverman, Art Smith, Ben Smith and The Stonewall Archives & Museum, Lori Tanner, Bobby Tvorsik, and AJ Wessen. We would also like to express our eternal gratitude to Eric Miller for his eagle eye as our proofreader. The authors would also like to express thanks to St Sukie de La Cioix and Ian Henzel from Rattling Good Yarns Press, for their dedication to and support of this project.

Additionally, thanks to the Stonewall National Museum & Archives, we had access to the following sources: *411, Alive!, Boyz, Celebrate (Key West), Community Voice, Cruise Magazine, Damron Guides, David Magazine,* Facebook, *Florida Knight Life, Fodor's Guide to Gay Florida, Fort Lauderdale News, Friendly Voice, Fun Maps,* GayBarchives.com, *Gay & Lesbian Directory, Gay Community Yellow Pages, Gay Rag, Gay Yellow Pages – Florida, Guild Guide, Hollywood Sun Tattler, Hot Shots/Hot Spots, In Town Exposure, Key West Life, Key West Pride Connection, Little Black Book, Lonely Hunters: An Oral History of Lesbian and Gay Southern Life, 1948-1968 by James Sears,* MiamiTodayNews.com, *The Miami Sun Sentinel, Michael's Travel Guide, New Times, Out Pages,* OUTSFL, OutTraveler.com, *Pulse, Q Magazine/Gay Rag, The Ranch, Rivendell Regional Maps, She Magazine, South Florida Gay News, South Florida Pink Pages, South Florida Pride Pages, South Florida Travel Guide, Time Out, Travel With Pride*

ABOUT THE AUTHORS

Rick Karlin has been a freelance journalist and editor for over 40 years. He is currently the Arts & Culture editor for Out South Florida and a contributing writer for The Bay Area Reporter and Grab Magazine Chicago.

His last book, *Last Call Chicago: 1001 LGBT-Friendly Taverns, Hangouts, and Haunts*, co-written with Sukie de la Croix, was published in 2022 and ranked number one in Amazon's LGBT Studies category. His memoir *Paper Cuts: My Life in Chicago's Volatile LGBT Press*, published in 2019, was about his life over several decades working in the Chicago LGBTQ press.

He has also written three novels: *Show Biz Kids, Tales of the Second City*, and *Death on the Rocks*. His musicals *Witches Among Us, Scrapbook, Ladies at Large, Musical*, and *Spin Cycle* have been produced in Chicago. His plays *Turning Tables, Gregg Shapiro '77*, and *Patient B: A Case Study*, based on the poetry of Denise Duhamel, have all had staged readings in Fort Lauderdale. He has also written numerous children's musicals.

Recognizing his years as an LGBT community activist and writer, he was inducted into the Chicago LGBT Hall of Fame in 1997. He wrote for nearly every LGBT publication in Chicago, starting with *GayLife* in the 1970s, followed by *Gay Chicago Magazine* (entertainment editor), *Outline/Nightlines* (now *Windy City Times*), *Chicago Free Press*, ChicagoPride.com, and *Boi Magazine*. He was also an on-air personality for LesBiGay Radio.

After too many Chicago winters, he retired to Fort Lauderdale, Florida, where he lives with his husband, poet and journalist Gregg Shapiro, and their fur baby, Miss Coco.

Fred Fejes moved to South Florida in 1986 from the Midwest, where he received his PhD in Communication Studies from the Institute of Communication Research at the University of Illinois. He is an LGBT community activist and professor emeritus in the School of Communication and Media Studies at Florida Atlantic University, where from 1986- 2016, he taught courses on LGBT Studies. He is known for his work on sexuality, media, and the history of the LGBTQ movement in America. From 2018 to 2019, he was a Fulbright-Palacky Distinguished Chair at Palacky University (Czech Republic). Fejes is the author of *Gay Rights and Moral Panic: The Origins of America's Debate on Homosexuality*, an account of the 1977 Anita Bryant campaign against gay rights in Dade County, Florida, and *Imperialism, Media and the Good Neighbor: New Deal Foreign Policy and United States Shortwave Broadcasting to Latin America*. In 2013, he received the Roy F. Aarons Award for "contributions to education and research on issues affecting the gay, lesbian, bisexual and transgendered communities." He is a Research Scholar at the Stonewall Library and lives in Fort Lauderdale, Florida.

www.ingramcontent.com/pod-product-compliance
Lightning Source LLC
Chambersburg PA
CBHW080955120626
46546CB00010B/2901